Positive Impact

Communicative Competence©

Keld Jensen

M☉tivational PRESS®
LEADERS IN GLOBAL PUBLISHING

Published by Motivational Press, Inc.
1777 Aurora Road
Melbourne, Florida, 32935
www.MotivationalPress.com

Manufactured in the United States of America.

ISBN: 978-1-62865-191-1

CONTENTS

ACKNOWLEDGEMENTS 9

FOREWORD 11

BEHAVIORAL ECONOMICS AND COMMUNICATION 17

The Three Chief Motivating Factors 17

Interactive Trio 18

Foundations of Success 19

Behavioral Economics and Irrational Behavior in Communication 19

Economic Irrationality 23

The Bottled Water Study 24

Irrationality as Seen from a Traditional Economic Viewpoint 25

Rationality, Irrationality and Brain Structure 33

Competence and Awareness 34

Perceptual Blindness 34

Are You a Level-10 Negotiator? 35

How do we learn? 36

Level 1 - Unconsciously Incompetent 36

Level 2 - Consciously Incompetent 36

Level 3 - Consciously Competent 37

Level 4 - Unconsciously Competent 37

Executive Competence 38

Rational or Irrational 40

Decisions Are Based on Information, Emotion, Personal Chemistry, and communication 41

Dollars and Hard Facts Aren't Everything 43

The Importance of a Clear Communication Strategy and Approach   45

Communication Code of Conduct 46

A Case History: Chancing Your Right Arm 47

CHAPTER 1 - COMMUNICATION..**51**

1.1 Correct Communication..**54**

1.1.2 Movement when looking 54

1.1.3 Use of hands..54

1.1.4 Movement 54

1.1.5 Use of humor 54

1.1.6 Facial expressions..54

1.1.7 Use of voice, volume, intonation, dialect...................55

1.1.8 Presentation structure, convincing or information 55

1.1.9 Body language..55

1.1.10 Behavior 55

1.1.11 Representation systems 56

1.1.12 Assertion 56

1.1.13 Nervousness 56

1.1.14 Dress code..56

1.1.15 Profiling 56

1.2 The use of audio visual aids **56**

1.3 Be sure that you have a dialogue **58**

1.4 Words are secondary **59**

1.5 The brain and memory..**61**

1.5.2 The sensory memory 62

1.5.3 The short-term memory 63

1.5.4 Filtering information...63

1.5.5 Long-term memory..64

1.5.6 How does the brain work?...65

1.5.7 Conscious versus subconscious...................................65

1.5.8 The subconscious mind 66

CHAPTER 2 - MAKING AN IMPACT ON PEOPLE **69**

Introduction and basic techniques....................................70

It is not enough to be a "good chatterbox" 70

2.1 Varying gaze – eye contact.....................................**72**

2.2 Gestures **74**

2.3 Humour - Don't take yourself too seriously **74**

2.4 Gesticulation – arm movements, use of hands **78**

   2.4.2 An open hand 79

2.5 Individual habits **79**

2.6 Use of feet **80**

2.7 Use of voice **81**

2.8 Use your whole body **84**

2.9 Look at yourself in the mirror **84**

   Good advice 85

CHAPTER 3 - THE FIRST SEVEN SECONDS **88**

   3.1 Facial expression **89**

CHAPTER 4 - NERVOUSNESS **91**

   4.1 Fear **93**

   4.2 Presentation, nervousness and anxiety **96**

      The 5 'belts' 96

   4.3 Visualization **97**

   4.4 Principles of visualization **101**

   4.5 Verbalization **101**

   4.6 Conversation **102**

   4.7 Ways of reducing nervousness: **102**

      The audience receives only what you give them 104

CHAPTER 5 - STRUCTURE **105**

   5.1 To inform **105**

   5.2 To entertain **105**

   5.3 To motivate **106**

   5.4 To persuade **106**

   5.5 Presentation **110**

5.6 The subject 110

5.7 Intention 110

5.8 Topic classification 111

5.9 Time 111

5.10 Questions 111

5.11 Presentation of problem 114

5.12 Needs analysis 114

5.13 Provide the solution 114

5.14 Document the payoff 115

5.15 Conclusion /summing up 116

5.16 Summing up, topic, intention and payoff 117

5.17 Questions 117

5.18 Conclusion 118

CHAPTER 6 - PREPARATION 129

CHAPTER 7 - TRUST 141

CHAPTER 8 – PACING, RAPPORT AND LEAD 148

8.1 You have a choice 148

8.2 Physiological matching 150

8.3 Voice matching 152

8.4 Language and representative system 152

8.5 Visual thinking 152

8.6 Auditory thinking 153

8.7 Kinesthetic thinking 153

8.8 Experience, common ground 153

8.9 Breathing 154

8.10 Belief and values 154

CHAPTER 9 - REPRESENTATION SYSTEMS **158**

9.1 Identification of primary representation system **160**

9.1.1 Visual (v) 160

9.1.2 Auditory (a) 161

9.1.3 Kinesthetic (k) 161

9.2 How rapport, pace and lead are used **165**

9.2.2 Why learn about representations and strategies? 166

9.2.3 Using ,the strategy 171

9.3 Eye movement **174**

CHAPTER 10 - ASSERTIVE BEHAVIOR **178**

10.1 Assertive body language **181**

10.1.2 Self-assessment questionnaire for assertion evaluation 191

10.2 Stress **196**

CHAPTER 11 - EMOTIONS AND MOTIVATION **200**

CHAPTER 12 - ASKING QUESTIONS **215**

12.1 Types of question **216**

12.1.2 Open questions 216

12.1.3 Closed questions 217

12.1.4 Leading questions 217

12.1.5 Follow-up questions 217

12.1.6 Questions for your audience 218

12.1.7 Questions from the audience 219

12.2 Listening **224**

12.3 Back door sales (information from third party) **226**

12.4 Look for the motives – "Where is the money?" **228**

12.5 Counter questions **229**

12.6 Being too open **230**

12.7 General behavior **230**

12.8 Breaking promises..**232**

12.9 Other people read you!..**233**

CHAPTER 13 - TECHNIQUES AT MEETINGS...**237**

CHAPTER 14 - PRESENTATION, NERVOUSNESS AND ANXIETY **276**

QUESTIONS: **334**

THE 'POWER OF WOW' **335**

ACKNOWLEDGEMENTS

Many people from all over the world have contributed to developing the content that is the sum and substance of this book. Many have also been sources of inspiration – either because they were very skilled communicators, or because they were quite the opposite.

A number of the ideas I've shared here germinated years ago, but only recently came to full fruition when I realized that communication, trust and behavioral economics are the cornerstones of any successful commercial transaction – in fact, of any successful human interaction. It would not be possible for me to fittingly acknowledge everyone who has played a role forming these ideas. Many were inspired by presentations, training sessions, advisory services, and the writings of scholars and thought leaders in the fields of negotiation, behavioral economics, communication and conflict resolution. Everything you'll read, though, is the product of hundreds of hours of solitary reflection, in which I sought to identify the variables that make some people "work" and others fall short.

There are several individuals who deserve special recognition for their contributions to this project. First, I want to convey my gratitude to Justin Sachs at Motivational Press, for recognizing the universality of the concepts I have developed. My editorial team made the manuscript process as painless as possible and offered exemplary suggestions for better readability, notably Russ Williams.

I have numerous professional colleagues in Europe, Asia and the U.S. who have provided support and wise counsel along the way: Tim Cummins from IACCM; Dr. Karen Walch of the Thunderbird School of Global Management; Dan Shapiro of the Harvard Program on Negotiation, and my PA, Mrs. Charlotte Nielsen.

I am very fortunate to have many many good friends who always supports me in my efforts – just to mention a few; My sister Anette, Antonis & Kib, Jesper & Anne and Clef & Annette. Paige Stover has partnered with me from the beginning of the project and played an invaluable role in providing structure to my thinking, developing ideas, and adding her own insightful perspectives.

I am deeply grateful to my lovely wife Keyanna for her wonderfully positive and inspiring behavior, and her willingness always be there.

Lastly, I want to thank my daughter Nadine. Any parent understands that the first twenty or so years of a child's life provide a continuous study in the art and science of communication. I freely acknowledge that Nadine has been my most instructive critic, and my least objective teacher. She is also the light of my life.

FOREWORD

Welcome to Communicative Competence*—an excellent opportunity to re-evaluate your own communication skills!

Over the past twenty years, practical experience in communication, presentation techniques, meetings, negotiations, training, and staff, etc. has led me to believe that no systematic study of communicative competence has yet been carried out in Denmark.

For over 25 years our international organization has dealt with over 25,000 negotiators from more than 30 countries. These negotiators came from both the public and private sectors and represented every level from Mid-level Managers to Chief Executive Officers.

We have trained, evaluated, measured and performed follow-ups of their negotiating skills and can now demonstrate that even the most seasoned and well-trained negotiators lack skills within the following four areas:

- **Personal impact**
- **Personal communication**
- **Techniques at meetings**
- **Presentation techniques**

Regardless of their function, position or task, every professional must be able to master these skills on a daily basis.

Have you ever been in a situation where you were faced with the kind of person who made you feel small? This could be either on a physical or a psychological level, and it is what is popularly known as personal chemistry. When confronted with this type of person at a meeting, he or she was completely disparaging about your thoughts, your attitudes, your ideas and your aims. You may well have been compliant, but you leave the meeting in an irritated frame of mind with the thought running through your head that "My idea was best!"

But for one reason or another, you failed to assert yourself. How do you manage to stand up for your rights, your ideas and your objectives without others infringing on you and your interests? That is what we call assertive behavior.

How did you react the last time your boss or your colleague asked you to present a new proposal to a client?

Did you think "Oh no, why me, what should I do?" Did you say to your boss "Don't you think it would be better for someone else to do it?" Were you unsure and unprepared, and had not the foggiest idea about the objective and how to go about your presentation?

Were you a bag of nerves beforehand, unable to sleep a wink and incapable of doing it without your hands trembling and your legs shaking?

Or:

Have you ever attended a talk where the speaker was an instant cure for insomnia? Someone who spoke in a dull monotone, stood there motionless, holding onto his chair while looking only at his manuscripts, and you thought to yourself "I wish he would hurry up and finish!"

During the break you meet a business associate who gives you a flimsy handshake, looks down on the ground and says, "It was great to meet you!" in a loud voice.

You were negotiating last month with your supplier. You agreed about the delivery, what it should contain and about the price.

Your supplier then supplied the goods to the wrong address, with the wrong contents and at a price that was too high. What went wrong with your agreement? You made an agreement, didn't you?

At the office meeting every Friday, you are used to Nielsen constantly interrupting everyone else. Olsen minds his own business and is never committed. On the other hand, Britta is particularly committed, but talks to the person sitting next to her, who thinks that Mike, the boss, is incompetent and his ideas are ridiculous.

No doubt you are also used to 8 out of 10 meetings producing absolutely nothing or at best a conclusion which is never implemented. What is missing?

The situations above are common to all groups of business people, no matter whether they are project managers, directors, sales staff, buyers or technicians.

The four areas described are not theoretical skills that we can learn at school, Business College, university or a postgraduate training institution. They are often learned through practice by "trial and error"–hopefully not too many errors, or otherwise you might lose your job.

In this book I will attempt to teach you procedures based on many years of practical experience with methods that work in many situations, though there is no universal solution to every situation and obstacle that will come your way.

Acquiring these techniques will improve and boost your own feelings of self-confidence and self-assurance and will give you better communication skills in a number of different areas. Far too often, good ideas and ingenuity are lost in the overall packaging.

So what is personal impact? Not everyone perceives it in the same way. If a salesperson can sell sand to the Sahara, is it because his behavior is convincing? Or because he has charisma?

What is manipulation? Almost always it is viewed in a negative light, but what it actually means is "change" or "influence."

For some people it has totally negative connotations, such as exploitation or abuse. Other people are drawn towards it. How do you acquire impact? What about persuasive skills? What does *impact* mean to you?

Throughout history people have used impact as way of controlling the lives of others, of implementing ideas and convincing others. In the beginning, this was done by means of physical force. Those who were physically stronger and faster had power over others. As civilization progressed, people came to inherit impact and authority. Because the king and his men symbolized power, they were able to make decisions for everyone else.

At the onset of the industrial age, capital became the decisive power factor. Without capital, you had no opportunities, influence or power. Capital was power. Those who had access to it were dominant.

The situations above still play a role in our lives today. It is better to have money than to be poor. It is better to be physically strong than small and weak. The greatest personal resource today, however, is knowledge.

We live in an age in which the world is changing almost daily due to new thoughts, ideas and opportunities. A huge and an incredible amount of information comes at us at the speed of light via books, TV, radio, the internet, newspapers, magazines, etc. In our world those who have access to information and understand how to process it possess what used to be the king's preserve: unlimited power and authority.

The truth is, however, that even in this day and age information is not enough. If our only need were for good ideas and creativity, our lives would be different. Results are generated by implementation and action. Knowledge is only potential power until it is in the hands of someone who understands how to use it effectively and correctly.

This book was written with skills training in mind. It can be used productively not only as a tool to improve our personal competence and ability, but also as an easily accessible work of reference.

Scottsdale, AZ 2015.

BEHAVIORAL ECONOMICS AND COMMUNICATION

THE THREE CHIEF MOTIVATING FACTORS

I am a curious researcher, deeply interested in learning what motivates people's decisions and actions. I meet a great number of people in the course of my work, and when the opportunity arises, I often ask them an unusual question: "What motivates you?" A strange thing to hear from someone you've just met. I receive a wide variety of answers – from things you would expect, such as "my family," "my career," or "freedom," to the somewhat less usual, such as "my boat," or "horseback riding," to the downright exotic, like "travel to Mars!"

I have found that when we get down to our most fundamental drives, there are three primary motivators common to most everyone. These are the things driving all of us, though not everyone is driven all three – at least not at the same time. The "big three" are *money, sex,* and *power*.

Now, in order to obtain any or all of these three things, I contend that you're going to have to engage in quite a lot of two specific activities: *communication* and *negotiation*.

If you want more money, for example, you're going to have to communicate about it. If you have a "regular" sort of job (one with hourly wages or a salary) it will be necessary to communicate with your boss about a raise – and perhaps with other people as well. If you run your own business, you're going to have to communicate with your suppliers, customers, staff and partners or colleagues about ways to increase production, revenues and profits. You may well have to communicate with lenders or investors, too. In your quest for more money, you might even have to communicate with your spouse and family about your household income and budgeting. And in *all* of these interactions, *negotiation* will come into play, to some degree, and in one form or another.

Do you want more power? More influence? Once again, you're going to have to communicate and negotiate. I meet people who claim that they *don't* want power or influence. They've almost certainly mistaken the meaning of the terms, for you exert some degree of power and influence any time you seek anything from another or others. Have you ever done that?

The third of Man's most prominent motivators is sex. Many people wonder what exactly I mean when I talk about this. It's not necessarily the sexual act itself that is the ultimate goal here. Contact and pleasant interaction with, as well as recognition, admiration and affinity from others of the sex one finds most attractive (or both sexes, in some cases) might be considered mere shadows of raw sexual activity – yet they still are craved and cherished by almost every individual. And obtaining these things requires, once again, communication and negotiation. In fact, I've met many people (usually male) who consider themselves masters of these two human arts, and practice them with the greatest of intensity, devotion and finesse nearly every week – even every day – all with sexual gratification as their singular objective.

INTERACTIVE TRIO

A colleague of mine, Peter Frensdorf, recently commented that if you've got plenty of just one of the three motivating factors – money, sex or power – you'll almost automatically end up with plenty of the other two! I think he's got that right, and history certainly holds abundant evidence to back the idea. With enough money in hand, power and sex can be acquired. If your sex appeal is strong enough, you don't even have to be terribly clever to leverage it into considerable money and power. And with sufficient power over others, money and sex are yours for the asking – or taking.

FOUNDATIONS OF SUCCESS

Social research on the subject of personal success has led to the conclusion that approximately 15% of a person's success is the result of his or her intelligence, experience and formal education. So what makes up the remaining 85%? **Human engineering.** Human engineering is the study and activity of human interpersonal relations in pursuit of any given objective. In other words, it is the science of how we conduct interpersonal communications and negotiations.

BEHAVIORAL ECONOMICS AND IRRATIONAL BEHAVIOR IN COMMUNICATION

Look at the book you're reading – the physical object. Whether you're holding an ink-and-paper printed edition or electronic device, its production involved a whole series of technical miracles, some dating back thousands of years. Now look at your surroundings, and all the marvelous creations we take for granted – from lamps and chairs to nuclear power and mobile phones, from aircraft to oil rigs. All are the products of human ingenuity.

And yet we forget where we put our car keys. We're late for meetings. We put on too much weight and can't seem to lose it. We smoke or drink too much, or indulge in even more harmful practices, knowing full well they could ruin or end our lives. So just possibly, we're not individually as smart as we like to think we are. There are even scientific research findings to the effect that most people consider themselves more intelligent, rational and reasonable than hard facts indicate.

Further, our conscious thought mechanisms aren't able to

handle large numbers of individual data – at least not all at the same time. Our top "data rate" is normally between four and nine bits (individual data) at a time. Here's a little demonstration of what I mean. Look at the string of letters that follows for about ten seconds. Then turn away or close your eyes, and try to repeat the letters aloud and in sequence. It's easiest if you have someone help with this – checking the string of characters as you try to repeat them – but you'll still get the point, even if you do it on your own. Here are the letters:

IBMIRSBBCCIAUSAKGB

How did you do? Did you get the whole string? If not, don't feel bad – very, very few people would. There's just too much data there to absorb and retain in so short a time.

Now watch what happens when we reduce the number of individual data and try the exercise again:

IBM IRS BBC CIS USA KGB

Same 18 letters, same sequence – but suddenly it's possible to remember them without much trouble. This is because you're no longer looking at 18 random letters; instead, there are *meaningful groups* of letters; six data instead of 18.

We carry on this same sort of mental processing all the time. As the world and people around us bombard us with by sensory input and messages, we automatically categorize and group what comes in, recognizing and paying attention to things which are important, and mentally filtering out the rest.

We see this phenomenon at work in other ways, too. For

example, in giving instructions on how to do a particular task, success is far more likely if you break the task down into small steps or sub-tasks, each one easy to understand and execute.

Looking at the emotional or "subconscious" side of your mental functioning, we find a totally different picture. Here we see fantastically complex tasks performed without effort, conscious thought or calculation. Activities like cycling, dancing, turning a somersault, walking on our hands, or typing just flow. They seem simple as we do them, and they look simple to anyone watching us perform them. Once we've learned them, we can do them without thinking, even while carrying on *other* complex activities, like having a conversation. If you break any of these activities down and imagine all messages that must travel to and from the brain to execute them (sensory inputs, messages to control muscle movements, etc.) you see at once that there are hundreds or thousands of individual data being processed and messages sent and received, almost instantaneously. It's miraculous.

For centuries now, Man has thought that he existed as what we might call *Homo economicus* – sensible, rational beings living in a well-ordered economic world, capable of rational thought and most often making rational choices. Over the last 20 years or so, scientific research in the field of behavioral economics has documented that this conception is far from accurate. We do *not* most often make good decisions. We are *not* rational in many of our conclusions. We do *not* live in an orderly economic world. We live instead in a *behavioral* economic world.

This world is one traditional economists do not like – in part because it threatens to deprive them of the dominant positions they've enjoyed for so many years. They also dislike it because it suddenly strips them of the ability to predict (or at least claim they can predict) a society's economic future. In an orthodox economic world (if one actually existed), people would do what one expected them to do. In a behavioral economic world, people's actions and reaction are far more difficult to anticipate or predict.

Another phenomenon I've observed is that we, as a society, do not seem to adapt to new ideas as easily as societies have in the past. This is perhaps because we have a society with an increasingly large proportion of older people. Birthrates are declining (in Western societies), while at the same time we tend to live longer. Older people tend to be more entrenched in their attitudes, beliefs and habits than younger people, and this factor is reflected in the way the society as a whole behaves.

For example, if you happen to be an older person, I may already have irritated you with what I've said in this book. You may disagree with a lot of it, to the point where you're on the verge of setting it aside and reading something more comfortable. If that's the case, you're certainly free to drop the book – but wait for a moment. Isn't that what we too often do? We choose to read or listen to things that support the views we've already formed. And we choose not to give much heed to anything contrary. We don't like being confronted with the possibility that conclusions we've formed might not be quite in line with the truth. We prefer materials that confirm what we know and affirm our beliefs.

An interesting experiment that documented this phenomenon was conducted in the context of a U.S. presidential election. In the months leading up to the election, researchers examined book sales on Amazon – specifically sales of books about Barack Obama. Among the available selections were books critical books of Obama, as well as favorable, positive works. It was found that books favorable to candidate Obama were purchased mainly be people who had already decided to vote for him. Most of the critical books were purchased by voters who had already decided to vote against Mr. Obama. Apparently buyers chose books that would support or confirm decisions they had already made.

Economic Irrationality

Professor Daniel Kahneman is one of the world's leading researchers in behavioral economics. In 2002 he was awarded the Nobel Prize in Economics for his work – an unusual honor, in light of the fact that he is a psychologist, not an economist!

In his prize-winning research, Kahneman concluded that Man's behavior is very often irrational, particularly in his economic activities. We will readily do business with someone we like and trust, even though their product is of low quality and overpriced. We will avoid dealing with someone we do not know, like or trust, even if their product is clearly superior and their price lower. That's not the sort of behavior that would occur in a strictly rational economic environment, and it certainly isn't what an orthodox economist would predict. Unfortunately for the traditional economic expert, concepts such as affinity, sympathy, empathy, confidence and trust can't be charted on a spreadsheet – yet they are integral in our economic behavior.

Kahneman further concludes that all our decisions have a significant emotional element, regardless of whether we're buying a new car, deciding which job offer to accept, choosing a major supplier for our business or finding a new partner (business, marital or otherwise). *After* we've come to an emotional conclusion, we begin listing facts to support it.

When I confront managers with this fact – that their decisions are based heavily on emotion rather than entirely on pure reason, I meet strong resistance. That isn't surprising, as few people recognize or are willing to admit to their own irrationality. There seems to be a general attitude in our society that irrationality is taboo, something to be shunned and avoided, as though it were some sort of disease. But I don't believe the irrationality I'm talking about is a bad thing. Further, I believe that only by confronting, understanding and embracing it (and the new view of the world that goes with it) can we use it to advantage in our lives and in the world of commerce.

If we accept Kahneman's findings as correct, we suddenly find ourselves in a new situation, business-wise. Product, price, quality, delivery speed and other such considerations are reduced in importance. What becomes the primary concern? YOU. As a business person, *you* create relationships. *You* inspire, earn and build trust. Relationships and trust carry more weight than product or price – at least to a far greater extent than we've previously thought.

THE BOTTLED WATER STUDY

I've conducted an interesting study, surveying more than 3,000 people. I presented each with a simple scenario:

You are a business owner; as part of your routine operations, you must keep a supply of bottled drinking water on hand, for your employees and for customers and other visitors. For the last five years, you have purchased your bottled water from the same company – we'll call it Supplier A. You've met the supplier and are familiar with several of her staff. You get along well, communication is frequent and friendly, and the trust between you is high. Your price for a single bottle of water from Supplier A is 10 cents.

Now a new supplier enters the market in your area – Supplier B. He can deliver a product that is identical to Supplier A's in every way. Quality, quantity, delivery cost and packaging (aside from labelling) are all the same. The only difference is that Supplier B's price is 2% lower than Supplier A's. You have no established relationship with

Supplier B. He seems friendly, but you don't know, like or trust him.

The question posed at this point is, "Who will you deal with? Supplier A, or Supplier B?"

At a price difference of 2%, **everyone** presented with this decision said they would stay with Supplier A.

Next I increased the price difference a percent or two at a time, and re-asked the question – stay with Supplier A, or switch to Supplier B – looking for the point at which the price difference overrode the trust-and-familiarity factor.

The threshold for the majority of the participants was between 10 and 20 percent. Some went as high as 30% before they would switch suppliers.

Further, based on this simple study, as well as years of experience in commerce and negotiations, it's my conclusion that the greater the complexity of the product or service involved, the greater the importance of friendly familiarity and trust in commercial decisions.

IRRATIONALITY AS SEEN FROM A TRADITIONAL ECONOMIC VIEWPOINT

Consider the following scenarios, which have been used in research with thousands of volunteer subjects. Ask yourself how you would act or react in each.

- You're dining in a restaurant, in a country and city to which you're certain you will never return. After the meal, would you tip the server?

According to traditional economic thinking, it would not be strictly rational to leave a tip. The server's wages are covered by what you pay for the meal, so there is no sound reason to leave an additional amount. Leaving a tip would be strictly altruistic – a friendly, human, emotionally-driven gesture.

- I offer you $50 in cash right now (for no particular reason), but say that if you will wait until tomorrow, I'll give you $100 instead. What would you do – take the $50 now, or wait a day and double your gains?

The majority of respondents say they would take the immediate $50.

- Which would you rather have: $50 after 30 days, or $100 after 31 days?

Suddenly the majority response shifts: the $100 in 31 days is preferred. Interesting! When it's a matter of today or tomorrow (a one-day difference), the response is the opposite of the 30-or-31-day question. Yet both scenarios involve a one-day difference, and the dollar amounts are the same. Strange.

- Scenario A: You have been employed by a company for several years. At the end of the current year, the company announces it has enjoyed 12% growth, and has shown a profit. The company gives you and its other employees a pay raise of 7% for the year to come.
- Scenario B: You are employed by a company which has had zero growth for the year just past, and has run a deficit. The company reduces wages and salaries by 5%.

Which of these two scenarios do you think is most unfair – A, or B?

If you think the wage reduction is more unfair than the raise, your thinking is not rational, according to traditional economics. In fact, both examples treat the employee equally, in terms of sharing the results of the company's performance.

- Scenario A: You are on your way to the theater. When you arrive, you discover that you have lost your ticket, worth $100. Would you buy a new one at the door, or go home?
- Scenario B: You are getting ready for an evening at the theater; you put $100 cash in your pocket, to pay for your ticket at the door. When you arrive at the theater, you discover that when you stopped for dinner along the way, you lost the $100 cash. Would you buy a ticket anyway, or go home?

There is a marked difference in the way people react to these two scenarios. In Scenario A (where the $100 *ticket* was lost), the majority would buy a new ticket. In Scenario B (where $100 *cash* was lost instead), most participants said they would go home. In both scenarios, the *value* of the loss is $100. So what makes the responses so different?

- Scenario A: You leave your home to do some errands. When you return home, you discover you've lost a $20 bill. "Well, that's too bad," you think. The next day you go for a walk. When you're back home again, you notice that once again you've managed to lose another $20 bill! You're amazed at your own carelessness.
- Scenario B: You go out for a walk; when you return home, you discover you've lost $40 in cash. Annoying.

Which of these two scenarios would you find *more* annoying – losing $20 two days in a row, or losing $40 on a single day? Keep your answer in mind as we go on to two additional and similar scenarios.

- Scenario C: You're out for a walk when you find $20. You think it's your lucky day! The following day you take your walk around the neighborhood as usual, and once again you find $20. Amazing!
- Scenario D: You go for a walk and find $40. Cheers!

Now, which of these fortunate scenarios would you prefer? Finding $20 two days in a row, or finding $40 on a single day?

When asked about Scenarios A and B (loss of $40), most said they would rather experience Scenario B – losing $40 all at once. Perhaps the thought is that it's easier to take the upset of the whole loss all at once, rather than having to go through the pain of loss twice.

The answers were reversed for Scenarios C and D (*finding* $40). The majority said they would rather find $20 twice than $40 all at once – perhaps to spread the excitement and sense of good luck over a longer period.

Conclusion: If we're going to experience loss or are otherwise "hit" by life, we'd prefer to take it all in one blow. If we're going to be rewarded or experience good luck, we'd rather "stretch out" the happy experience.

This suggests some useful applications for business owners and managers. If your business is having a rough year, and it looks like you're going to have to cut wages or salaries (or even downsize), making the cuts all at once – and making it clear that it's a one-time action – will have less negative impact overall than if you were to prolong the agony by stretching out the reductions over time. Conversely, if things are going very well and you're thinking of making promotions and pay increases, spread them out for a cumulative and lasting positive effect.

Are these things rational? Not according to traditional thinking. But if you understand this one principle of behavioral economics, they're rational indeed; you're using what you know to achieve the best possible outcomes.

- One of the better-known experiments in behavioral economics is a version of a classic game theory experiment called "The Prisoner's Dilemma." There are two test subjects involved. The experimenter hands the first subject (we'll call him Subject A) $100 in $1 bills. The second subject (Subject B) knows that A has been given the money, and its amount. Both are told that Subject A must now decide how much of the money he will share with Subject B. They are also informed that if Subject B is not happy with the amount he is offered, he may refuse it – but in this case, all the money will be taken away, and neither subject will have any.

If you were Subject A, how much would you offer? 10%? 30%? 50%? 70%? After running this experiment on thousands of participants, it was found that if Subject A offers less than 20% of the money, Subject B will reject the offer in the majority of cases. In other words, if he is offered less than 20%, Subject B would rather punish Subject A, even though it means forfeiting all monetary gain of his own. A strictly rational choice would be to take any amount offered. Subject B might dislike Subject A afterwards, or even seek some sort of revenge after the fact, but at least he would end up with more than he had at the outset. But again, a different sort of rationality is in play here.

In a modified version of the same experiment, Subject A is dressed in various styles, to represent his economic status: as an affluent business person, for example, or as a college professor, clerk, or construction worker. When Subject A appears to be more affluent, Subject B's minimum acceptable offer increases. When Subject A is perceived as being less affluent, the "minimum requirement" tends to be lower. Here again we see choices influenced by emotion or empathy, rather than strict rationality, in the traditional economic sense.

- You're sitting in your office, working late, when the phone rings. It's your wife, asking you to bring home a marking pen and a stack of copy paper from the office.

You promise to do so and end the conversation. When you go to the supply room to get the pen and paper, you find neither item is in stock. "Terrific management!" you think. You know your wife is going to be upset if you show up without the pen and paper – she needs them to complete an important school assignment, due the next morning. Then you remember that on your way home, you'll pass an office supply store that stays open late. "Problem solved!" you think – until you discover you've left your wallet at home, and have no way to make a purchase. Finally you remember that there's a coffee can in the break room where people put change and small bills – the office "kitty" to buy fruit, pastries and other snacks for everyone to share. You check out the kitty and discover there's more than enough there to buy the things you need. Do you take the money?

The majority of the participants in this experiment would not take the money, even though they would willingly take the office supplies. What's the difference? Both would be petty thefts, both with the same dollar value.

- A similar experiment was made in a college dorm's shared kitchen. Six cans of soda were put in the fridge, each labelled with a fictitious name. Within a week, all six sodas had disappeared.

Next, a jar was placed in the fridge, labelled with the same name and containing the cash value of six sodas. A week later, all the cash was still present.

This last example suggests something unexpected: One of the reasons trust is in decline in today's world is that we have moved further and further away from using cash. Most transactions today are made without any physical money changing hands. It's most often done with the click of a mouse or the swipe of a card. For some reason, we tend to be more honest when real, physical cash is changing hands.

- The following experiment was conducted with groups of students who were about to take an exam. They were told that for each question they answered correctly on the 50-question exam, they would be given a token valued at $1, redeemable at the school snack bar for food or beverages. They were also told that they would be grading their own exams, and that their grading would be accepted without cross-check or verification by the teacher.

The same experiment was conducted with separate groups of students, but this time the students were told they would receive $1 in cash for each correct answer.

All participating groups were as close to identical as possible in terms of grade level, age, past scholastic performance, etc.

In the token-reward version of the experiment, the students averaged 47 out of 50 correct answers, by their own evaluation. In the cash-reward version, the average was only 39 out of 50.

Were the token-reward students smarter than the cash-reward students? No, not according to their past performance. So it can be concluded that when cash was involved, the students were more honest than when they knew they would be receiving not cash, but tokens. I've conducted this experiment several times myself; other researchers have run it countless times, with consistent results.

- In the 1960s and 70s, Walter Mischel of Stanford University conducted a series of experiments in which he offered children treats – marshmallows, cookies or pretzels. The children were seated at a table, upon which were a plate of goodies. They were told that they could choose to have one treat right away – but that if they would wait two minutes without taking one, then they would be allowed *two* treats.

Some of the children went for the single treat, with little or no waiting. Others looked longingly at the goodies but maintained control for a while, but finally relented and gobbled one. Many fidgeted and writhed in frustration, sometimes coming out with strange noises, but managed to restrain themselves for the allotted time, to be rewarded with the promised two-treat prize. Though the test was a strain for all participants, a few sat more or less patiently throughout. In the end, 33% of the children tested proved unable or unwilling to endure the delay in order to double their reward.

Mischel went on to follow the children who participated in the experiment through their school years, through college and on into their adult lives, with jobs and children of their own. What he found was interesting indeed. When they reached high school age, the children who had been able to restrain themselves scored an average of 200 points higher on the SAT examination. On the whole, they also exhibited better self-control later in life, and were more likely to make decisions that led to greater rewards. Among the group who had been unable to restrain themselves, there was a greater tendency to exhibit character flaws and behavioral difficulties as the years went on.

Rationality, Irrationality and Brain Structure

When we make business decisions, whether we're making a purchase, choosing a supplier or sitting at the negotiating table, feelings and emotions are far more potent factors than we might suspect or care to admit. When we choose to do business with Supplier A rather than Supplier B, the decision-making process is strongly affected by unseen and often irrational-seeming factors stemming from the subconscious mind, outside the awareness of the "rational brain" of which we're so proud.

The reason for this behavior has its roots in the physical structure of our brain. We each have, in effect, *three* brains. There is the "reptile brain" – the most primitive of the three, tracing its evolutionary origins back many millions of years. It operates on a rather crude, stimulus-response basis and is the seat of instinctive reactions rather than rational thought. Next there is the "limbic brain" – more advanced in structure and function, and the seat of our feelings and emotions. And finally there is the neo-cortex –

the "rational brain." It is the largest and most complex of the three, and the most recently developed in terms of human evolution. If there were a "traditional economics brain," this would be it.

Research has found that among the three brains, the limbic brain has the final say in decision-making – not the neo-cortex, as might be expected. People who have sustained injuries to the limbic portion of the brain commonly exhibit severely reduced decision-making abilities.

An understanding of rationality, emotions and game theory – and the ability to put your understandings into practice – can have huge impact on your success in business. You have much greater understanding of your own decision-making process and tendencies, and a heightened ability to predict and control them. Perhaps even more important, you'll more easily and accurately understand and predict the actions of those with whom you do business and negotiate.

COMPETENCE AND AWARENESS

PERCEPTUAL BLINDNESS

Back at the turn of the 15th century, when the first European explorers and settlers arrived in the Caribbean, the native tribesmen were amazed at the sight of the newcomers' ships. Terrified at what appeared to be clouds come down from the sky, they believed the heavens were about fall. They simply could not comprehend the sight of a ship, with its enormous, billowing sails, riding on the sea. Why not? They had no prior experience with such an imposing object, and so were unable to recognize it for what it was.

The same sort of thing happens to us today, when we're exposed to something completely new and outside our experience. A true expert in any field is aware that there are things of which he has no knowledge. When he sees something totally novel, his impulse is to inspect it closely and find out all about it. In contrast, an amateur often has a seriously inflated opinion of what he knows; when confronted with a completely new thing or concept, he imagines (or pretends) that he already knows all about it and makes no attempt to find out more. A person completely unfamiliar with the field, confronted with something totally new, may not even register it at all.

Are You a Level-10 Negotiator?

You would be hard pressed to find a negotiator who would tell you he didn't really know how to do his job. Why would he? No one readily admits to incompetence in his chosen field; most rate their own competence as "above average." This is very consistent in the responses I get at the start of managers' negotiation training sessions. I ask such groups this question: "On a scale of 1 to 10, how would you rate yourself, where 10 is the perfect negotiator and 1 is completely inept at negotiating?" The majority respond a 7 or an 8 – a pretty high self-evaluation.

Two to three days later, nearing the end of the session, I repeat the question. This time the average response is 3 to 4. What happened during the three-day training period? Did I somehow make the trainees stupid, or crush their confidence? Did I de-motivate them and degrade their abilities as business people and negotiators? Or had they generally over-estimated their knowledge and skills at first, but found a new understanding and respect for negotiation as an activity – as well as a more realistic evaluation of their own competence? For an appreciation of the answer, let's examine what goes on in these training sessions.

HOW DO WE LEARN?

During the sessions, the executives were gradually made aware of mistakes they hadn't realized they were making, and brought to an understanding of *why* they were mistakes. This is a crucial part of any learning process where participants are already experienced in the subject being taught. There is actually a definite learning pattern in play, with four distinct levels or phases of competence:

LEVEL 1 - UNCONSCIOUSLY INCOMPETENT

Imagine a typical two-year-old girl; we'll call her Nadine. She has spotted the milk carton on the table during breakfast, and decides she wants to pour some milk into her glass. She has seen Mommy and Daddy do it many times, and it looks easy. Her first few attempts are quickly stopped by her parents, to prevent a flood of milk across the table and onto the floor. Nadine is *unconsciously incompetent*. She thinks she can carry out the task with ease, not realizing that at present she is actually incapable of doing it without assistance. Many video-recorded negotiations have captured similar situations, wherein the negotiators are unaware that their attempted strategies and tactics are wrong-headed and doomed to failure. Only when they see themselves on video playback does the truth begin to dawn on them.

LEVEL 2 - CONSCIOUSLY INCOMPETENT

Nadine is not the type of little girl who abandons an idea easily. Mom and Dad's backs are turned, and she seizes the opportunity: grabbing the milk carton, she lifts it up, starts to tilt it, and ... SPLASH! The carton slips from her tiny hands, falls to the table and splatters milk far and wide. Nadine has suddenly gone from Level 1 to Level 2. She now realizes that she is unable to pour the milk on her own without making a mess. Our negotiator trainees experience this sort of revelation when they see themselves in action on video. They become aware of their mistakes and the areas where improvement is required.

Level 3 - Consciously Competent

Nadine practices, under her parents' careful guidance, until she is able to pour the milk on her own without a messy disaster. She is now aware of her new skill, but exercising it requires total concentration – to pour milk on her own, she has to focus all her attention and carry out each phase of the operation with utmost care.

Level 4 - Unconsciously Competent

Nadine is now six years old. She can bike, climb trees, and swim. She pours milk for herself several times a day without even thinking about it. Through practice she has acquired a solid skill – a competence that no longer requires much concentration or conscious effort.

This is similar to the way we learn the arts of communication and negotiation. We begin with limited theoretical and practical knowledge; then, through practice and further study, we gradually develop competence with the tools and techniques, and their use becomes second nature.

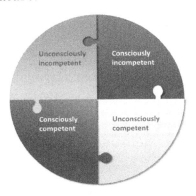

EXECUTIVE COMPETENCE

Great demands are made of people at the top in the business world; they find themselves in the limelight more than ever before. As competition intensifies, there are those who choose to resort to dishonesty and unsavory practices in order to win.

In today's world of commerce, the jobs at the top have become increasingly complex and demanding.

Motivation vs. complexity

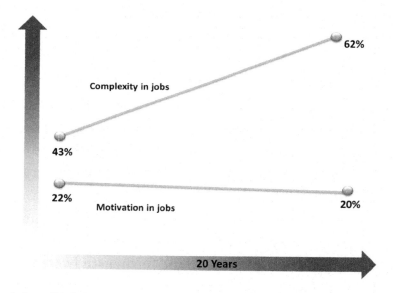

A job which just 10 or 15 years ago involved, let's say, 400 important tasks and responsibilities each month may involve 600 today. Just as the scope and complexity of the work demanded of top executives has grown, the competition for such positions has intensified. Research shows that a typical job's complexity has increased by approximately 50% over the past 20 years. Over the same period, people's personal motivation to perform well has *reduced* by 10%. Higher demand and lower motivation – a nasty cocktail!

Earlier social-scientific theories about leaders sought to isolate and measure universal traits which characterized a good executive. Numerous managers were sounded out, evaluated and put through batteries of psychological tests. However, attempts to identify characteristics common to successful execs proved to be completely off the mark. No one ever succeeded in establishing a defining set of traits or characteristics.

Instead, it was found that each efficient, competent executive seemed to have unique characteristics which made him or her the ideal person for one particular role, at one particular time. A deep understanding of collaboration and the ability to make it work, personal magnetism or charisma, great skill at motivating others – these characteristics and many more were commonly found, but no definite, universal set of traits or abilities could be named.

Motivation and complexity aren't the only factors that have changed markedly within the business world. Just compare the 1990s, when profits were soaring and everything seemed so simple, with the early 2000s with their terror attacks, wars, weakening dollar, economic recession, and disease epidemics. The whole business landscape changed. Public perception of and attitudes toward top company executives also shifted. In the 1990s, many CEOs and other top managers were looked on as celebrities, almost rock stars. Today they face distrustful markets and investors, suspicion and criticism of their motivations, increasingly strident demands for transparency, and close, critical scrutiny of everything from balance sheets to bonuses.

If two people with the same education, the same qualifications and comparable backgrounds were to submit identical presentations on a given subject, invariably the person who conveyed the greater air of authority, self-confidence and credibility would be the most successful at putting his ideas across

Rational or Irrational

People are not rational. Interpersonal communication is frequently played as a sort of game in which people attempt to fulfill their psychological and material needs. The thoroughly rational person does not exist.[1]

The fact that you prefer doing business with the people you *like* may not seem strictly rational. It might seem misguided, petty or even foolish that you would rather deal with people you trust and with whom you share a sense of identity, rather than doing business strictly on the basis of your technical and financial needs. However, your *psychological* needs outweigh your material needs – and your preference for dealing with those you like is, from your point of view, completely rational.

Further, there is no such thing as an absolute objective truth. Your perceptions and assessments are no more inherently true or correct than anyone else's. There are countless different ways to describe and evaluate past, current and possible future events. Each individual negotiator works on the basis of different "maps" or conceptions of past, present and future reality than those followed by any other. To negotiate effectively, the parties at the table must have a common perception of the reality upon which they will be negotiating – that is, a shared perception, as close to identical as possible. In order for one party's decisions and conditions to be perceived as rational by the other, his assessments and experiences must be well aligned with theirs – or at least thoroughly understood by them.

To one party in a negotiation, decisions made by the other party often seem irrational.

---

1   In 1978 Herbert Simon won the Nobel Prize in Economics for demonstrating that the concept of the decision-maker as superhuman was nothing more than an illusion.

Example:

As a supplier, you might want to sell only the most recent model of a particular item –the model that demonstrates your technical superiority over your competitors. You take pride in the most recent design as the state-of-the-art industry leader. Much to your surprise, your most prominent buyer wants to purchase the model you launched five years ago. You think you have a very strong case for convincing the buyer to take the most recent model instead. Its performance is superior, and you can demonstrate its strong profitability. Nevertheless, the buyer insists on purchasing the old model.

As far as you're concerned, the buyer's decision is irrational. You think he is being bullheaded (if not downright stupid), and doesn't know what's good for him. You try to convince him that he is making a bad decision. However, in the buyer's eyes *you* appear to be stubborn, and unwilling to take the least interest in a customer's needs and wants.

The buyer sees the five-year-old model as the best solution to his specific needs and assessments. He does not *want* the newest technology; his staff is not trained on it, his customers aren't asking for it, and he can't see how he could viably take advantage of its finer points. What *you* consider to be rational arguments might be counter-productive nonsense, from his point of view.

DECISIONS ARE BASED ON INFORMATION, EMOTION, PERSONAL CHEMISTRY, AND COMMUNICATION

It is extremely difficult to get a complete, pure, unbiased overview of almost any situation. There is too strong a tendency to overweight your own experience, to pay little or no attention to alternatives to your favored solution, or to consider others' viewpoints. Further, though your information and views aren't necessarily wrong, there may also be unrecognized, intangible needs or motivations influencing your thoughts and opinions. Even if you were to become aware of these, you might not willingly acknowledge them.

You have a need for power, security and acceptance. You don't want to lose face. You may be seeking good, tangible results – but you might just be out for revenge and retaliation. Such deep-seated motivations might arise from childhood events of which you're not consciously aware. There may be other factors underlying your unsuspected needs or desires, and limiting your ability to make rational decisions based solely upon facts.

People are not machines. The idealized image of Man as a coolly rational decision maker, governed by the rules of logic and the laws of the physical sciences, is part of an obsolete school of thought. Understanding that such a concept of humankind *is* obsolete and unfounded, your approach to human and business relationships should include awareness of emotional reactions and motivations. Put personal chemistry to work; use your common sense to create a positive atmosphere in which mutual understanding and respect for the needs and viewpoints of all concerned foster cooperation and mutual benefit.

Often one of the parties in a negotiation offers more facts, figures and other details than the other party needs or can absorb and use. The added, unnecessary information serves only to create confusion, insecurity and even suspicion. Bear in mind that you can easily talk a deal to death; be very alert to any indication that you're heading in that direction, and when you've said enough, shut up.

Many people, particularly those working in technical or engineering enterprises, are completely absorbed and involved with the intricacies of technology. They mistakenly assume that purely factual and precisely-ordered technical reasoning will bring the results they desire at the negotiating table. Such people do well as long as negotiations are centered on specifications, testing results and other purely technical matters. But when the tech arguments have been presented and commercial considerations and bargaining come into play, technicians and engineers are outside their comfort zones. The cool confidence they exuded in the technical phase evaporates.

A superior product that dominates its sector puts an enterprise in a strong negotiating position, allowing that business to dictate terms and conditions even though its people lack negotiation skills. However, it is dangerous to be satisfied with commercial success based only upon technical superiority. As soon as that power position is seriously challenged or lost, negotiation skills become crucial to continued success – as any enterprise that has been so challenged will attest. Without an effective negotiator, they cannot navigate the shift in market realities, and so they watch their market share dwindle right along with their technical leadership.

DOLLARS AND HARD FACTS AREN'T EVERYTHING

In negotiation, sooner or later you're likely to find yourself suddenly unable to understand the other party. He appears to have ceased operating rationally, making decisions, statements or proposals that give more weight to value judgments (which you don't fully understand or accept) than to financial concerns and measurable facts.

Decision-making and negotiations cannot be fully analyzed or explained by mathematical, economic or technical calculations alone. They involve an additional dimension, not subject to precise measurement and often difficult to understand. We have to learn to perceive this factor in action and seek to understand it, irrational as it may seem when first encountered.

Let's look at an example. Two hotels are situated on the same street, some hundred meters apart. Both offer all the services a businessman might need. Both give top priority to guest comfort and safety. Yet the difference in *price* between the two is more than $100. Still, both hotels enjoy a high rate of occupancy. Many of the more expensive establishment's guests could not imagine choosing the cheaper alternative. Why? The answers would vary, from guest to guest:

- They find the less-expensive hotel's atmosphere disagreeable in some way.
- They feel the cheap hotel's profile does not fit the image they wish to present, and wouldn't want anyone to associate them with such a low-priced or "lower-class" establishment.
- They once had a bad experience at another hotel in the cheaper hotel's chain, and ever since have associated the company with bad food and poor service.
- The more-expensive alternative is part of a well-known chain which invests heavily in its brand, working hard to foster the image of being the first choice of the wealthy "beautiful people."

If a company whose employees must travel on business attempts to restrict those employees to lower-priced hotels, it is likely to face objections. To the company finance manager, this seems irrational – but only because he does not share the others' value norms. A company finance manager might believe that lodging employees in expensive hotels would signal that the company is not cost-conscious. The traveler might argue that clients would see the modest accommodations as reflecting poorly on the company's standards or financial health.

Neither of these possible assessments is necessarily more correct than the other. However, an understanding of these key terms *is* vital:

- Status, profile and class
- Design
- Credibility
- Brand
- Experience
- Safety
- Closeness
- Language and cultural community
- Atmosphere
- Political value norms
- Ethics
- Fairness

These terms and the concepts they represent have strong emotional connections. Failure to take them into account can result in unsuspected but powerful negative perceptions and associations, leading to difficulties in earning and retaining the respect of those with whom one negotiates.

The Importance of a Clear Communication Strategy and Approach

Successful businesses have and follow strategies for virtually everything they do. They allocate resources to creating, developing, and fine-tuning a marketing strategy, a product development strategy, an HR strategy, a media strategy, and a R&D strategy. Can you imagine Apple or Toyota operating without clearly defining such strategies, and then setting a budget for their implementation? It's almost unthinkable.

I have asked countless business leaders in many cultures, across several age brackets and genders: "How many people have an individual communication strategy?" The responses are consistent: almost no one has a defined communication strategy or articulated approach for relating to partners, suppliers, customers, or other stakeholders in their organization. Despite the fact that all business is human, rarely does a company have any policy in place establishing guidelines for dealings with strategic partners. As a result, relationships and connections commonly operate at inadequate levels of openness and trust; consequently, the full potential of such relationships is not realized.

Similarly, few people have any defined strategy in place when they sit down to make a deal. They rely on their "gut feelings" and allow emotions to drive their demands and concessions. It becomes nearly impossible to develop the open, honest, transparent communications necessary to creating added value.

"How should we communicate and negotiate?" This is the first question organizations and business leaders must ask themselves.

COMMUNICATION CODE OF CONDUCT

A Communication Code of Conduct can be developed and used to create a cooperative climate, and to serve as a tool for implementing strategic choices. The code I use in my own practice establishes rules of behavior between delegates, and guidelines for facilitating cooperation even in the most challenging situations. It includes statements of what we will and will not do, under any circumstances, to preserve the honesty and integrity of the meeting or negotiation. When I sit down at the table to conduct a meeting or negotiate, I introduce the code and ask the opposing delegation to sign it, just as my delegation has. This establishes a positive environment from the outset – a climate that fosters open communication.

A CASE HISTORY: CHANGING YOUR RIGHT ARM

A couple of years ago, while in in Dublin on a business trip, I had an afternoon free to indulge in a bit of tourism. I find it easiest to get the feel of a town by just strolling about, so stroll I did. By chance I walked past Saint Patrick's Cathedral, one of the largest and oldest of Dublin's historic cathedrals. I went in and admired the fascinating architecture, including the enormous vaulted ceiling. Suddenly I found myself in front of an old door, set up on an exhibition platform. The massive door was, rounded at its top, and had an opening at its center, several inches wide and more than a foot tall. A sign above the door proclaimed it as "The Door of Reconciliation."

Naturally I was curious to know the story behind the door. This is what I learned: in 1492 this had been the cathedral's main door. At that time, two major Irish clans – the FitzGeralds and the Butlers – were in the midst of a bloody feud, with severe casualties on both sides. After a time, the Butlers began feeling the strain of their losses and sought sanctuary in the Chapter House of St. Patrick's cathedral. The FitzGeralds quickly surrounded the holy place and settled in to wait.

The FitzGerald chieftain and elders discussed the situation, concluding that the feud was senseless. No one would ever truly win, and both sides were suffering hideous losses. But what could be done? There was no trust between the two clans, and there seemed no way to establish any.

The chief of the FitzGeralds pleaded with Black James, head of the Butler forces, through the Chapter House's barred door, asking him to come out and negotiate peace. James refused: "I do not trust you or your people. Your proposal is nothing but a crafty trick. If I came out, you would attack us."

What now? FitzGerald understood Black James' distrust. How could he breach this invisible barrier? Then he had a brainstorm. He had his men cut a hole in the heavy oaken door. Thrusting his right arm through the opening – utterly vulnerable to the swords and axes of the defenders inside – he called to James: "Look! This is my sign of trust! Will you accept my trust, give me yours and agree to end this madness?" Black James shook the offered hand, and the feud was ended.

This is the origin of the expression, "willing to chance your right arm."

One of our world's biggest problems is the lack of trust. For twenty years, Dr. Karen Walch at the Thunderbird School of Global Management has conducted an ongoing study on negotiations. She asks each new group of students to answer questions about how cooperative and trusting they are personally, and how they feel about those they deal with.

"What we've generally found so far is that 40% of people surveyed believe that they are cooperative and trusting," says Dr. Walch. "Yet, when asked about their negotiating counterparts, they generally believe that the other party is just looking to win. It's this type of mentality that causes negotiators to take a defensive strategy, which tends to leave a whole lot of value left on the table." Low trust makes truly productive collaboration impossible!

Compounding this problem people's tendency to act irrationally, overvaluing our like or dislike of those with whom we negotiate, rather than remaining purely objective. Just as Nobel Prize-winning psychologist Daniel Kahneman has proven, our decision-making is largely guided by emotion and intuition.

This book will offer you simple yet useful tools to improve your ability to convince, present, conduct meetings and negotiate. It will help you to become more successful.

CHAPTER 1 - COMMUNICATION

I had a retired uncle who was in his early seventies. He used to be a lawyer with his own practice. My uncle had two passions in life—his summer house and his two dogs. They were big dogs, Great Danes.

My uncle had a flat in Copenhagen, Denmark, but he wanted to drive himself, his wife and his two dogs to the summer house whenever the weather permitted.

In order to be able to do this, though, he needed a new car. The old one had very much outlived its usefulness with more than 13 years of faithful service.

My uncle thought: *I know that I want solid quality.* But unfortunately he did not know much about technical things, not to mention cars. *Volvo,* he thought, *has always been associated with quality. That is what I want!*

He went along to a Volvo car dealer, walked around a bit and looked at the models. He found a big, spacious estate car, as they call it, and looked contemplatively into the boot. A salesman rushed up to him and asked: "Well, looking at the lovely new model, are you?" What could my uncle answer but "Yes! But I am wondering whether there is room for ...."

The salesman interrupted: "This new model is equipped with standard ABS, power steering, airbag, air-condition, and if you buy this week you will get an extra boot!"

"Will I get an extra boot?" my uncle asked, surprised, "Do you extend it or??" The salesman answered: "No, no, we fit a luggage box on top of the car with room for 450 liters extra without cost!"

My uncle asked: "How big is the boot?" He imagined the two Great Danes in there and could not really assess whether there was enough room. "According to Autograph there is room for 1,118 liters in there," the salesman answered quickly and confidently. "But why do I not mention some of the most recent technical gadgets which are included in this S80?"

My uncle gave up. He could not take in all the technical terms, and when the salesman started talking about liters, he imagined his two dogs submerged in a bath to measure how much water came out.

When my uncle left, the salesman called out after him: "Take a brochure with you and call me when you want your old Audi assessed!"

My uncle continued his search and happened to end up at a Renault car dealer.

A salesman came over to my uncle, who after an introduction asked: "How big is the boot?" The salesman answered: "As you can see, it is big, but what do you need room for?"

My uncle told him about the dogs and the summer-house and all the problems and his thoughts on this. The salesman asked: "Where do you live?" My uncle answered and the salesman said: "Do you know what? That is not so far from here, so why don't we drive to your place? That will give you a chance to test the car and find out whether there is enough room for the dogs."

The dogs fit into the car without any problems, and my uncle bought a Renault.

In what way were these two salesmen different? Was the Renault salesman more skilled technically or a better salesman? Was it the offers or ...? The Renault salesman *listened*. He asked questions and showed interest in what it was that my uncle needed.

This Renault salesman was the company's best, won all

competitions and was always in the top league. When you asked him what he did to sell so many cars, he answered: "Well, I do nothing in particular, I am just myself talking to my customer!"

This example illustrates very well the simplicity of communication. Listen and talk.

Be dedicated and be interested. Be yourself and be honest.

Have you ever seen a locksmith in action? It seems a bit like magic. He tinkers with a lock, listens for things you cannot hear, sees things you cannot see, feels for things you cannot feel, and suddenly he succeeds in a remarkable way in opening the lock and the door to the safe.

Perfect communicators operate in the same way. They can work out people's mental idea, objectives, ambitions, motivation and wishes. You have to look for things you have not looked for before, feel things you have not felt before, hear things you have never heard before, and ask yourself questions you have not asked before.

If you can learn to do this elegantly and effectively, you can influence any person's strategy in any situation. You can learn how to accommodate people's objectives, give them what they want and, at the same time, give yourself what you want—a win-win situation.

The secret is to listen to what people tell you. They most often do tell you what their objectives, strategies and ambitions are. They say so with words. With the way they use their hands. With their body language. With their facial expressions and with their eyes.

Before you can use the tools to read another person, you need to learn what to look for; what are the clues that tell you where a person is heading, and with what feelings are attitudes and ideas expressed?

1.1 CORRECT COMMUNICATION

In order to be sure that you create an impact, communicate effectively and establish the foundation for making your recipient understand your message, we have divided the book into a number of different areas. We will cover the following:

1.1.2 MOVEMENT WHEN LOOKING

Eye contact—why is this so important? How do we knowingly use this to create a greater impact and make our opponent understand us?

1.1.3 USE OF HANDS

A wise man once said: "The most difficult thing for most businessmen is to make a speech! The second most difficult thing is for them to decide what to do with their hands."

1.1.4 MOVEMENT

Bodily activity, movement and the use of feet are central elements in sending a message. How, why and with what will be described.

1.1.5 USE OF HUMOR

Humor or anecdotes and examples are ways of adding a picture to our message. A sense of involvement is created by means of examples, demonstrations or stories we can relate to.

1.1.6 FACIAL EXPRESSIONS

We all have different faces. Here I am not thinking of beauty, but the design. How the face is used and what result comes out of it will be dealt with in this paragraph.

1.1.7 Use of voice, volume, intonation, dialect

The voice is an effective means when it comes to persuading other people. Often we can tell by the voice alone whether our opponent himself believes what he is saying.

How do we become conscious of our voice? How is it to be used actively in the effort to create optimal communication?

1.1.8 Presentation structure, convincing or information

No matter whether we speak in front of 1 or 500 people, structure creates the governing idea for the listener—and for ourselves, by the way. It helps the recipient understand contents, message and purpose.

1.1.9 Body language

How do people react when they tell a lie? How do you react when you are stressed or nervous? How do we reveal ourselves in these situations? We read others in the same way that they read us.

1.1.10 Behavior

There may be a number of basic elements which cause our actions. These elements create our image for others to read. We have to be able to understand and interpret other people's behavior and understand what model they represent.

1.1.11 REPRESENTATION SYSTEMS

All human beings have some guiding channels, representation systems that control us. These systems are a decoding of our experience of the world. If we can understand and interpret other people's primary channels, we will be able to increase and facilitate communication with those who are different from ourselves.

1.1.12 ASSERTION

Assertive behavior is a theoretical description of the "perfect human being." We can understand and handle different situations by analyzing and drawing conclusions on our own conduct and that of other people.

1.1.13 NERVOUSNESS

Who does not become nervous in one situation or another? How can we control this nuisance? Or do we need to control it?

1.1.14 DRESS CODE

Different cultures, different rules: How do we present ourselves? How do we create respect and authority for ourselves?

1.1.15 PROFILING

This paragraph deals with how we are perceived by the surrounding world. How are we "read"?

1.2 THE USE OF AUDIO VISUAL AIDS

Let me say this immediately. This book is *not* a private study in the use of audio visual aids, but we try to provide a quick overview on how we can support our own message by means of these components.

Only 15% of your success is based on your professional/technical knowledge and about 85% is based on knowledge of human behavior ....

This is the surprising result of a study carried out by The Carnegie Institute of Technology which supports the importance of effective communication.

The characteristic of functional communication is primarily that it is two-way. The parties listen to each other, ask questions, answer questions, make use of the answers and discuss alternatives. They avoid strains and instead of fighting about proposals and demands which need to be met, they try to make themselves acquainted with each other's viewpoints. Listening implies that you respect your opponent.

If communication does not function satisfactorily from the beginning of the conversation, you will find no common ground or openings, and it becomes difficult to evaluate your opponent's intentions. This leads to continuous withholding of information and to a situation whereby the parties become locked in their own proposals. You recognize that the opponent has locked himself into his own proposal. He shows no interest in listening to you and is unwilling to negotiate.

This is how communication reaches a deadlock and interest in further co-operation dies, not because the parties have different values, interests or proposals for concrete solutions, but because they have missed the point of what they are both trying to say. Efficiency in communication is to a large extent determined by whether the parties exchange enough credible information. Whether the information is credible or not is always determined by the opponent. A statement like "It does not seem as if he believes me, so that is his fault" shows that the message has not reached its target. It is, however, not the recipient's fault, but the sender's. It is he who has been unsuccessful in getting his message across.

One-way communication leads to misunderstandings and prevents the parties from understanding one another. You can study the effects of one-way and two-way communication by carrying out the following simple experiment.

*To ensure good communication, a two-way
process is necessary*

On a piece of paper you have drawn a circle, a triangle with different sides, and a rhombus. A test subject who sits opposite you has to try to reproduce the figures and their place on the paper based on your oral description. He is not allowed to ask questions. You are the only one allowed to talk. Do you think it is an easy task for the test subject?

Do the experiment a couple of times, and you will find out how hard it is to make yourself understood.

Next, do the experiment again, but allow the test subject to ask questions which you answer. In a much shorter time, you will get good reproductions of the picture you have communicated to your test subjects. If you want them to understand you perfectly, you have to transmit on several channels. You have to combine words and pictures.

1.3 BE SURE THAT YOU HAVE A DIALOGUE

Two-way communication requires that you take part and ask questions and sum up instead of listening passively. You ask to make sure that your picture is equivalent to the picture which the sender wants to communicate. You ask when you do not understand, when you are interested, when you want more information, or when you want to test ideas. Your questions are answered.

"You have two ears and only one mouth in order to listen twice as much as you talk!"

Studies show that we use 45% of our time listening to other people. Thus, listening is an extremely important part of our communication. When it comes to powerful and persuasive communication, you have an advantage that nobody else has–yourself.

You have the resources to make an impression. Emphasize your ideas and achieve your goals in co-operation with people, talking and presenting ideas in a manner which can impress even the most arrogant person.

We have to be intelligent speakers, and this also means intelligent listeners.

There are two fools at every market: one who asks
too little and one who asks too much.
Russian saying

1.4 WORDS ARE SECONDARY

Professor Albert Mehrabian from UCLA has carried out ground-breaking studies which show communicative correlation with the following result:

Body language is our non-verbal behavior. It is the way in which we move our arms, our facial expressions, our gestures, where we put our legs, etc. Do you stand with your arms crossed? Is your face a happy and open face?

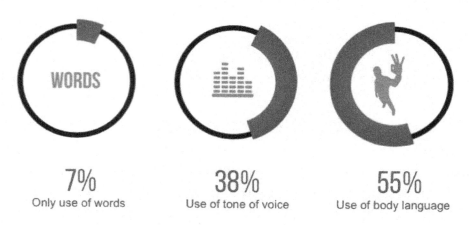

MEHRABIAN'S RULE OF COMMUNICATION

7%	38%	55%
Only use of words	Use of tone of voice	Use of body language

It is not what we say, it is what we do!

The word is the verbal expression, the meaning of the very word.

Intonation is volume, speed, accentuation and stress.

Surprised? When these three parameters are combined optimally, we create congruity in our communication. Not only do we become trustworthy, but we create thrust.

To substantiate this, you can try to say: *"**I** never said that you had taken from the till!"*

Here you stress the first word, *"I."*

Then you can try to say the same sentence by stressing differently, e.g.: *"I never **said** that you had taken from the till"* or *"I have never said that you had **taken** from the till!"*

As you can see, you convey three different meanings. Perhaps you mean the same, but subconsciously you may happen to place the stress wrongly. Misunderstandings arise. This shows the value of intonation!

Imagine that you meet a person you have never seen before. He stands with his arms crossed, his side towards you and a moody, sad, closed face, down in the mouth, without a spark in his eyes. Then he says with the same body language: *"I am very pleased to meet you!"* Do you believe him? Hardly a person you will find inspiring and interesting, is he?

You are in a stress management course. The teacher bites his nails, twists his hair around his fingers and shouts at people. Or you go to a weight watchers' class where the teacher weights 140 kg. and eats Danish pastry during the break.

The above-mentioned examples are what we call *incongruous behavior* or behavior where what we say and what we do are contradictory. In most cases, humans have an in-built "lie detector" which sends signals to the subconscious saying that something is wrong!

Always tell the truth. There is an old saying that says: *"If you tell the truth, you do not have to remember what you have said!"* Be yourself and do not put on airs or behave in an artificial manner.

1.5 THE BRAIN AND MEMORY

Not all of us are good at listening. Before we start this section, it is important to understand how our brain works when registering and receiving information.

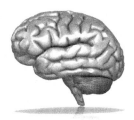

Our sensory organs and sensory center

All external signals you receive are at first registered by your sensory organs. (The five traditional senses are sight, hearing, smell, taste and touch–but there are more: balance, muscle, temperature and pain.)

The signals you receive are sound, light or influences of a mechanical, thermal or chemical nature. When the signals strike the sensory organs, the message is coded and stored.

The signals move on to the brain, where they are transformed into conscious and subconscious sensory impressions by means of different sensory centers, and these are later stored in your sensory memory (the sensory register). The information is stored the same way as the working memory in a computer.

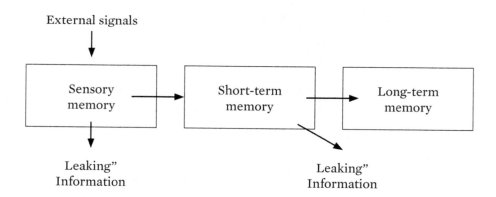

1.5.2 THE SENSORY MEMORY

The sensory memory has a very limited storage capacity. It does not hold more information than you are capable of registering during approximately half a second. New information constantly enters the sensory memory, pushing the previously stored information on. This information then moves on to the next memory unit, the short-term memory.

1.5.3 THE SHORT-TERM MEMORY

Not all information moves on from the sensory memory to the short-time memory. Large parts are filtered away and leak. Signals such as light and sound cease to exist. That information is gone for all eternity. Approximately 50% of the original sensory impressions are filtered away at this stage. The filter is on all the time. It is active and functions without your conscious influence.

1.5.4 FILTERING INFORMATION

Information which at first moves on from the sensory memory to the short-time memory is believed to be information which you are prepared for, which is positive, which is connected to your needs and which concerns you emotionally. Quite simply: You hear what you want to hear. The information which you exclude is everything which you cannot interpret: foreign languages and terms, facts which you cannot relate to your needs, unpleasant information.

If you receive too much information at the same time, there will be competition between the messages. Even though you try to participate actively in filtering the messages, it is difficult for you to distinguish between the important and the less important. Certain signals influence your feelings and previous experience so strongly that your emotional commitment prevents you from picking up new signals.

Try a thought experiment: You imagine that you are sitting next to a person in the theater who has forgotten to wash himself and who smells of sweat. You get very little out of the theatrical performance, and later you will not be able to explain to others what it was about. The sense of discomfort stemming from your sense of smell has ousted other information.

Even short-term memory has limited storage capacity. The amount of information which you can store depends on the type of information in question.

Some information is not intermediately stored in short-term memory; instead, it moves directly into the long-term memory. Here all signals attached to our experiences are stored—for instance, all the signals we have learned to perceive as threats. We are out driving, for instance, when an obstacle appears on the road. We react with lightning speed to the danger which we have registered, step on the brake and steer clear.

1.5.5 LONG-TERM MEMORY

New information that enters the short-term memory pushes old information out. It has to move on to the long-term memory, but at first it passes through a new filter which functions in the same way as the filter between the short-term memory and the sensory memory. Approximately 25% more signals which your sensory organs originally registered and turned into impulses are leaked. Only about 25% of all signals arrive in the long-term memory. There the stored signals are transformed into chemically stored signals, which cannot be leaked. All information stored in the long-term memory will remain there as long as we live. The information can disappear only if we suffer physical brain damage.

If someone asks you what you did on the 3rd of February, 1988, you may claim not to know, but that is wrong. You know, but cannot remember. To remember and to know are two entirely different things. If you do not associate the 3rd of February with a special event in your life, it is a date without content, a date which you have excluded. You do not register all dates, and information in the long-term memory is not stored chronologically. For this reason, no date can be used as a search word in your memory, but you do know exactly what you did that day.

The less frequently you use previously stored information, the more difficult it is for you to find it again and thus make use of it. Finally, the information is so fragmented that you can recall only parts of it.

1.5.6 How does the brain work?

Your brain consists of approximately 10 billion nerve cells (called neurons). Every neuron is attached to neighboring cells with a network of fibers of up to ten thousand per cell. Because of the enormous complexity of the brain, possible interaction between the cells is far greater than there are atoms in the entire universe.

Brain researchers believe that the human brain is capable of working with up to 10,000 separate factors at one time, just below our level of consciousness when we make decisions.

When you get into a plane, you put your life into the hands of a computer which is smaller than an enlarged flea brain compared to your own supercomputer between your ears. Perhaps we should trust our own intellect somewhat more. Are you willing to trust your own brain when it comes to communication?

1.5.7 Conscious versus subconscious

Imagine a golf ball placed on top of a football. This illustrates the difference between the subconscious in the shape of the football and the golf ball in relation to consciousness. The two levels of consciousness are very different from one another, but at the same time very dependent on each other.

The conscious mind can, at a maximum, contain seven thoughts or actions at a time. Consciousness is used to identify information received through the six senses, vision, sound, taste, smell, touch or feeling.

The conscious mind registers and categorizes everything that goes on around you. Imagine that you are walking along a forest path, deep in thought. Suddenly you hear a hissing sound and look down on the path in front of you in order to identify what has made the sound, and you see a snake.

The conscious mind now makes a comparison. The hissing sound you have just heard and the snake you have seen go to your subconscious mind, where they are compared with previously stored information and experiences with snakes.

If the snake is four meters away and not very big, your subconscious mind tells you that there is no danger and that you can scare it away.

If the snake, on the other hand, has risen up, with its teeth showing ready to bite, you will receive a "warning" message, which will stimulate your body's further action. The conscious mind has thus made an analysis before a decision is made. The conscious mind accepts or rejects data in connection with choices and decisions.

1.5.8 The subconscious mind

The subconscious mind is one big memory hard disk. The capacity is basically infinite. The subconscious mind stores everything that happens to you. When you are 21, you have already stored the equivalent of more than 100 times the contents of the entire Encyclopedia Britannica.

The purpose of the subconscious mind is to store and retrieve data. Your subconscious mind is subjective; it does not think and act on its own, but acts on the basis of orders from your conscious mind. Your conscious mind decides, and your subconscious mind obeys. Your subconscious mind has registered and stored that your body temperature is as it is and where your comfort zones are and how they function and work in order to keep you within your boundaries. Your subconscious mind makes you feel out of balance when you try something new or change the pattern of your behavior.

You can feel that your subconscious mind pulls you back to your comfort zone when you try something new, change job, call a new customer, meet a new person, etc.

The decisive difference between successful and less successful people is their ability to go further, to go beyond their comfort zone. They are aware of how quickly the comfort zone becomes a habit, and they know that enervating behavior is an enemy to creativity and future possibilities.

In order to develop and change, you must be prepared to feel strange and different during the preliminary phase. If you are not prepared to feel clumsy or bad at the beginning of a new job, sport or in personal relations, you will be locked into a low success level.

Any idea or thought produced in your conscious mind will, without being questioned, be processed towards realization by the subconscious mind.

When you begin to believe that something is possible for you, your subconscious mind will begin sending out mental messages and energy. E.g., if you decide to buy a red car, you will begin to see red cars everywhere and on every street corner. If you prepare a trip to a foreign country, you will begin to see articles and information about the country everywhere. Your subconscious mind draws your attention to the information, which may be necessary in your decision-making process.

When you begin to think of a new objective, your subconscious mind will take that as an order and begin to work towards fulfilling the objective. It begins by adjusting your words and actions in order to aim your behavior at the target and become one with it. You are in fact working out a new comfort zone, or rephrased, a new habit.

Are you a wandering generality
or a meaningful specific?

CHAPTER 2 - MAKING AN IMPACT ON PEOPLE

What does it take to make people want to listen to what we have to say, and why do we need to capture their attention?

Presenting favorable news is easy–you don't need much in the way of presentation techniques if you announce to your colleagues that they are going to have a 25 per cent pay raise, or if you tell them that they are going to have an extra week's holiday. The message in itself will have an impact on them!

Sometimes presentations can be powerful in themselves. However, the ways in which you deliver your message are normally crucial for your recipients' acceptance and understanding of it.

When you talk directly to people with the aim of making an impact on them and motivating them, in addition to words, the following are also important:

- **Varying gaze**
- **Gestures**
- **Humor**
- **Gestures**
- **Use of feet**
- **Use of voice**
- **Image**

The facets mentioned above are among the most basic elements, regardless of whether we are giving a talk at a gathering, making an announcement, selling a product, conveying an idea, telling people about our objectives, or having a one-to-one conversation.

INTRODUCTION AND BASIC TECHNIQUES

Say you need to introduce a case to a committee or at a meeting, or you need to explain a project to a work group, to an individual, to a manager, to your employees or to one thousand people in an auditorium. If you want to give a good impression of yourself and your organization, you must be capable of presenting your objectives well in gatherings, no matter whether to one individual or to a large plenary group.

IT IS NOT ENOUGH TO BE A "GOOD CHATTERBOX"

You need to acquire skills and techniques in effective presentation in order to communicate professionally and effectively.

To start with, you must learn about the use of your voice and the use of gestures.

The spoken word, or verbal communication, is always more flexible than the written word, so why not use it?

The English language has thousands of words at its disposal.

The average sixth former has a vocabulary of approximately 2,000 words, whereas the vocabulary of a university student can reach up to 4,500 words. A businessman uses around 1,000 words daily.

Familiar words and phrases inspire confidence and have more impact on our audience. Recreate or repeat special expressions or words which may be appropriate to your target group. You must not talk down to your audience or use sophisticated words. You must not give the impression of being supercilious about your area of knowledge.

Use short, concise words. Shorter words tend to be the most powerful.

At the same time, remember that you are speaking because you want to convince your audience about something: You want to entertain, you want them to buy something, or you want to manipulate them into accepting your message in some way or other. Think in the same way as your audience. They are thinking:

- **What am I going to get out of this?**
- **Make me feel important.**
- **Give me confidence.**
- **Is this relevant to me?**
- **Show interest in me. Show that you are talking to me.**

We are living at a time when people of many age groups are used to 30 seconds' input ranging from MTV to news with more than 100 sequences per minute and party political broadcasts which become shorter with each campaign. This kind of audience is particularly demanding.

Research has shown that people remember:

- **10 per cent of what they read**
- **10 per cent of what they hear**
- **30 per cent of what they see**
- **50 per cent of what they see and hear**

It is tempting to spend all the time you have available preparing a manuscript; however, tone of voice and body language are important aids, so you should use these in your presentation.

2.1 Varying gaze - eye contact

You will capture the attention of your audience only if you look *at them,* so don't look up at the ceiling, down on the ground or out of the window.

Don't fix and hold your gaze on one particular person in the audience. It will make that person feel uncomfortable, no matter how agreeable or approving that person may seem. Distribute your attention evenly and give everyone the impression that you are talking directly to them.

It is a good idea to start a sentence by looking directly at one person or a group and finish by looking at another group or another person as if what you are saying is directed especially at them; it does not make any difference whether you are sitting or standing.

At a smaller meeting or talk, you should maintain eye contact for up to **five seconds** per participant. This is identical to the average time it takes a person to process a thought. It also increases the chances of people remembering what you have said.

Make eye contact with several people during your presentation, long enough for individuals to perceive personal contact, but remember not to stare anyone down, as that can make an individual feel very ill-at-ease. Calmly turn your face round the room; do not twist your head, and do not shuffle from one side to the other, but move calmly.

The demands of your audience are like those of a child who says "Mummy, look at me."

Eye contact is a vital component for establishing rapport and pace.

When it is time for your presentation to begin, just walk calmly to your place; you should then look around at all the participants in a serene manner while maintaining an air of composure. Spend a few seconds calmly looking at everyone. Not only does this make you seem more assertive, it also makes you come across as open and relaxed. If you don't do this, participants will continue with their internal dialogue, as they will not be sure when you are going to begin.

A speaker who does not look directly at his audience will be perceived as not being serious.

Why doesn't he look? Isn't he sure of what he is saying? Is he frightened of us?

Eye contact is an effective method of obtaining and maintaining control of a group. At the same time, it enables you to register how attentive people are to what you are saying and helps them to feel part of the performance.

When someone asks you a question at a larger meeting, you must look directly at that person, after which you should start to glance around at everyone in the room. If you look only at the person asking the question, there is potential risk that one or several of the participants will "switch off" because they feel that neither the answer nor the question relates to them.

When you feel that you have finished answering the question, you should look at the person who has asked the question again in order to elicit from them acceptance of your answer.

At the conclusion of your presentation or the meeting, you should repeat the eye contact which you used in the beginning. Conclude by spending a few seconds looking around at each participant.

2.2 GESTURES

An interesting piece of research has classified human beings into three groups.

- **Those with closed, almost angry-looking faces**
- **Those with neutral, almost indifferent facial expressions**
- **Those with open, cheerful facial expressions**

Take a long look around you! People look angry, neutral or optimistic, not necessarily because their emotional expressions reflect their inner feelings, but quite simply because we are all born with different faces and for this reason exude different expressions.

With me, I know that when I am really concentrating on something I come across as withdrawn or angry. Because of this, I do not naturally come across as showing very much interest or openness towards other people.

Our 80 facial muscles enable us to create approximately 7,000 different facial expressions!

In itself this provides a number of options for combining expressions. When we introduce a speech or a presentation at a meeting, we must try to relax, as our facial muscles particularly tend to stiffen up when we are nervous. We should bear this in mind before we open our speech and concentrate on our eyebrows, our mouths and our eyes.

2.3 HUMOUR - DON'T TAKE YOURSELF TOO SERIOUSLY

A few years ago I was invited to a wedding. There were more than 100 guests present, all of them in a festive mood and well-dressed. Both the bride and the groom were absolutely charming, and they both looked really stunning, absolutely gorgeous.

The weather was marvelous, the sort of beautiful weather that seems to come only in May, and the whole ceremony had gone perfectly. There we were, sitting down at the table elegantly laid out for the festive meal.

There had been the usual series of speeches, some more interesting than others, and then one more speaker raised his glass. This was Erik, noted for his wit. Everyone had been waiting for this moment, and there he was about to begin! Everyone went quiet as they turned to him. He cleared his throat and began. Evidently Erik had read, learned, or been told that humor is a good "ice-breaker." He actually started his speech by telling a joke about a man who stuttered.

Normally when someone starts to tell a joke, people begin to chuckle. That did not happen on this occasion. There was just an embarrassed silence, and not a single trace of a smile was on anyone's face.

This gradually dawned on poor Erik, who by this time had started to sweat, fiddle with his tie, while continuing to tell his joke faster and faster. Finally he got the message; no one would smile. All the guests sat there in embarrassed silence and either looked down at the table or at each other. In order to compensate for this silence, Erik broke out into hysterical laughter, after which he promptly sat down again, quite unable to complete his speech. What had happened? Was it a bad joke? Did he tell the joke badly? What this speaker had not realized was that the bride's father stammered, a fact which naturally changed what could have been a funny joke into something insulting.

This story illustrates very clearly that humor can be as dangerous as it is effective.

In situations where you are very agitated and nervous before an important meeting or presentation, you must consider whether it will be of any significance in 100 years' time. Will people remember your presentation or your meeting? Will it go down as one of the greatest presentations in history?

No way!

The Chinese have a saying—*"There are three mirrors which form a person's reflection.*

The first is how you see yourself. The second is how others see you. Then the third one is how you really are."

Humor is a tool worthy of special respect. If you can master this area, you have every chance of creating rapport and softening people up. To have the inspiration to be entertaining, you need to read literature, and by this I mean literature other than the literature that relates to your job.

If you are a technical engineer and you build bridges, it is most unlikely that you will be met with enthusiastic applause and roars of laughter from your audience if you read and quote *Technical Principles of Suspension Bridges* or the equivalent. If you seldom introduce or use humor when communicating with people, it may be difficult to jump right in and begin to use it as a starting-point.

Start by considering your favorite film stars in relation to humor. What do you think is funny about them? Watch Breakfast Television. What do you find funny there? What is it people usually laugh at? Which comments are relevant and funny?

Make humor relevant. Make it relate to the situation. One little word of warning, which is well worth remembering, is that you must not make jokes about the following:

- **Religion**
- **Sexual orientation**
- **Job**
- **Skin color**
- **Disabilities**

If you do include these subjects, the risk you run is that you unwittingly offend one of the participants directly or maybe someone whose partner is associated with the subject of the joke.

Now you may well ask, "Well, what is there left to make jokes about?"

Well, there is self-depreciating irony, which is an excellent harmless source of humor.

Use well thought-out humor, relevant to the situation. On a course about questioning techniques, a joke like this one can seem funny:

A young man goes into a bar and sees an old man sitting at a table with a dog at his feet. The young man goes over to the man at the table and asks him "Does your dog bite?" The old man looks at him sleepily and says "No!" The young man stretches his hand down to the dog on the floor to pat it on its head, and it growls at him, nearly biting his hand off. The young man jumps back quickly, turns round to the old man and says "You said that your dog didn't bite?"

"That is not my dog," the old man answered.

The problem was, of course, that the young man did not ask the right questions in the right order.

With 70 per cent of all people who lose their jobs, the problem is not lack of talent, but lack of communicative competence.

People who take themselves too seriously are easily recognizable. In general they tend to talk an awful lot about themselves. A large ego is good, but one that is too big can be disastrous. When it comes to communicating, genuine emotion can be of considerable and overriding importance. Emotions can arouse sympathy, compassion, enthusiasm and a sense of participation.

There are two types of emotional behavior: rational behavior guided by the head and irrational behavior guided by the heart.

When we talk about the budget, taxes and government dues, we think with our heads. When we talk about illness, child welfare, lack of day nursery places, hospital waiting lists, we think with our hearts. People become involved.

2.4 GESTICULATION – ARM MOVEMENTS, USE OF HANDS

Use your arms or your hands to emphasize and stress facts, whether you are seated or standing up.

 Don't stand there "slouching"; never keep your hands in your pockets, do not fold your arms over your chest, and never put your hands behind your head or on your hips.

Neither should you nervously "click" your knuckles or a pen. Calmly place your hands in front of you for the first few minutes or on the table if you are seated (you can place them over your stomach, but you must not keep them folded).

Once you get going, you can begin to use them to emphasize points.

Normal gesticulation may vary quite a bit from one person to another. To what extent do you use your hands during a normal conversation when you are relaxed?

A general rule is to try to avoid folding your arms, as others perceive this type of posture as isolating and uninviting. Use of hands is very important. Hand language is very effective, and your audience will be able to ascertain whether or not you are using your hands correctly.

Don't be tempted to pick up things which are within your reach. Many speakers lean up against the arm of the overhead projector—that is not what it is made for. Avoid using objects as psychological props.

For your recipients, draw your message in the air. If you are talking about filling your lawn mower up with petrol, you can show how this is done quite clearly with your hands.

Because body language shows action, you can train your hand movements when you use a verb. Let your elbows hang loosely by your side, as this seems less threatening to spectators.

Your arms signal superiority and self confidence. Folded arms can be an obstacle to communication

2.4.2 AN OPEN HAND

When you need to draw the attention of someone in your audience, you must not do this with your index finger, as this will be perceived as aggressive. Instead you should do this with an open hand as if you are stretching out towards them.

The open hand is an historical phenomenon which came about in the Middle Ages when two horsemen passed each other on the road. Showing an open hand illustrated that they were unarmed and that they did not have hostile intentions.

2.5 INDIVIDUAL HABITS

Do not adopt distracting habits, such as shuffling your notes, changing weight from one foot to the other, folding your arms over each other or stretching them out, running your hands through your hair, stuttering, coughing, fiddling with rings, etc. Habits like these can be very distracting for an audience and may divert people's attention from your message.

2.6 USE OF FEET

When you want to deliver a message while standing up (something I always prefer), it is essential to have an air of composure when using your legs and feet and always have them under control.

Rocking backwards and forwards (men often tend to do this, but I do not know why) or women twisting their legs reflects nervousness and insecurity and makes you immobile at the same time. You should point your feet forward, neither inward nor outward. When you stand, are you upright and determined, or are you slouched and unsure of yourself?

At the introduction your position should be balanced, with your legs slightly spread out and loose at the knees (figure 1). After a few minutes you may start moving. As with hand gestures, you can use your feet to support your presentation.

Every time you move on into a new section of your speech, you can mark this by making a movement.

When you want to emphasize a point, consciously move towards your audience without confronting them closely, but respecting their need for personal space. This grabs their attention.

When you invite questions, you may move slightly backwards. If you are talking to a gathering seated in a semi-circle, you should attempt to ease yourself into the center. For some people this can be really difficult the first time, but it comes quite naturally the third or fourth time. This signifies self-confidence, involvement and interest. Have a look at the following drawings and see which one is most like you:

2.7 USE OF VOICE

Volume

Most people talk too softly. Speak louder than you would if you were having a conversation with a person sitting right at the back. Speak loudly to give the impression of authority and enthusiasm. Emphasize points by increasing volume or by *decreasing* volume to get your audience to listen carefully to what you are saying. If you are one of those people who tend to speak too loudly, you should make a special effort to decrease volume.

Speaking too loudly is unpleasant for your audience as it wears them out, and in order to protect their ears they will stop listening to what you have to say. Using the volume of your voice correctly gives your presentation vigor.

Tone

A bad speaker will come across as boring and monotonous. By varying your tone, you put life into your presentation.

Speed

The majority of us have a tendency to speak too fast, especially in stressful situations such as giving presentations. Speak more slowly than you would in a normal, everyday situation. This will give your audience sufficient time to think about the message you are communicating to them. By doing this, you yourself will have the advantage of having more time to think; that will make you feel more confident, and this is beneficial both to you and to your audience.

Pauses

The pause can be one of the most effective tools you have at your disposal. You should make short pauses to dramatize or to emphasize the point you have just made—or the one that you are about to make. A reasonable pause ought to last a little longer than you feel necessary.

Breathing

Many people who have tried to give a presentation without having prepared properly know the problem of lack of air, especially during the introduction or when the situation is stressful.

Give yourself a few days to learn this simple breathing technique. Say to yourself 1, 2, 3, 4, 5 and inhale. Repeat 1, 2, 3, 4, 5, and inhale. Continue this exercise about 5 times, 3 times a day for about one week and then you will begin to have your breathing under control.

Image

Before drawing up our plan, I gave a great deal of thought to dress, its significance and what it tells us about other people. I decided to carry out an experiment:

I got one of my good friends to stand outside a major train station in the center of Copenhagen and ask people passing by for money. The first day he stood there dressed as a successful businessman in a smart suit, newly pressed shirt with an elegant silk tie, wearing well-polished shoes, carrying a fashionable and expensive attaché case. He asked for money, telling people that he had accidentally left his wallet at the office and needed some money to get home. Several business people and office workers stopped to give him money, quite considerable amounts. Several people suggested that he should take a taxi. At the end of the day, my friend had collected over 200 USD.

The next day my friend stood at the same spot with the same purpose in mind. This time he was wearing ordinary jeans and an ordinary light windcheater. Just as he had on the previous day, he asked for money, saying that he had accidentally left his wallet at work. The reaction was different on that day. People who passed by were not as generous as the day before. They suspected him of having some sort of ulterior motive. At the end of the day he had collected 40 USD.

On the third day my friend stood there dressed as a tramp. His clothes were really shabby and dirty, and he looked scruffy. He had not combed his hair or shaved. Just as he had done on the previous days, he asked for money. Very few people stopped on that day, and the money he received was far less than the other two days.

Image is sometimes misunderstood. Your image is not how you see yourself, but how others see you!

If you do arrive at a meeting or at a presentation one morning and you tear your jacket on the way there, you should start by telling people at the gathering what had happened.

The alternative is that people will find out anyway, as the participants will sit there and wonder why you are dressed so badly and why you don't want to show them any respect.

Our image should correspond to the message we would like to convey, and it should be commensurate with the intended target group. Appropriate behavior is everything. If I need to address my clients directly in a hut on a building site, I would probably not come dressed in a suit. If I am to meet the managing director of the Construction Company, I will at least make sure that I am dressed to the appropriate standard.

A good bit of advice: It is best to be slightly better dressed than normal. This is an expression of respect for your opposite number.

Not very long ago I was at a presentation in Odense. The lecturer was eloquent and entertaining and knew his subject well, but the whole time he kept "fiddling" with his clothes, straightening up his collar, adjusting his tie, hitching up his trousers and patting his jacket. This continued throughout the whole presentation, one and a half hours. Just like everyone else in the audience, I became really distracted by this, so much so that I did not take in much of what he had to say.

There is a direct connection between the words you use and your body language. Here are a few tests:

- Imagine that you are a football referee and you tell a player: "YOU ARE SENT OFF!!!!" You immediately get the urge to raise your arm.
- Put your hands behind your head and say to your husband/wife: "I love you!" Again, body language is lacking.

2.8 USE YOUR WHOLE BODY

Use your whole body. If you tell a story about getting something down from a shelf which is two meters high, you need to use your body to mime the actions made when trying to bring something down from a shelf. Don't be afraid of stepping forward towards the group, as being physically open towards them gives the impression of self-assurance.

2.9 LOOK AT YOURSELF IN THE MIRROR

Look at yourself in the mirror. Think of a presentation you gave recently to the board of directors, to investors or to staff. Try to put yourself back into that situation. Resume the posture you believe you had when you had put forward your proposals. Take a look at your shoulders. Are they tense or are they relaxed? Stiff, tense, nervous, hands on hips?

GOOD ADVICE

- Always point your feet forward. This reduces the risk of talking at the flipchart after you have written something on it. Remember to turn around.

- Don't adopt an aggressive stance. Rest your hands calmly at your side, keeping your legs a reasonable distance apart.

- Don't use your body in an uncontrolled manner. Keep your movements under control.

- Since your audience tends to imitate your body language, make sure that your movements are calm and balanced.

Through conscious body language you may produce situations which are perceived as very stressful and frustrating. Silence and physical encroachment, i.e., sitting or standing too close to your opposite number, can disrupt their equilibrium. By establishing eye contact, raising or lowering your voice and touching your opposite number, you can build their trust and make them more attentive.

How closely do you hold your arms to your upper body? Do you tend to place your arms on your hips (this can express superiority, like a "head teacher syndrome")? Look at yourself sideways on. Are your shoulders raised, or are they slouched?

In a negotiation team, unconscious gestures can mark acceptance, support, distance or tension. People who convey these signals are not aware that they are revealing themselves in this way. The speaker unconsciously turns his back on a member whom he does not like in his own delegation. He positions himself further away from him, does not give him the same support through eye contact and short nods, as he does with other participants.

He may shake his head when that person speaks. Once I

participated in a discussion when a woman in my opposite number's delegation was an observer and took down precise notes. When we commented on the requirements that had been specified, I found that she gave a satisfied nod each time our suggestions seemed acceptable and shook her head whenever they seemed superfluous. Her co-representatives commented on all the points by saying: *It is not enough; we must have more!* When this discussion was over, I asked her if she had intentionally tried to manipulate us by nodding and shaking her head. She was really taken aback by this and said that she did not send out any signals.

It is not easy to decipher another person's body language. A single gesture does not mean anything. There are countless stress signals, but all these are unique to that individual, and people use them in different ways. Not until you have come to know your opposite number and his usual pattern of communication can you benefit from being aware of his body language. People have different ways of communicating their attitudes:

Openness

Open hands, unbuttoned jacket

Defensive posture

Arms folded over the chest, crossed legs, gestures with clenched fists, gestures with index finger, karate chop

Concentration

Hands placed on face, head turned from one side, a hand put on the bridge of the nose

Suspicion

Looking away, folding the arms, increasing the distance from the opposite number and buttoning up jackets

Co-operation

Open hands, sitting forward on the chair and reducing physical distance

Stress/nervousness

Coughing, puffing noises like "puh," holding the hand in front of the mouth when talking, sweating, not looking at the person being spoken to

Frustration

Letting out short puffs, tightly clenched fists, massaging neck, aimlessly kicking with feet

NB: This is not a complete list. In many situations all these signals may be empty gestures or express completely different attitudes.

As a communicator and a negotiator, you should develop insight into this area.

Book recommendations:
- Desmond Morris: *Manwatching*
- Desmond Morris: *Gestures*

CHAPTER 3 - THE FIRST SEVEN SECONDS

Try to think about a meeting with another person who has made an impression on you over the last month. This may be a business associate, a friend, or someone completely different. How did you "read" that person? What did you experience?

It is an established fact that people read each other when they first meet, and after just seven seconds they have formed an impression and made up their minds about whether or not they wish to have more to do with that person and whether or not they want to continue talking to them. People scan one another in many ways and according to:

Sex:	Which sex? Which one is preferred?
Age:	People feel more comfortable with their own age group.
Facial expression:	How does the person look? Angry, happy, enthusiastic?
Posture:	Upright or limp? Upright posture symbolizes high self-esteem, assertive behavior.
Bodily hygiene:	Extremely important in our culture. It is very off-putting if a person does not attend to his or her personal hygiene.
Contact:	Firm or limp handshake.
Appearance:	People rely on dress, mannerisms and expressions to appraise each other's social status and

cultural identity.

Skin color: Individual assessment.

Every time we meet a new person we unconsciously appraise and prejudge that person. If the other person is untidily dressed or is untidy with his possessions, we believe that this person is untidy. If the other person is bombastic and ostentatious, we are convinced that this person is superficial.

In this life the only person who really needs changing
is a baby with a wet nappy!

Image is the picture which you project or would like to project to other people with whom you come into contact. Image has been likened to a toothpaste tube. If you see an unattractive toothpaste tube on the supermarket shelf, you are probably not going to buy it if there is another one which is colorful and attractive-looking. On the other hand, you need the packaging of the colorful toothpaste tube to correspond with its contents, or you won't be buying that brand again.

Try to think about how you present yourself to other people. How do others perceive you? Is there anything that you would like to change that you *can* change? Try to cast your mind back to a recent meeting you have had with a new person. Was there anything you would have done differently? You should always remember that a first impression always sticks in the other person's mind and that people are rarely consistent in their behavior during the first seven seconds.

3.1 Facial expression

Children are born with the ability to read other people. They know when to ask their mother or their father about something, and they know when not to ask. They know when to leave the room and when there is conflict or when their parents are having a row. They "read" people on a different wavelength than adults

Most of us can read ordinary facial expressions–happiness, sorrow, anger, disappointment–but what about all the other nuances? Try to train yourself to interpret different expressions.

Place yourself in front of a mirror and concentrate on a really sad experience, a very happy experience and a very surprising experience. Look at your eyes. When your eyes smile, your face lights up, when your eyes are sad, your whole face looks sad.

You can also try this out with your television set. Turn on your television set and turn the sound off. Sit down for half an hour and look at the presenter's facial expression. Can you "read" what is going on? A good rule of thumb: If you find the host's facial language and body language so interesting that you want to turn the sound up, it indicates that this person is skillful and his ability to inspire others is of a high standard.

CHAPTER 4 - NERVOUSNESS

According to a survey carried out by Wall Street Journal, 97 per cent of all managers are afraid of giving a presentation. How serious is this? In The Book of Lists, *fear was delineated in the following way:*

1. Public speaking 41 per cent
2. Heights 32 per cent
3. Insects 22 per cent
4. Financial loss 22 per cent
5. Deep water 22 per cent
6. Disease 19 per cent
7. Death 19 per cent

I can remember one of my first presentations on management and counselling. The Marketing Association had invited me along to make a speech in a huge conference venue.

The event was scheduled three months before it was held, and the closer it got, the more nervous I became.

I thought long and hard about why I was in the management sector and what it was that made me concentrate on courses, training and counselling, topics which require public speakers. It was just as though the managing director of the American Butchers Association was a vegetarian or as if Budweiser had a managing director who did not drink beer, or as if the British American Tobacco had a managing director who was a non-smoker.

The day arrived. I stood up and went through my two-hour presentation, shaking like a leaf. When the meeting was over, I did not have a clue about how it had been received. My presentation was being recorded on video, and when I watched it I saw a self-confident, skillful, articulate speaker who with a great deal of energy, enthusiasm and motivation projected his message, attended to questions and tackled the whole presentation with great adeptness. That speaker was me, and in no way did I come across in the recording as a bundle of nerves. There was a huge difference between the way I felt and the way I looked! Nowadays I know what the antidote is: Practice elementary ways of keeping nerves at bay and maintain a constructive stress level.

The conditions mentioned above are affected by nerves. It is natural to be nervous, and the fear of making a fool of yourself can actually improve your presentation.

Nervousness can also make you speak too fast, prevent you from pausing because pauses seem to last forever, and prevent you from emphasizing things with gestures or a varied tone of voice.

A well-known speaker once said: *"I don't know why it is called stage fright; it is usually the audience people are frightened of!"*

In our training seminars on communicative competence, since 1999 we have taken surveys of the way in which participants perceive themselves. The participants carry out 4 presentations over 2 days and are assessed in the following way:

	presentation #1	Presentation #4
Beaming with self confidence	45%	87%
Perceived self-confidence	12%	92%
Were nervous before they came on	97%	97%

Typical signs of nervousness can be:

- Voice cracking
- Wringing and stretching of hands
- Hands in pockets
- Fiddling nervously with pen, buttonhole, a piece of paper or another object.
- Shaking legs
- Gaze does not vary, or eyes focused on one person
- Dry mouth
- Trembling hands
- Agitated and uncontrolled gestures
- Rocking ones feet (men) crossing legs (women)
- Tugging at skin or flattening hair
- Clearing throat

4.1 FEAR

People who are not frightened of making mistakes learn very fast. They do not allow themselves to be inhibited by fear. A potential error does not bother them. Fear of speaking in public is a combination of a number of different factors. It is important to understand that primary fear entails making yourself vulnerable to others; on top of this there is the fear of messing things up, and when all these factors are combined, fear grows out of proportion. Your hands sweat, you cannot think clearly, you secrete adrenaline, and your throat feels tight.

This is called primal fear, and psychologically speaking it is beyond your control. It is produced by a type of stress called the fight-or-flight syndrome (see also assertive behavior) and is based on mankind's age-old survival instinct. If you met a sabre-tooth tiger in the jungle in prehistoric times, you would not have stopped to discuss the situation. To survive you would have had two choices: fight or flight.

Physiologically speaking, the fight-or-flight reaction is functioning when we secrete adrenaline which sends blood to our muscles, but nowadays the problem is that we have a greater need for our blood to flow to our brains.

The chances of you meeting a sabre-tooth tiger on the way to a presentation are very remote. It is in this way that a natural survival mechanism, which once benefited our ancestors, now limits our productivity and restricts the way in which we express ourselves, including our ability to give our best at a presentation.

Consider what you really are frightened of when you speak in public? Is it the way in which the spectators will judge you? Are you frightened of what other people may think of you? Are you frightened of messing things up or being humiliated? Are you frightened of not getting the credit for what you say?

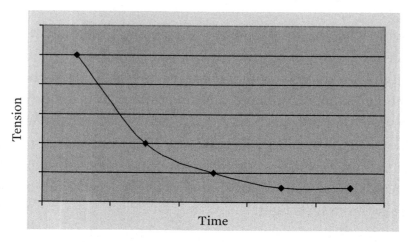

The graph illustrates tension versus time in a presentation. You are nervous when you introduce your presentation; you feel a great deal of tension, which gradually eases off as you warm up. What you are probably most frightened of is that you might dry up. Provided you are properly prepared, this won't happen. *Remember that in most cases the audience will be on your side.*

Another common cause of nervousness is the fear that you may not be competent enough. What do I do if there is someone in the audience who knows more about the subject than I do? This may well happen, but remember you are the world's greatest authority in one area—*your own personal experiences.*

None of us has exclusive rights on the way the world is perceived, and no one has a monopoly of the truth. Add facts, knowledge and details to your personal experiences and you will suddenly become the authority people are expecting.

Why not introduce your presentation with the wording *"I am aware that you know considerably more about building than me because ...."* In this way you have already signaled that you are not going to infringe upon your participants' areas of expertise.

One of the most important conclusions that have emerged in research on personal development is that people who attempt something new carry it out successfully in the vast majority of cases. In cases where satisfactory completion is not achieved, it is seen as a flop. This is due to the fact that most people's minds are set on things going badly rather than successfully; they focus their minds on fear rather than their chances of success.

For many years Wilson Kipketer, the runner, has performed some of the best athletic feats in Danish colors. What goes on in the head of someone with such talent? Is he held back by thoughts of a defeat? Or survival? Or by what people thought of his presentation? I don't think so. I think Wilson has self-confidence, but is he nervous? Quite definitely. There is no doubt that Wilson is anxious and nervous before every single start, but he has learned to focus his nervousness in a constructive way. He makes use of the adrenaline-pumping flight-or-fight tactic and channels this energy into his running.

Public speaking entails speaking while under stress. There is no easy way around it, and that is why you should learn to lose your presentation nerves and achieve an appropriate balance between composure and apprehension before your presentation. A sense of apprehension will be a great asset to you during your presentation.

4.2 PRESENTATION, NERVOUSNESS AND ANXIETY

THE 5 'BELTS'

Based on my experience going back many years in public presentations, I have categorized speakers and communicators into 5 "belt-categories."

1. White belt – the untrained person

The untrained person never holds presentations or gives speeches and tries at all costs to avoid such tasks. The very idea of giving a speech inspires a considerable degree of fear and anxiety in this type of person. Even on courses where a plenary session introduction is required he gets nervous. Often the untrained person is extremely shy.

2. Yellow belt – the casual speaker

This could be a salesperson who once in a while finds himself in a situation where he has to give a speech or a presentation. He is not overcome by fear at the thought of speaking in front of a group, but would not volunteer to do this. The casual speaker has tried to give speeches, maybe in private, on several occasions.

3. Blue belt – the experienced speaker

This speaker has just moved from the yellow belt up to level 3. He has given quite a few presentations and/or speeches with a certain amount of success. He feels he is on reasonably safe ground when he has to give a presentation, but he needs to spend a long time preparing. He does not have a grasp of the relevant techniques and does not understand the finer details of the task.

4. Green belt – the willing speaker

This speaker gives many presentations and is self-assured, capable and experienced. He is happy to volunteer when people want a speech or presentation, and his extensive experience has taught him the basic techniques necessary for giving successful presentations. He feels tension when he has to give a presentation, but he uses this tension constructively. He has a wide vocabulary and is articulate. His job is likely to be that of manager. Given motivation and experience, he can enter the next level, the black belt.

5. Black belt – the communicator

Communication here is best described as the task at hand. This speaker feels stimulated, enthusiastic and at ease when he talks. He welcomes more or less continuous and positive feedback from the audience. This is someone who is completely competent at turning flight or fight to his advantage. He is always ready and enthusiastic about introducing himself and his ideas. He knows that tenacity will be rewarded. His typical work-area will be management, but he is primarily a person who is respected as a motivator as he inspires others through his techniques.

4.3 VISUALIZATION

The creative side of our brain has difficulty distinguishing between fantasy and reality. This is why we are frightened when we see an unpleasant film or shudder at the thought of something we do not like. Scientists have found that people can increase their self-esteem by inner visualization. This enhances self-confidence and people's belief in their ability to carry out the task at hand.

*Self-confidence is built upon experiences
with success.*

Imagine that you are going to speak in front of 200 important people. These could be clients, colleagues, people from your department, or people who are important to you. First of all, start by considering how your life would be different if you were capable of successfully carrying out a presentation. Think about how much more confident you will be and about all the respect that will surround you.

Concentrate on the room where you will be holding your talk. It is actually best if you have been into that room, touched the tables, the chairs, noticed its smell, seen the lighting and absorbed the atmosphere.

Cast your mind back to a time when you had a casual chat with friends or family. See yourself as relaxed and happy. Summon up feelings of self-confidence, pride and composure. Every time you think about yourself speaking at a presentation, you must retrieve that mental image and see yourself as being calm and collected with the people you are talking to.

Visualize yourself next to the overhead projector in front of 200 people. See 200 happy, eager, appreciative faces, each of them waiting with great anticipation for what you are about to say, because you and you alone have a message that is going to interest them.

Visualize yourself starting to talk and using your first transparency. Notice this transparency between your fingers, switch on the projector and imagine beautiful graphics. Give your talk and conclude it. See your audience responding, watch them as they applaud you, and notice that warm feeling of enthusiasm rushing through your body. Now if you have made a good presentation, you must always recall it every time you give a talk. The process of creating visualized repetition practically enables you to program yourself. You have in fact carried out your first successful communication presentation.

There are four elements to visualization. Strengthening each of them will accelerate the speed with which you will achieve your main objective. The first element is **frequency**. How often do you visualize your future objective, your behavior or the task? People who achieve outstanding results continually visualize what they intend to do. They keep thinking the whole time about what they are going to achieve. They play "the film" over and over again, and by doing this they imagine the final result. The second element is **precision**. How precisely do you visualize your objective or your task?

Less successful people have a vague picture of their objectives. Your initial thoughts are likely to be vague, but as time goes on and you frequently "replay" the film, the concepts will become much clearer in your mind. Finally you will be capable of closing your eyes and seeing a clear and precise goal.

The third element is **intensity**. What degree of feelings do you combine with your mental image when you really want to achieve something? When you are enthusiastic, looking forward to reaching your goal, and believe that you will achieve it, the final result will be achieved more quickly. When the degree of feeling is identical to your mental picture, then you will achieve your result. Unsuccessful people are normally unenthusiastic and unmotivated. They are quite pessimistic, and their low energy level is low.

The fourth and final element is **period**. How long are you able to keep the picture of what you want in your mind? The longer you are able to do this, the greater your chances of success. If you have a specific picture of the thing you want, for instance a car, you should get hold of a picture of this car. Put this picture in a visible spot, where you can often look at it. I have heard quite a few people say that visualization is pure humbug, black magic or something supernatural. No, it is not really.

What is the difference between daydreaming and visualizing? Daydreams are a substitute for work. Visualization is work, hard work. For visualization to be successful, you must take care of the basics. It is important that you have prepared your speech, either all of it or some of it. You must know where and when you are going to deliver this speech. It is important that you have some idea about the audience which is going to come and listen to you.

There is a simple reason why visualization is successful. Researchers have noted that our subconscious *is not capable of distinguishing the difference between a real experience and one which you have creatively invented.* Visualization is not in itself a guarantee for success, but it does give you a visible goal.

I frequently use visualization myself. Before a seminar or a lecture, I run through the procedure 20 times. The first 20 times are inside my head. The last time is reality. This means that I have run every single course many times before it is carried into effect.

What happens if reality does not equate with your visualization?

The one thing you can be sure about is that you have done a better job than you would have done if you had not done any visualizing, and not only this, it has given you some additional training.

Do you know what it was that gave Albert Einstein the ability to discover the theory of relativity?

He told people that one of the chief reasons was his ability to visualize:

"What it would be like to ride on the end of a beam of light?"

4.4 PRINCIPLES OF VISUALIZATION

1. Make your visualization realistic. Think about a real event. Use all your senses to help you get an idea of the location, the spectators, the weather, the lighting, and well, yes, even the food.

2. Make it positive. Hear the applause. Listen to your enthusiastic audience. Notice their friendly response.

3. Do this often. Visualize often, preferably every day. The more often you try to train yourself, the better. Think of an event immediately before you go to sleep. By doing this your unconscious mind will carry on working on the project while you sleep.

4. Use visualization everywhere. People who are successful within their field visualize either consciously or unconsciously. Use visualization every day and in many different situations.

4.5 VERBALIZATION

Verbalization means expressing a purpose or a vision out loud. Standing in front of the mirror and saying *"I can do it! I can do it!"* several times over is a good way of building your self-esteem. Every time you say this consciously with self-confidence and enthusiasm, your belief in yourself will become stronger. If you watch a high jumper preparing himself for the championships, you will often see him talking to himself. Any tennis star who has just missed his opponent's serve will go around in deep dialogue with himself. A girls' handball team will stand around in a circle before the important match and have group battle cries and slogans. All this is verbalization, which enhances motivation and the objective.

4.6 CONVERSATION

Think about your presentation as if you were holding an intimate conversation with your audience—not as a performance. Think about how you speak to individuals in the group. When you concentrate on a conversation with individual members of the group, do you begin to talk in a calmer and more relaxed tone of voice? When our clients start doing this, their presentation gradually changes.

4.7 WAYS OF REDUCING NERVOUSNESS:

- • Analyze your audience
- • Research your audience
- • Prepare possible questions
- • Read through the guidelines and the work structure
- • Visualize a successful presentation
- • Prepare yourself physically and psychologically

They no longer worry about uncontrolled body language, and they move about in a natural way.

They look participants straight in the eye and avoid any audio visual aids, which they would otherwise find indispensable. Instead of focusing on fear, you should learn to see yourself being met with nods of recognition, smiles or good eye contact from the participants. Imagine your participants as being warm and appreciative and that your presentation finishes with rapturous applause.

Find a friendly face in the group, someone who is nodding and giving you a friendly smile.   React to this person's messages and reactions. Look at them often, focus on everything that is positive, send your energy in that direction and remember—do you use your smile?

Try it out. It works miracles!

There are several grades in presentation technique (you can obtain belt grades depending on how skilled you are in this area). Do not throw yourself into large and difficult presentations if you have never done one before.

Begin in a small way: Do short presentations. After that, you can move up a level. If you have tested out your presentation level and found that your standard is high, you could soon take on one that is difficult. Presentation technique, level of proficiency and nervousness are very much related to training and training alone. If you would like to increase your level of proficiency, you should set yourself targets according to the degree of difficulty you dare to embark upon.

Nerves before an important presentation will never disappear completely. You will always be nervous. It is important to handle your nerves by making the fullest possible use of them for your presentation. When you are nervous, your mind concentrates on the task at hand. There is a lot of positive energy in your nervousness, and this can be turned to constructive use when faced with an audience. If you find yourself in a situation where you are not at all nervous about your presentation tasks, I am afraid to say that you probably run a great risk of giving a bad and boring presentation.

*"Before they get up they do not have any
thoughts about what they are going to say,
when they speak they do not know what they
are saying and when they sit down they do
not know what they have said."*

—*Lloyd George*

THE AUDIENCE RECEIVES ONLY WHAT YOU GIVE THEM

Even though it does not seem like this to you, your audience does not have supernatural powers or telepathic abilities. **Always remember that:**

They cannot see through you and your papers. They cannot hear your thoughts. The audience accepts only what you give to them.

What does that really mean?

- They are not aware of your shaky legs or the butterflies in your   stomach.
- They don't know how nervous you feel.
- They don't know how you feel.
- They are not aware of the thousand and one thoughts that are racing through your head.
- They don't know what you are going to say in 30 seconds' time.
- They don't know anything except what you tell them.

CHAPTER 5 - STRUCTURE

When we talk about structure, we mean a planned approach for delivering your message. This is regardless of whether your message is intended for a small number of people or for a large audience.

This particular model has been thoroughly tried and tested at thousands of meetings, presentations and events, and we have found its basic approach to be simple and easy to understand.

When you begin to prepare your presentation, you should have one or several of the following objectives:

5.1 To INFORM

You want to give information about a process or a procedure, whether about how the new IT-system works, about what is necessary for the new campaign or on working hours in August. The purpose of a report-presentation is also to inform. Informative presentations instruct and give guidance by answering the "wh" questions: where, who, what, why as well as how. Ideally the participants should go away with the impression: "I learned something new."

5.2 To ENTERTAIN

You could be asked to give a light and entertaining speech at an office party or at a function for clients. Remember that this is not just about telling jokes. Talk about yourself in an ironic way. You will discover that the best jokes and stories are those with you as the main character. At the same time, you must be very careful not to include subjects which may offend participants, for example, religion, weight, skin color, etc.

American researchers asked a number of top managers about their reaction to a typical business presentation.

The result: Stimulating 3%, Interesting, 52.2 %, Boring 43.5 %, Unbearable 1%.

5.3 TO MOTIVATE

Anything that can encourage participation and motivation is always particularly appropriate at any presentation. As an inspiring speaker, it is not your duty to talk to your participants about their faults and shortcomings, but to direct attention to new methods.

5.4 TO PERSUADE

Persuasion may involve changing a procedure or selling an idea or a product. Persuasion involves using material that is related to fact. It is important that the speaker come across as being honest and open, someone who participates in the result in addition to being enthusiastic and confident about the new idea or product. In your discussions you may need to broach the subject of negative aspects, challenges or objectives.

A well-structured presentation contains three main parts:

- Beginning/introduction
- Middle part/main part
- Summing up/conclusion

Beginning/ introduction

A good introduction has three primary purposes:

- To give participants the chance to settle down. Participants need to listen for a few minutes before they begin to concentrate.
- To capture the attention of the participants and guide them into the subject you want to talk about.
- To create an atmosphere and tell the participants why they should listen and what the advantages are of being present.

Welcome everyone. Start with a quip if you are able to, or begin by introducing a particularly interesting point about your subject. Don't begin with a question to which you might get an unexpected answer. Do use humor, but be careful. Humor can bring life and vigor to your presentation, but with humor you can unintentionally cause offence.

Misplaced humor can ruin the whole of your presentation, no matter how fantastic your message may be. If you really need to use humor, you must make sure that it is a benign type of humor. Never exaggerate humor. One good tip is to use self-irony. Very few people will be offended if you make fun of yourself.

Introduce yourself and your company, and state your credentials. Give a clear description of what your aims are with the presentation. Let your audience know as early as possible what you are going to say.

You ought to have reminders on the topics you are including in the middle of your presentation.

It is also a good idea to mention how long your presentation is going to last, whether you are going to use any visual aids, and what handouts you are going to distribute.

Mention when you intend to answer questions and any other "rules" which may apply. If you would like to give a little more "prominence" to your introduction, you could start by making an apt remark such as:

"Last year you lost USD 2,400,000 because of bad presentations."

"Did you know that the Danes are only in the 17th place when it comes to public health?"

"Development requires change."

"Would you like to make my work twice as easy?"

"When I began this project I felt very optimistic. Now I am over the moon!"

You could tell a story related to the subject or about yourself.

You could tell a joke or an anecdote.

Speakers have used various recordings to capture people's attention at the beginning of their presentations, ranging from the sound of roaring elephants to motorway noises and light shows.

Middle part /main part

While you are talking you should use memory aids, i.e., let your audience know when you have finished one topic and are moving on to the next one. With each topic you should order your ideas in a logical sequence. It is quite appropriate to answer questions when you have reached the end of each topic.

Conclusion /summing-up

Sometimes it happens that a speaker spoils a good address by saying something like "That's it," or "I don't think there is any more!" The conclusion may be a type of summing up (though not a repetition of the whole presentation), or quite simply it may be a rounding off of the presentation. Clearly indicate that you have come to the end of your presentation and don't just let the presentation degenerate into an apologetic anticlimax. Quickly remind your audience about the points you have made. Thank them for coming along.

Other alternatives are:
- Conclude by telling a dramatic story.
- Quote something.
- Look forwards.
- Appeal to the participants.
- Obtain acceptance and commitment for further action.
- Motivate your audience.
- Just say "Thank you for letting me come along."

Introduction

The introduction is the first 2 to 5 minutes of the presentation. Use it to establish your credentials, to verify your expertise in the subject, and to give an outline of your talk. Compare your introduction to the chapter divisions in a book. This helps the reader who is in the process of building up an overview of the task at hand. We have divided the introduction in the following way:
- Presentation
- The subject

The opening sells your message to the audience, introduces the subjects, and establishes expertise.

The main part conveys the message in your presentation and gives the necessary details to your audience.

The conclusion gives you the opportunity to sum up and elicit reaction from your audience.
- Intention

- Topic classification
- Time
- Questions

5.5 PRESENTATION

The first thing is to introduce yourself. Who are you? Which company/organization do you represent and what your justification is for being there?

For example, *"Good morning, my name is Keld Ianen. I am the director of MarketWatch Management, the Management Company. MarketWatch specializes in negotiation and communication and has more than 25 years' experience behind it!"*

5.6 THE SUBJECT

Here we describe the subject of our presentation. Do this even though it is probably written on the invitation, a leaflet, or something similar.

For example, *"The subject of my talk today is the importance of communication. It also covers the way in which we can increase our profit contribution by increasing and optimizing our communicative competence!"*

5.7 INTENTION

The intention is the aim of the entire presentation. Here it is also worthwhile to consider what this will mean to the recipient. What value will this be to the recipient?

For example, *"In today's talk my intention is to help you to understand why communicative competence is essential for generating financial earnings in your branch and to show you how easy and simple it is to generate growth through communication!"*

5.8 Topic classification

Topic classification is an outline of the different areas you would like to cover on the subject. This gives your recipients an idea of the areas you are going to deal with and an indication as to when you reach certain points during your presentation.

For example, *"First I will tell you about deciphering body language; after that we will cover structured methods of conveying messages, and finally we will talk about representation systems!"*

5.9 Time

We should make it quite clear how much time we are going to spend. Your time schedule should be reasonably precise. If you say you are going to spend 20 minutes, you must definitely not spend 40 minutes; neither is it a good idea to spend 10 minutes. If you take longer than you said you were going to, your participants will often feel cheated.

For example, *"My talk today will last approximately 15 minutes!"*

5.10 Questions

Finally you should announce how you would like to deal with questions. Depending on experience, contents, presentation and aim, you can plan this strategically. If you want to have a more dialogue-oriented presentation or meeting, it may well be an advantage to invite questions during the presentation; however, if you lack experience or if you are going to talk about something that is not intended for debate, it is best that you leave your questions to the end. By specifying when the questions should be asked, you take control and have the upper hand. This means that you do not get distracted.

For example, *"I prefer questions to come last!"*

An example of an introduction could be as follows:

"Good morning, my name is Keld Ianen. I am the director of MarketWatch Management, the management company. MarketWatch specialises in negotiation and communication and has more than 25 years' experience behind it!

The subject of my talk today is the importance of communication. It also deals with the way in which we can increase our contribution margin by increasing and optimizing our communicative competence! In today's talk my aim is to help you to understand why communicative competence is essential for generating more income for your departments and show you how easy and simple it is to instigate growth by means of communication.

First I would like to talk about deciphering body language; after this we will touch on conveying messages in an organized way, and finally we will talk about representation systems! Today my talk will last approximately 15 minutes! I would prefer to leave any questions you may have to the end!"

Middle part /main part

Once you have gone through the general introduction, you should move straight on to the message—the reason why you are there.

At this exact point, it can be effective if you change your position on the floor, or move a slide, the overhead projector, the PowerPoint presentation or demonstrate that you are about to move on to another section in some other way. Essential categories have been allocated to the structure so that participants may follow the lecture or the meeting as a systematic procedure. These categories are as follows:

- History
- Present

- Future
- Presentation of problem
- Needs analysis
- Show solution
- Substantiate the payoff

History

The purpose of describing the history is to give an outline of the actual story. That is, what things were like before, or how things were done earlier. To give an example I will continue with the presentation which I made earlier.

For example. *"In this company people were not sufficiently aware, nor did they use sufficient resources to improve their employees' insight and understanding."*

Present

The present reveals the actual situation. The presentation at hand could easily be woven in with the problem presentation which comes afterwards.

"A number of leading companies have recognized that they have an overwhelming need for communication training which as yet has not been met. Now they have implemented both training programs and skills assessments for employees. Likewise, in this company, we are aware of this need, and this is why we are all here today!"

Future

This part draws a picture of the future, plans that have been initiated, items on the schedule, management decisions etc.

For example, *"After 1ˢᵗ August we have the opportunity of*

initiating an epoch-making era in our company's history! If we make a decision on this today, we can get a training program under way. This will give our most prominent project managers training in communication with a good solid program lasting just 3 days."

5.11 PRESENTATION OF PROBLEM

Outline the problem as if your participants are not aware of its magnitude or significance. Convey to everyone the actual significance of the problem. How much does it cost? Which tasks does the problem disrupt?

For example, *"The problem of not having been trained effectively in communication is that our project managers do not succeed in making an impression on people when they need to get a message across. It is evident that this affects disciplinary matters when a client, for example, complains about an assumed error with a delivery and our project managers give in. This costs our organization more than 2 per cent of our net contribution each year."*

5.12 NEEDS ANALYSIS

Needs analysis is a contemporary description of what is needed in order to solve the problem. At this stage, we are not ready to advocate or provide the solution.

For example, *"Quite clearly what is needed is communication training, which should include training to enhance the project manager's ability to decipher body language, understand human behavior, show empathy and adopt a structured approach when presenting information"*

5.13 PROVIDE THE SOLUTION

Because the presentation of the problem and the needs

analysis were previously mentioned separately, we have outlined a problem but no solution. The solution is introduced here. Hopefully we have captured a sufficient amount of attention from our participants for them to be focusing on this problem area to the full.

For example. *"The solution is the training module Communicative Competence, which stretches over 2-3 days. This product will actually counteract the main defects in communicative competence."*

5.14 DOCUMENT THE PAYOFF

The result of the solution is finally introduced and documented in the main part of your talk.

For example, *"As previously mentioned our expenditure is 2 per cent of our net contribution. This loss may be reduced to less than 0.5 per cent, when the project managers have been sufficiently trained in communication. The result of this will show at the latest 14 days after the seminars have taken place!"*

My example of a medium/main part can be as follows:

"Previously people in our company were not sufficiently aware, nor did they use sufficient resources to improve employees' understanding and insight. A number of leading companies have become aware of a serious unmet need for training in communication and, consequently they have implemented training programs and ways of assessing the skills of their staff. Likewise we are aware of this need in our company, and that is why we are gathered together today!

After 1st August, we have the opportunity of initiating an epoch-making chapter in the history of our company! Provided that we reach a decision on this today, we can set up a three-day intensive training program to qualify our key project managers in communication. The problem with project managers being insufficiently trained in communication entails that they do not have an impact on people when they need to communicate a message. This clearly affects disciplinary matters, for example, in cases where the client complains about an assumed defect in a delivery and a project manager gives in.

This costs our organization more than 2 per cent in net contribution per annum. Clearly there is a need for communication training, which would include enhancing project managers' ability to decipher body language, strengthening their ability to understand human behavior, improving their ability to empathize with people and adopt a structured approach to the presentation of information.

The solution is the training module Communicative Competence, which stretches over 2-3 days. This product will effectively remedy the primary defects within the area of communicative competence.

As previously mentioned, our expenditure is 2 per cent of our net contribution. This loss can be reduced to less than 0.5 per cent once the project managers have been sufficiently trained in communication. The results can be measured at the latest 14 days after the seminars have taken place!"

5.15 CONCLUSION /SUMMING UP

A wise man once said, "If you want to convey a message to people, you should first explain what you are about to say. Then you should say what you want to say. Finally you should repeat exactly what you have said. In this way there is some chance that people will have actually understood you!"

With this sentence in mind, you will then be able to conclude your speech and sum it up. This will be done in accordance with the following:

- Summing up

- Topic
- Intention
- Payoff
- Question
- Conclusion
- Do's and don'ts

5.16 SUMMING UP, TOPIC, INTENTION AND PAYOFF

Summarize the primary and most important points in your speech.

For example. *"Finally, let me briefly recap on what we have looked at today. We have spoken about deciphering body language, a structured approach to conveying messages and representation systems. In my speech today, my intention was to help you all to understand why communicative competence is essential for your departments so that they can generate an increase in profit and growth.*

As mentioned previously, our expenditure is 2 per cent of our net contribution. It is possible to reduce this loss to less than 0.5 per cent!"

5.17 QUESTIONS

The time has now come when you should invite questions if you have chosen to keep them to the end of your presentation. This can be done by asking an *open question* such as: *"What questions do you have for me?"* Never say *"Are there any questions?"* since some people are shy about opening up and asking questions. If there are no questions, this type of pause may seem rather embarrassing. On these occasions I sometimes say, *"In actual fact, I have often wondered why people don't train department managers? My answer to this would be...." By doing this I ask myself a question, which I also answer. Watch your audience. If they are interested, they will nod when you ask the question.*

5.18 CONCLUSION

When we conclude, we must clearly indicate that we have finished. This is done either by moving about or changing something around in an ostentatious manner. Thank everyone for their time and tell them who the next speaker is going to be.

For example. *"On this final note, I would like to thank you for your time today so I could give you my side of the story!"*

Do's and don'ts

When your meetings and presentations are of a persuasive nature (i.e., where you assert your ideas), you should never leave without having received some type of approval from your audience. I have often met people who left meetings with the impression that everything had gone perfectly and thought that their ideas had been accepted, when in reality it was the exact opposite and the proposal was outvoted by a large majority. For this reason, we should ask participants a final question *"Does everyone agree that we should commence the training course on 1ˢᵗ August?"*

My example of a conclusion /summing up could be as follows:

"Finally, let me briefly recap on what we have covered today. We have spoken about deciphering body language, structurally conveying messages, and representation systems. The intention of my speech today was to help you all to understand why communicative competence is essential for your departments, as it enables them to generate increased profit. As previously mentioned, our expenditure is 2 per cent of our net contribution. This loss can be reduced to less

than 0.5 per cent! What questions do you have for me? On this final note, I would like to thank you all very much for giving me your time today so you can look at the situation from my angle. Does everyone here agree that we should commence training on 1st August?"

Summing up of the structure

Introduction – Greet everyone, introduce yourself and say whom you represent.

- Identify the subject.
- Justify your credentials.
- Make the purpose of your presentation clear.
- Let people know how much time you are going to spend.
- Let everyone know how and when you will answer questions.

Contents - Outline the situation as it is at present.

- Outline the presentation of the problem in light of the situation.
- Sum up all problems and arguments.
- Outline the solution (ideally alternative solutions).
- Identify advantages and disadvantages of each solution.
- Demonstrate that the advantages of your solutions are that they achieve the best results.
- Briefly sum up (ideally you should repeat the topic categories).
- Repeat intentions.
- Invite questions.

Action – Involve your audience.

- Identify who does what, when, time, etc.
- Reach a final agreement and thank everyone for coming.

Structure – persuasive presentations

Since approximately 80 per cent of all communication between people is of a persuasive nature, i.e., A tries to convince B of an idea, a product or something similar, we will look into this area more deeply. When you are going to introduce a scheme which could involve the use of financial resources, or where there may be an alteration of objectives (or both), you should make an extra effort to prepare your presentation thoroughly and introduce it in a professional manner.

What is a persuasive and convincing presentation, and does it work, you may ask. One of the best examples is of course the world of advertising. If you smoke or have smoked in the past, which applies to about half the population of Denmark, you can probably remember the first of the many cigarettes that you smoked. Did it taste nice? I doubt it—quite the contrary, your body protested and told you quite plainly that it would prefer to be spared such a thing. Why did you do it? You were "The Marlboro Man" or you were taken in by an image, persuasive marketing from manufacturers who told you that it was smart to smoke.

A good persuasive presentation will correlate with the three representative systems described in communication: visual, auditory and kinesthetic. If it is cogent and contains elements of the three representative systems, it will be immensely effective and add weight to what you are saying. This type of presentation is structurally the same as an informative presentation. The difference lies in the way you process the contents while going over the presentation of problems and discussing solutions. For example, it can be an instance when you try to persuade a person or a group to accept actions, which you would like them to perform. This covers everything from selling life insurance to persuading employees about new strategies and agendas. The order of the topics should be "Structure – persuasive presentation technique."

Improvisation

It has been said that a visitor once witnessed Winston Churchill walking backwards and forwards talking to himself. The explanation was that he was preparing an improvised speech. If you have reason to believe that you will be asked to say a few words, try to prepare something beforehand. Unfortunately, the nature of surprise is such that you cannot always prepare yourself, as you may suddenly find that you are in the midst of the situation.

Here are three tips:

Firstly: With an improvised speech, no one expects pearls of wisdom or invaluable information. They will be perfectly satisfied with a little bit of friendly small talk (talking about the weather, as we call it). For this reason you can be quite vague and unspecific without suffering loss of credibility.

Secondly: You can often jog your memory by using mental images which go as far back in time as possible and after that bring the story back to the present (the structure is used in the same way as with an informative presentation). You can, for example, ask yourself when you first heard about this product/firm/subject and in what context. Can you recall anything happening after that? Where are we now? What about the future?

Thirdly: Remember to take all the time you need. At a maximum you should spend two to three minutes. On such occasions what you say is normally forgotten after a short time.

Reading a speech

The best advice we can give to those who are planning to read a speech is – don't do it. The spoken word and the written word are two completely different things. When someone reads out a speech, it sounds inauthentic and artificial. Out of habit, people speak much better on the basis of what they understand than directly from detailed and thorough notes. There can nevertheless be occasions when you need to present a document on behalf of another person. This is an incredibly difficult task, as you need to look at the audience as often as possible in order to put life into your presentation. It means that your eyes should be five to six words ahead of your voice—a very difficult technique to master. If this applies to you, you can practice by reading out loud from a book or a magazine while looking up as often as you can.

Persuasion: reasons for buying – features and benefits

The art of persuasion

Telling someone something is not the same as selling them something or persuading them about something. It is important to be aware that there is a huge difference between informing people and selling them a product, a service or an idea.

Reasons for buying:

People buy anything, including ideas, for one or several of the following reasons:

- Finance
- Durability
- Utility value
- Image/appearances
- Reliability

- Productivity
- Safety
- Security

They buy because the idea, the service or the product meets a need and gives them an advantage. No one buys products because of their features; they buy them because of their benefits. It is for this reason that when you want to sell something or introduce an idea, a product or a service, you should mention their benefits.

Features and benefits

Definition: A feature describes what things can do

A benefit describes what a feature can do *for* someone

1. Qualify

In order to avoid losing the thread of what you are saying, wandering off the subject or repeating yourself, you should make sure that you talk to the right people. Ask yourself "Who are they," "Which department do they come from," and "Do they know who I am and what my occupation is?" Do tell them that you know that they already have quite a bit of knowledge on the subject. This helps you to make contact and establish a rapport.

Remember that you will need to explain any technical details which some of your audience may not be familiar with.

2. Define needs

At least a quarter of your presentation should be confined to defining needs. So as to give yourself the chance of persuading people, you must make sure that everyone agrees on the problems or disadvantages of the situation at hand. Many ideas are lost because the speaker does not attach much importance to such matters. Before you go on to the next stage, you should ask your audience whether they accept that these problems exist.

3. Meet needs

At this point your audience will be very keen on hearing how you believe you can solve their problems. You will have built up their expectations. Tell them about your solutions. These solutions ought to be features or descriptions instead of benefits, which will come later on in the structure.

4. Mention benefits

Then explain what your solutions entail and how the company can benefit from them. Attempt to make each benefit an answer to the problems which were defined in step 2. This is often a good moment to mention expenses—not just costs, but savings. Make sure that you are prepared for objections regarding an increase in costs in your preparation.

5. Action

You are ready to recommend how it ought to happen. When all is said and done, this is the intention of your presentation. Be as positive as you can!

Interruptions

These situations can be difficult, but they can be handled in a professional manner. Never show irritation towards the person who has interrupted. Tell him or her that you will answer the question at the end or comment on the question as mentioned above.

If a member of the audience is difficult or is making a fuss, you can refer that person's points to another member of the group or to the whole group for comments. If you have good eye contact, you will already know which members of the group are amenable. You should use gentle tactics before you demand change. It may be that you will need to rebuke this person about their behavior (this is rare), and you may also need to define your limits, preferably in a positive way.

Perhaps you could have a break (even though this may appear unnatural, everyone will know why you are doing it) and see to the person who has interrupted. Acknowledge this person's enthusiasm, but say quite clearly that it really disturbs your presentation. Ask this individual to control his enthusiasm. If this person is downright rude, you may ask him to leave the room. If he is really making an awful nuisance of himself, the rest of the audience will thank you for sending him out.

This is important for you so that you may proceed with the rest of the presentation and also for your audience, who find interruptions and moaning just as frustrating as you do.

Use of Language

Anyone can make things sound complicated. A skillful speaker gets the whole of his audience to understand what is being said. Be yourself and avoid coming across as pompous. Use a short word instead of a long word if they have the same meaning. Use precise expressions instead of unclear phrasing. As a general guideline, we can say that provided we use words (not slang) which you use in everyday speech, you will do well. Don't use technical jargon without explaining it unless you are 100 per cent certain that your audience understands what it means. You have perhaps been brought up with technical expressions without realizing that they are peculiar to your occupation. It is pointless to talk if your audience does not understand what is being said.

Level of attention

In the beginning the level of attention is very high, and then it falls relatively slowly during the first 10 minutes. After that it falls abruptly until after an hour it reaches its minimum. It then increases quickly, and during the last 5 minutes it is high again. Your audience's attention will not increase towards the end unless they are informed that the end is approaching.

The main points which the audience needs to remember are placed at the beginning and at the end. With each topic, the final sentence or illustration is particularly important. Presentations lasting 25-30 minutes have the greatest effect. These receive more attention, though topics that are too short can also impair the presentation.

Be enthusiastic

Enthusiasm, involvement and empathy are key words when trying to use your demeanor to inspire your audience with enthusiasm. I believe in feelings during presentations, as these are natural. When you reveal your inner being, your real self, your audience will automatically find congruence in your demeanor, find you credible and listen to you. Find 2-3 areas in the presentation, which really inspire you. Use these actively to improve your own presentation.

Be active

Make demands on your participants. Ask them to participate in physical activity and get them to move about, ideally after lunch. Have a few quick games or challenging tasks to encourage them out of their chairs.

Tell stories

Every presentation, regardless of whether the subject is budgets, product descriptions, sales meetings or courses, will be considerably improved by stories, preferably personal stories. The purpose of your story is to help people come to grips with the subject and make it simple to understand. They also help you to relate to your audience, create rapport, and make your presentation one to be remembered. Where does the story come from? Your everyday life. Each and every day something happens in your home, at your office, in the club or in a shop, which can be converted and used as a story or an anecdote. Your own stories should contain situations that your participants can relate to, a story where the audience will say "Me too!"

8 ways of making your presentation more interesting:

- Humor
- Remarks
- Personal stories
- Examples and illustrations
- Statistics
- Graphs and graphics
- Expert opinions
- Involving the audience

Always relate your substance to your agenda

"My next theme is ...."

"The new development affects ...."

"After this comes ...."

"This leads me on to ...."

This is the way in which we change over to a new section in our presentation. The audience must know with absolute certainty that the former section has finished and that you are continuing onto a new subject area. Instead of saying "OK ..." and continuing, these suggestions are relevant.

> *Effective presentations do not just have powerful openings and main points—they have a powerful ending and cogent main points!*

CHAPTER 6 - PREPARATION

*80 per cent of your time should be spent on
preparation and layout. You should spend
only 20 per cent of your time on its actual
contents!*

Before you start, find out whether a presentation is the proper forum or whether a telephone conversation, a letter or another means of communication would produce a better result.

Bad presentations cost billons!

"The cost of a bad presentation is horrendous. When participants lose interest, important messages are lost, sales are lost, training programs go wrong, company policies are badly implemented, and productivity and efficiency are undermined."

When you deliver a bad presentation, you may well waste just one hour of your own life; however, you also waste something like one hour in the lives of, say, 45 participants—thus a total of 46 hours at USD 200, plus expenses such as transport, lost work time, room hire, and equipment. This loss can amount to more than USD 20,000 for just one hour.

Gathering information

Form your opinions on the subject and write them down on a large sheet of paper (preferably with an asymmetrical pattern, brainstorming). Note down anything that comes to mind regarding the subject you want to talk about. The advantage of an asymmetrical pattern is that it is a working method adapted to the brain's creative way of thinking. In most situations, our brains do not work in a strictly logical or systematic way.

Not preparing is the same as preparing for a mess-up.

Ask yourself questions such as:

- Who are the participants?

- How much do they already know about the subject?

- What would I like to tell them?

- How much time do I have available?

Define your goals

After that, you can reject everything that is not relevant to the notes you first prepared. Decide which headings and sub-sections you would like to use and arrange them systematically. The structure in your presentation gradually begins to take shape. Remember that you do not have time to talk about everything that you know about the subject. Include only the relevant points which can be included within the time you have available. That is very important. If you want to come across as professional, bear in mind that if you are allotted thirty minutes, you should keep to thirty minutes.

Principal points

- Why are you doing a presentation?

- What reaction would you like to have from your audience?

- What action is the audience going to take after your presentation?

The purpose should be written out so that it is clear and easy to understand, as in the examples below:

"The purpose of this presentation is to make people aware of the company's new bonus incentives" or "My aim with this presentation is to make all employees aware of customer relationships."

There is a tendency to confuse the objectives of the presentation with the objectives of the project. They are not the same. In order to understand the objectives of the project, you must ask yourself, "What will happen if the project is a success?" In order to understand the objectives of the presentation, you have to ask yourself "What happens if the presentation is a success?"

One example of the project's objective could be: "We will complete the building by 15th December at the latest." The presentation's objective could be: "To convince the board of directors of the need for extra subsidies for the building."

Preliminary plan

Here we have an example of a preliminary plan. It is based on reorganization of middle management in the company *AYZ Machines*. We are already aware that we need three meetings, and we have identified the principal ideas for the first presentation followed up by supporting information.

First meeting: Principal idea

1. Changes in the contracting market will considerably affect our income potential.

2. We will look into our organization's structure to reduce operational costs.

3. We will not reduce staff numbers.

4. Based on the proposed ideas, each department manager will present his own recommendations for cutting costs.

First meeting: supporting information (Changes in contractors...)

Principal idea no 1

- Sales figures for the last 4 years showing reduction in earnings.
- Information regarding our competitors' price structure with bargain prices and turnover.
- Market assessment carried out by market research companies, describing future prospects.

First meeting: supporting information (We will look into.....)

Principal idea no 2

- Expenses over the last 4 years, which show a constant rise
- Estimated expenses in the future, as long as existing administrative expenses are maintained
- Detailed expense factor for a department which has the greatest increase in expenses

First meeting: supporting information (We will not reduce....)

Principal idea no 3

- Departments where employees will be involved and how they will be moved
- Plans for further training of extra personnel

First meeting: supporting information (Based on the......)

Principal idea no 4

- Areas where expenses can be reduced or eliminated

- Type

Schedule for the presentation

As a result of several years' experience with professional speakers and with others giving commercial presentations, both as a participant and as a consultant, I have drawn up a *Schedule for presentation,* based on my work on negotiation techniques (see appendix A).

The schedule is a simple method for organizing your presentation, since you can see at a glance that the main themes are supported by gestures, notes, visual aids, examples, etc. This is particularly suitable for people who frequently find that they have too much information and find it difficult to be concise.

At the same time, the schedule has been organized so that the principal points in the presentation are listed. In addition to this, you can also use this schedule as a tool to develop your ideas. Do not use the schedule for the presentation itself. It is not a substitute for notes or any other kind of aid. One of my clients told me that he works best on his schedule on his way to and from his office. During this time he is capable of compiling a one-hour long presentation in less than 20 minutes. First of all, you should write out the aims of your presentation: "My aims are ...." The written objective is there as a focal point. Remember that the driving-force behind the presentation is the result. Try not to write sentences into the settings, but use only one or two words per setting.

Principal message

As there may be only 3-4 principal messages in your presentation, you can use the remaining spaces in your schedule for sub-sections.

Visual aids

This column enables you to describe which visual aids you are going to use for the occasion. Allow for only one transparency for two minutes, or at the most, ten transparencies for a 20-minute presentation.

Examples

In order to make your presentation as lifelike as possible, you should introduce actual examples from everyday life, preferably from your own. It is at this point that you can weave in anecdotes, examples and stories which you are going to use in your presentation.

Body language

Very few people are aware beforehand of the need for congruent body language throughout the communication process. Including simple, expressive mannerisms will make your messages appear even clearer to the gathering. Since approximately a third of the gathering will be visually orientated (see communication), exhibiting an expressive body language will help quite a few of the audience to understand your presentation. As we notice in other places, congruence, i.e., the correlation between verbal and non-verbal communication, is produced when body language and words convey the same meaning. In this way body language supports the spoken word.

Many well-prepared presentations have failed in their objective when the speaker has not attempted to pre-pare for the reaction of his audience.

When we ask participants what they remember about a presentation they had attended the day before, all of them seemed to say that they remember a person with cogent body language.

Notes for distribution

For some presentations, especially very technical ones, you will need to distribute notes. Perhaps you may need to distribute an actual example of the product you are talking about.

Who is your audience?

I will never forget one of my early presentations. I was working as advisory consultant for a large organization, and I had to hold two identical presentations for two different groups on increase in value and how it is generated. The first group was easy—they were keen and asked relevant questions. They were also very open and interested in what I had to say. The second group had critical comments about everything that I said; they were negative about the whole idea. By the end of the day I was absolutely shattered. Just as I stood packing my things, the department director turned up and asked "How did it go?" I answered, "It was awful! The first group was understanding and keen to listen, but the second group was churlish and unmotivated in every respect."

"I am not surprised" he answered, "They are our most difficult employees!"

"What do you mean?" I asked.

I was then told that the organization had intentionally put these people together to see whether they could acquire this particular technique. The alternative would be to dismiss this mistrustful group of participants. After careful consideration, I suggested repeating the presentation for this group. The department director accepted this, so I restructured the program for this group.

Experience had told me that the entire group of twelve were uncooperative because of individuals the rest of the group looked up to. I focused my energies on these people with the amended presentation, which emphasized self-esteem, feelings of value and their own sense of involvement. My idea bore fruit. The presentation went fantastically well with magnificent results. The experience taught me to ask questions, many questions, about the group I am is going to give a presentation to. For big events, courses and conferences, I send out questionnaires which have to be returned to me. Alternatively, I am physically present in the company and speak to representatives of the group which the presentation is geared for. I make it clear to my clients that every answer I receive will be treated with the greatest confidence.

Asking the right questions

The more you know about the situation at hand, its physical location, the client's requirements, background information and the type of audience, the greater your chances of a successful presentation.

The location

Find out about all relevant data regarding the physical location for the presentation and any contacts that you may need. This information should help to alleviate any feelings of stress and help you to deliver a top quality presentation. Being prepared for emergency situations is vital. You can never tell what might suddenly happen.

- Where is the meeting actually held?
- Who can you approach within the organization if there should be a problem?

- Where will I stay?
- Are there any participants from outside the organization?

The Program

I usually hold a pre-analysis day in consultation with one or several of the client's representatives. On that day the company clarifies its core motives, possibly situations even they themselves are not familiar with. The objectives of the pre-analysis could be:

- What are the actual objectives with the presentation?
- Are there subjects which ought to be avoided?
- Are there other speakers? Should I finish by a specific time?
- Have there been training programs in the recent past?
- Why interest in this particular program?
- What will happen if this training is not provided?

Background information

This establishes the actual tasks/problems which the client has, i.e., situations which we can relate to and thereby use in the presentation.

- What are the actual problems/challenges?
- What are the 3 biggest problems?
- Please give me 10 trade expressions.
- How were the participants informed about this program?
- Please attach the notice to attend.
- How are they expecting the program? Happy about it or ...?
- Have they volunteered to come along or have they been sent?
- Who poses the greatest problems in my group?

Participants

Knowing who the participants are going to be will help you to target your message accurately, and combined with that you minimize the chances of the group asking tricky questions.

- Please send copies of the most recent internal newsletters or other printed matter.
- Who is your main competitor?
- Compared to other organizations, what are the special qualities of your organization?

Remember that knowledge is power!
- And this comes from asking questions.

Many questions.

Some people send questionnaires out to participants beforehand in order to gain an insight into aspects such as the client's expectations and anxieties and the typical presentation environment. This information helps clarify relevant and important information when planning the presentation. Four basic questions and answers are of interest to you when you hold a presentation:

- How nervous are they about holding talks or presentations?
- Who is their typical audience?
- What is their level of previous training?
- What would they like to get out of the presentation or the course?

Those participating in the presentation or the course can benefit tremendously by having material sent to them before the presentation takes place, perhaps 1-2 weeks beforehand.

This is what we call pre-training, thus training before the presentation or the course itself. The course itself is the principal part, and we call the follow-up "post-training." Why is it an advantage to have material sent out with a view to pre-training? The participants have a chance of getting to know me and my methods and log onto my way of thinking, as well as familiarize themselves with the purpose of the presentation. All necessary information is distributed, and the motivation of the participants is heightened.

Each presentation situation is unique. The agenda varies, speakers are different, and so is the audience; the primary target group varies from one event to another. People's reactions fluctuate because of mood, attitudes and many other things. So ask questions – a lot of questions.

Based on experience, here are a few examples of presentations:

- An overview of a company
- Presentation of an offer to management
- Participation in client presentation
- Internal presentations for departments or staff groups
- Product demonstrations for clients
- Presentation of data for clients
- Welcoming suppliers and introducing company needs and requirements
- Actively participating in negotiations
- Submitting reports on projects

There are of course thousands of other examples.

Notes

Why not use a "post card"? Write the main heading in capital letters (You should be able to read these from a distance.) Under each of these headings, write two key words which will remind you of what you are going to say. Use a short introduction for each subject, one for summing up and one for your conclusion. Make sure that the order is logical. If you have prepared your ideas correctly, words will just come naturally to you. If you need quotations, these should be written on a separate card. Another good technique is "mind-mapping." Use large sheets of paper and colors. This is a slightly more difficult technique to apply because for most people it is a completely new way of thinking. We can, however, recommend this technique, as it is particularly effective once you have the hang of it.

Regardless of which method you use, you should be able to use catchwords. If you have to distribute technical drawings or specific data, you should use hand-outs.

CHAPTER 7 - TRUST

Imagine that you are a member of a football team. Neither team knows the rules or the point system, and no one knows which team is winning. During the break, the coach says to you that you should just concentrate on playing with the ball. What will that do to your motivation and trust? Nothing of course, both with regard to the coach and with regard to the task. The same also applies in the commercial world. If people do not know the goal or even whether they are winning or losing, there is a risk that all motivation and enthusiasm will be lost completely.

Imagine you are taking part in a very arduous expedition in the Amazonian rainforest. Every morning you are told how far you have to walk and what you should carry. When you ask the leader about the destination, he answers, "I am afraid I cannot tell you, it is classified information, and anyway, it does not concern you!"

There are four levels of trust-relationship which need to function in companies and between individuals:

- Relationship to clients
- Relationship to suppliers
- Vertical relationships between management and staff
- Lateral relationships between departments and divisions

In our courses on negotiation technique, we operate with a win-win concept based on foundations which presuppose confidence in each party producing an increase in value.

Research carried out with more than 25,000 negotiators in more than 1,000 negotiations shows that in traditional negotiations, distrust results in a potential increase in value being lost in more than 40 per cent of cases. Or to re-phrase this, a business with an income of one million kroner loses a potential DDK 400,000 because of lack of trust and lack of communication.

Try and imagine that you could rely on everyone.
The artisan who says he is coming on Friday actually comes on Friday. Your colleague, who promises to have the report ready for Monday, actually has the report ready for Monday. The person who says you will have the check tomorrow actually sends it.

The greatest problem for all negotiators is relying on the other party, i.e., opening up and giving information.

The fact that you prefer to do business with the people whom you like, those whom you trust and get on with rather than people who are better suited to your technical and financial needs, can appear irrational; however, it does show that your psychological needs are more important to you than your material needs and that in your own eyes, your decision to work with those whom you trust is extremely rational.

The person who endeavors to create a positive negotiation climate and openness and who wants to win his opposite number's trust aims to:

- Listen
- Answer questions
- Be open and show body language
- Express interest
- Respect opinions of his counterpart

Unfortunately, it is normal for negotiators to work with unnecessary expensive solutions. Resources go up in smoke, and neither party benefits. Not only that, defective relationships where each party shows lack of trust and openness towards the other bring about a bad negotiation climate.

Lack of openness entails that the negotiators see only what the consequences will be for themselves when they make decisions on the conditions they need to ask for or accept. They have failed to and have not tried to obtain information on what the conditions will entail for the other party.

Their decisions lead to sub-optimization. People do not make use of the opportunities that exist for rationalization, for optimal distribution of costs, and for payoffs. Do not treat the demands made by people as if they were threats. Behind these demands, you may find there are opportunities from which you can generate an increase in value if you make use of them in the correct manner. In order to find out if this is the case, you should use another technique rather than resistance. For this you should encourage productive discussion.

A study recently carried out at the University of Virginia in the United States shows that a fifth of every ten-minute conversation consists of lies. However, if you look only at participants from the educated middle class, lies are told more frequently than that: On average, with this group one in every three conversations consists of lies. It is thought that this difference has a lot to do with the fact that the better educated a person is, the wider the vocabulary.

Not only that, people in this group tend to be self-assured, which means lying comes easier to them. People with a higher level of education can more easily see the advantages of a well-placed fabrication, and that is why they are more likely to elaborate a little on the truth.

This research also shows that men in 68 per cent of cases would lie or cheat at a job interview, whereas 62 per cent of women would do the same. American psychologist Poul Ekman has studied lies for 25 years and finds that on the whole, it is easy to find out if a person is lying. Video recordings have shown that the body gives people away again and again. Only about 5 per cent of people have such a great talent for lying that they are not found out immediately. Of course there is no idiot-proof way of identifying a liar, but we do have a checklist which can be used as a guideline.

A liar may display the following types of behavior:

- Lack of eye contact
- Increased frequency in blinking
- Looks over onto his right (recourse to the creative part of the brain)
- Raises eyebrows
- Consciously smiles, but the smile does not reach the eyes
- Smile is fixed
- Eye contact more concentrated than normal
- Lips moistened
- Touching the nose
- Hand held over mouth when the person speaks
- Sweating and flushed skin
- Head movements not corresponding with verbal utterances
- Extra nodding
- Hands are either completely still or excessive gesticulation
- Fiddling with hands, a comfort gesture for the person
- Rubbing neck
- Fiddling with collar

- Rubbing ears, but absent eye contact
- Tapping feet on the floor
- Pressing legs tightly together
- Standing with weight on the instep
- Breathing more rapidly and more gasping

Speaking versus writing

Many people write a letter when they should have been physically present, and many people begin to talk when they should have written a letter. But when should we do what?

Written communication goes straight to the brain's cerebral cortex, the highly developed analytical part of the brain. Oral communication consists of emotions, impressions and energy and is therefore received in the creative part of the brain.

Written communication is one-channel communication. We satisfy only the visual sensitivities. We absorb written communication one word at a time, one line after another. Oral communication plays on several channels, visual, auditory and kinesthetic (emotions). Written communication is best suited to specifically factual information, such as data, details and other exchanges of facts. Your reading speed is approximately five times faster than your speaking speed. You can focus all of your concentration on the factual contents and not be distracted by a person's behavior.

You can read material again and again without fully understanding it or you can archive it for later use. If you want to make a real impact on people, have influence on them, have a powerful affect and persuade them, this should be done cogently with verbal communication.

Written communication is almost the opposite of oral

communication, and it rarely has the ability of convincing people, thereby changing people's attitudes and values. Approximately 80 per cent of a person's communication is thought to fall into the category of "persuasion."

This is also called action-orientated communication, which is used at presentations, sales talks, meetings and in all situations where person A wants something carried out by person B.

When a salesperson wants to sell a new type of product, he does not write a letter. He makes personal contact, and by doing this in a bona fide and sound manner that inspires confidence, he gets his messages across. Which prominent business people or politicians do you know who sound credible or come across as bone fide and able to inspire confidence?

When you meet a new person or you see someone making a statement on television, in the vast majority of cases, you will perceive that person either as having credibility or lacking credibility. We cannot impart information and communicate without inspiring confidence.

People must have confidence in our statements, their contents and their purpose. Our behavior should make them feel at ease, and they need to understand the values we represent. This is achieved when communication is congruous and backed up by enthusiasm, self-confidence and energy.

Imagine that you are at major marketing presentation. There are just over 350 people present. The first speaker is introduced and gets started. He comes forward on the stage, straightens his papers, many papers, and begins to read his speech. He looks down at his papers or down on the ground as if he is afraid that a large trapdoor is going to open and suck him down a deep hole.

He speaks with a monotonous, dull tone of voice, and he does not use body language. You look at him in surprise. He is recognized as an expert of note within direct marketing, but he does not sound like one.

Neither does he come across as being particularly sure of his material, and he really does seem unenthusiastic. It is as if he would prefer not to be there. Nevertheless, this speaker is a renowned expert within his field.

Immediately before his presentation he had exuded great charisma, self-confidence and enthusiasm when speaking to another colleague about new initiatives within the sector, but really, up on stage he has quite a soporific effect.

The next speaker is introduced. He uses beautiful large transparencies with colors and graphics. He has a powerful voice which varies in tone and exudes both empathy and self-confidence. While he talks, he goes around the stage expressing himself by using appropriate gestures. You had not expected this when you read the agenda.

He is a market analyst and an expert in market prognoses and statistics. Later on at the break you meet a new colleague, shake his hand (limp handshake), speak to him briefly and have minimal eye contact with him. Your conclusion is quite clear: He will not last two months in the company.

You do not register this consciously, but his posture, body language, and eye contact tell you a great deal. We are constantly judging each other by our utterances, statements, appearance and behavior, and we refer back to these.

CHAPTER 8 – PACING, RAPPORT AND LEAD

Think back to a time when you and another person saw completely eye to eye about something and were completely in tune with one another. This may have been a friend, a colleague, a member of your family or someone you had met by chance. Cast your mind back and work out what it was that gave rise to those feelings of absolute concord and unanimity.

Perhaps the reason for this was identical thoughts, or you had the same views on a book, a film or a play. Perhaps you did not notice this, but you are bound to have had identical breathing patterns, body language and manner of speaking. No matter what it was, the thing you experienced was something called *rapport*. This is called being "in rapport." What is rapport? Rapport is a harmonious, empathetic or sympathetic relationship or connection between two people. Rapport means identifying the ability to perceive the world as another person. In other words, it means communicating on the same channel as one's opposite number and thereby being better at communicating with that person.

8.1 YOU HAVE A CHOICE

You can consciously choose to establish rapport. The activity of establishing rapport is called *matching*.

Rapport is the ultimate tool for producing results with other people, no matter whether they are individuals or groups. The ability to establish rapport is one of the most important talents any human being can have in life. You can achieve amazing results by utilizing rapport.

Rapport can be the mediator in nonverbal communication. One word of warning: Rapport must be used in an ethical manner. Manipulating another person with dishonest or unfair motives can cause havoc. In most cases, body language is a give-away, and that is why rapport should also be used scrupulously.

To achieve rapport, you need to maintain a consistent speed when you are speaking and breathing. Notice people who agree on the subject they are discussing. These could be your colleagues standing round the coffee machine or a married couple in a restaurant.

They will either sit or stand in a more or less identical fashion. If one of them has arms crossed, it is likely that the other will be doing this too. If one of them is leaning up against a wall, it is likely that the other one will be doing the same. This is called pacing, i.e., conscious or unconscious imitation of the opposite number's total communication pattern, body language, verbal and nonverbal behavior.

By establishing rapport with another person we can create a basis for effective exchange of thoughts and ideas regardless of whether you are negotiating, giving a consultation, selling something or whether you are talking to someone who you know. There is often natural rapport between close friends or between husband and wife. They automatically complement each other. As humans, we tend to be attracted to those who are nearly identical to ourselves. How do we build up a rapport with another person? The most crucial factors are as follows:

- **Physiology, i.e., posture and movement**
- **Voice, tone, speed**
- **Language and representative system (auditory, visual, kinesthetic)**
- **Experience, common background**

- **Breathing**
- **Beliefs and values**

It is important to behave naturally, i.e., use our innate qualities when we match rapport. Each and every one of us has our own ways of sitting, standing, and reclining. We should be true to ourselves; otherwise the person who we are communicating with will perceive us as being affected and insincere.

One well-known cliché is that opposites attract each other. Just like the majority of clichés and myths, it is incorrect, but it does have a grain of truth. In your mind, who is the most appealing? Who would you like to spend time with or do business with?

People who you completely disagree with and who have completely different interests and goals? Of course not—you want to be with people who are similar to you. When people are similar, they tend to like each other. Are different people with different interests involved in the same type of club work, for instance?

The flimsy evidence about opposites attracting one another is based on the fact that two people who agree on most things can find that there is an element of excitement with their differences. Think of someone you really do like. What makes you like this person? Isn't it because this person is like you? Or is this person a prototype of how you would like to be? You perceive that person to be clever and smart. He perceives the world in this same way. Then think about someone who you do not like. You think to yourself, *what an idiot*. Does he think in the same way as you do?

8.2 PHYSIOLOGICAL MATCHING

Very often physiological rapport occurs automatically without us realizing it. Should we intentionally acquire the physiological characteristics of the other person and match them? For example:

- Adopting a similar way of standing or sitting, following suit if people lean up against a wall on one arm
- Crossing arms or not crossing arms, depending on the other person, and the same applying to legs
- Using the same gestures with arms and hands and assuming an equivalent facial expression
- Adopting the same posture
- Hands relaxed or stretched out
- Eyes—open or screwed up
- Eye movements (see section on representation systems)
- Shoulders raised or slouched

With matching you should never mirror another person exactly. Do it at a steady pace, one thing at a time. An example could be body language. Notice the tone of voice and the speed of voice. We should try to match and establish rapport early on in a dialogue in order to create a common basis for further communication. There is also the concept called "crossover matching," which means that what we do is equivalent, but not exactly the same.

If the person you are speaking to crosses his arms, you should cross your legs. If they fidget with a cup, you can click your pen, etc. A good way of establishing rapport is to have the same document, page, diagram or flip-over chart. This object creates a neutral basis and brings you closer together, as both of you are responsible for the development of the writing or the drawing on the paper or the flip-over chart.

What happens if the person you are talking to becomes aware of what you are doing? This happens very rarely and hardly at all if you follow my advice to do things at your own pace in a respectfully serious and scrupulous manner.

If the person you are communicating with is familiar with this technique, he will often be able to acknowledge your efforts and is likely to recognize your professionalism in communication as a goal for a win-win situation.

8.3 VOICE MATCHING

Physiological matching is not possible on the telephone. You cannot see each other. That is why we need to find other areas where we can identify each other. These could be:

- The volume of the voice—do we talk loudly or softly?
- Tempo—how fast do we speak?
- Tone of voice—what emotions does tone conjure up? Is your voice high pitched or low pitched?
- Phrases—what expressions does the other person use?
- Rhythm—does the voice flow, is it a steady or a jerking voice producing words in groups, and is it legato or staccato?

Avoid imitating dialects or other ways of speaking which could come across as if you were extemporizing and being amateurish.

8.4 LANGUAGE AND REPRESENTATIVE SYSTEM

You can establish a good rapport if you match the other person's representative system. In actual fact this complements the other person's way of thinking (see the chapter on representative systems).

8.5 VISUAL THINKING

People who think visually use expressions like "I can see it in front of me" and "Let us have a look at this."

8.6 AUDITORY THINKING

In the same way, these people use expressions like "I hear what you are saying" or "That sounds good."

8.7 KINESTHETIC THINKING

These people use expressions like "I feel this is going well" or "Things are running smoothly!" By matching and using equivalent expressions, you achieve rapport with the person in question.

8.8 EXPERIENCE, COMMON GROUND

If two people from the same profession meet each other, for instance two nurses or two lawyers, they will strike up a friendly conversation and build some rapport. Their situation is identical in many respects. We can consciously use the same basis to establish rapport with other people whose background we are not familiar with. If we arrive at a meeting or a presentation, there is every chance that each participant has:

- Driven through the traffic to reach the meeting.
- Had to leave the office with unfinished work.
- Been motivated in a specific way and has reasons for attending.
- A need to talk about "the weather."

If you are the chairperson, it is a good idea to make use of this common ground by saying something like, "Now you are all going to need a day to ...." You generate a type of parity with everyone present and by doing that establish rapport. Other statements may include:

- "Since we would both like to achieve a beneficial result, we prefer to have a win-win dialogue with our negotiations."

- "I believe we can reach an agreement very fast, since neither of us should lose out."

Skillful salespeople take note of the surroundings of the person they are speaking to. These may include pictures of their children, boats, or something else that is of interest to the person they are speaking to.

8.9 Breathing

Some people breath quite overtly; you can see their chest or their shoulders moving. When you have established eye contact, you can easily identify the other person's breathing pattern by looking at their shoulders. Then you can establish rapport by matching or by crossover matching, by nodding your head in accordance with their breathing.

8.10 Belief and values

The level of common values is determined by matching the effect. If you can establish that each person has the right, or a common set of values about money, honesty or friendliness, you have already created a platform for imparting other methods of rapport. Other expressions could be "We had better not waste any more time" or "We should all participate in the project." A good introduction for establishing rapport is to speak about a subject which we know will interest the other party. Create what we call a "yes stream." A "yes stream" consists of some well-chosen questions, which we know the recipient will probably say "yes" to. For example. *"Did you all travel here by car?" "Did you all receive the course book?"*

How to use rapport, pace and lead

Imagine that you are having a discussion with a rather aggressive person. He attacks you continuously and acts very angry. When you have identified this character's behavior, you can actually pace this person by mirroring his aggression (e.g., excessive use of kinesthetic words and phrases). Having done so, you now gradually tone down your use of body language and verbal expressions.

If successful, you can now lead the person into another lead channel, e.g., visual representation, and make him or her see the situation from your point of view. The previous aggression is now no longer present, nor easy to recall.

Try to think back on a situation where you were particularly agitated or very angry with another person. Recall the pictures from the tense situation and listen to the voices. Feel the anger that you reacted with. The feeling is now gone because you lead your emotions onto another channel. Try smiling at the same time. This can be very hard because your state of mind is changed immediately.

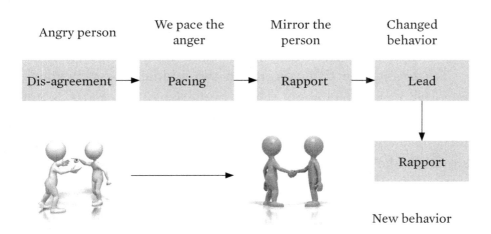

Try to test this behavior. Try to change your behavior slowly and see if the other person follows. Try to see and listen to whether they follow your behavior and adopt body language, voice speed and tone. If they don't, you need to go back to the beginning and try to establish rapport again.

You can use lead as a tool when you have a desire to influence other people's emotions, opinions, decisions and attitudes.

For instance, if a person's body language indicates a bad mood or depression you will by using this method achieve psychological and emotional harmony. After this you can again try to change your body language and express bigger joy and enthusiasm.

When to use rapport, pace and lead

You can use this technique in multiple situations:

- Conversation with your superior
- Handling of a difficult customer
- In negotiations
- When convincing others to your ideas
- Building team spirit
- Cooling down a tense situation
- Deliver bad news

Try to imagine that you are in the middle of a very tough negotiation and facing an angry counterpart. The cause is not really of any importance, but very often in negotiation feelings tend to take over. Many communication experts claim that in a situation like this, you must speak slowly and act calmly to cool down your counterpart.

But what happens? We all know the situation where being at home privately discussing with the husband or wife and the other party just remains calm. We get even more agitated and angry. We need to develop as the discussion proceeds. Therefore you need to pace the other person's body language, tone of voice and speed. When the person registers the empathy from your side, you will build rapport. For instance you could say "I know exactly how you feel; I would feel the same."

You build rapport, and hereafter you can lead the person in the direction you want, using a lower tone of voice and a more calm use of body language.

Numerous studies made on very successful people show that consciously or subconsciously, they all have a strong talent for building rapport with other people. Those who are flexible in all three areas can influence people regardless of whether these are public people, business people or "just" regular people. You will never be a natural talent or gifted with this talent from birth. All you need to master these skills is a little silent training where you measure your own success.

When do we want to break rapport?

Rapport can be put to an end where we wish to:

- End our relationships
- Get attention
- Move attention to other areas

How do we break rapport? Everything should be done opposite to the approach previously taken. Take on another body language, use another level of voice, and use conclusive words. We all know the situation where the counterpart looks at the watch or puts his or her palms to the table. Now, breaking rapport can damage the trust, so it is imperative that your mismatching actions are carried out in a calm way. **Do not break it off abruptly!**

CHAPTER 9 - REPRESENTATION SYSTEMS

Some people are better at communicating than others. This is partly due to differences in the way they perceive the world and partly because everyone has different ways of sensing the environment. When we meet another person who perceives the world in a similar way to us, we feel a certain amount of sympathy with that person.

American research scientists Richard Bandler, a gestalt therapist, and John Grinder, a linguist, established NLP (Neuro-Linguistic Programming) in 1975. Our perceptions are processed by our nervous system (the brain), via our five senses:

- Visual
- Auditory
- Kinesthetic
- Olfactory
- Gustatory

Representation systems are the processes whereby we sense the world we live in, and these can be divided into the following main categories, though numbers 1-3 are predominant:

Linguistic, language and other non-verbal communication systems through which our neural representations are coded, ordered and thereby given meaning:

- Pictures

- Emotions
- Sounds
- Taste
- Smells
- Words

Programming is the ability to discover and apply the programs we use in our neural system in order to achieve specific and desired results. People have been found and described as essentially made up of several possible representation systems: auditory (hearing), visual (sight) or kinesthetic (emotions).

The senses function as filters through which we receive information. On the whole people are aware that they utilize all representation systems, though with most people there are one or two that they tend to use more often than the others. The dominant and primary system represents the way in which we systematize our own thought-processes. For instance, if we want to recall last year's holiday in Crete and we are visually represented, we will see the waves, the sea and the hotel in front of us. This does not mean that we are not capable of recalling the smell and the sensations that we experienced when we were there; it means we are more likely to see things in front of us. If we are primarily auditory, we will hear the waves, the sea and hear sounds from the hotel. If our primary thought-process is kinesthetic, we experience the sensation of the sun and the waves, and we can possibly recall how it felt to touch things there.

*Presumption is the hallmark of the lazy
communicator*

If you are capable of identifying a person's representation system, your chances of communicating on the same wavelength and establishing a good rapport are excellent. You will be able to "speak the same language" as that person. If you need to match a whole group, you will have to use the whole breadth of representation systems in order that everyone may participate and establish a good level of communication.

9.1 IDENTIFICATION OF PRIMARY REPRESENTATION SYSTEM

If you can identify a person's primary preference, you can match it and establish rapport. Typical characteristics which indicate their favorite representation system are as follows:

9.1.1 VISUAL (V)

People who primarily use visual methods normally sit very upright and tend to blink fast and look up slightly. They speak fast, their breathing is shallow, and their voices are high-pitched. They tend to sit forward in their chairs, and the overall impression they give is that of being organized. When they visualize, they see pictures and often have difficulty remembering verbal instructions. They express themselves by using visual phrases such as "Can you see what I mean?" These people are interested in how things look, and they often think in pictures. People in this group normally think fast and are quick when it comes to making decisions. They base their decisions on how things look. Visual people will use expressions such as:

- I can see it in front of me.
- I see what you mean.
- Now I see the light.
- See you later!

9.1.2 Auditory (a)

Auditory people look to one side when they think. They breathe from the center of their chests, with rapid puffs. They speak in a tone of voice lower than visual people. They like music and talking on the telephone. Very often they tilt their heads sideways when they speak. They remember things in sequence. Auditory people like hearing feedback in conversations. Their hands are often folded, and they sit hunched up with drooping shoulders. They generally think in sounds, stressing words and sentences. When they listen, they often tilt their heads sideways. Auditory people often make decisions based on whether the suggestion sounds good, whether things have been explained well, or whether people have been listening to them. Their language includes phrases such as "That sounds OK!"

Generally these people are good listeners. They use expressions such as:

- Listen.
- Speak louder.
- Could I have a word with you?
- That rings a bell!
- Sounds great to me.

9.1.3 Kinesthetic (k)

Kinesthetic people draw deep breaths, really deep ones. You can usually see their stomachs moving up and down when they are breathing. Their sentences are often complex and contain a lot of detail. During conversations and when in thought, they often look downward, slightly to the left. They say things like, "That feels right!" Their vocal pitch is deep, and they speak slowly with a tone of voice that is low. Their shoulders hang down, and their posture tends to be good. They talk slowly, pausing a lot of the time.

People who are kinesthetic like to try things out for themselves. For them, it is not enough to have something demonstrated or to be told something! Kinesthetic people make decisions by weighing up the pros and the cons. It is important for them that the decision feels right.

These profiles mentioned above illustrate stereotypes. Even people with strong preferences do not need to match all the points, but gradually, as you train yourself to recognize these traits, you will be able to recognize each type and character quite clearly.

Kinesthetic people use expressions such as:
- I have a strange feeling.
- I feel you are right.
- I feel disorientated here.
- I love it here.
- That film was sensational.
- Let's just stick to the point.

Typical phrases and sentences

Following are typical sentences from different preferences. Listen carefully and see which type it is:

"You can hear him think."

"He wound me up."

"I cannot focus on the problem."

"Everything was blacked out."

"She always sees the bright side of things."

"She sounded really angry."

"I must look ahead."

"I have put it behind me."

"The way you go about things ...."

"I don't feel there is any need to be hard on him."

"She lit up at the thought."

"There is something in what he says."

"I don't care for that tone."

Examples of choice of words dependent upon representation system

Visual	Auditory	Kinesthetic
See	Hear	Feel
Look	Listen	Touch
Perform	Harmony	Letting go
Show	Tune in	Catches
Reveal	A bell sounds	Make contact
Obviously	Loud	Hard
Clouded	Deaf	Numb
Performance	Questions	Sacrifice
Depict	Accent	Active
Perception	Alarm	Gentle
Aspect	Articulate	Soft
Picture	Observation	Sloppy
Look	Narrate	Carry
Notice	Roar	Shock
Consider	Jarring	Established
Dream	Discuss	Grope
Colors	Subdue (sound)	Permanent
Focus	Declare	Fish
Evident	Audible	Seize
Inspect	Interview	Hold
Clarity	Converse (verb)	Cold
Light	Oral	Dark

What is your primary representation system?

Which primary representation system predominates most with

you?   Do the test below, and you will gain an insight into which one matches the way you are. For each statement, write 3 next to the sentence that is most true of you. Write 2 next to the sentence that is the second most true of you and then 1 next to the sentence that is the least true of you. Do the same with all 6 statements.

1. I think this is important:

a. being surrounded by pleasant music in my home

b. feeling the texture of the rug on my sofa

c. the colors on my sitting room wall

2. It is easy for me:

a. to adjust the volume of my television

b. to choose nice material for my sofa

c. to choose the right colors for my wall

3. In meetings the things that have greatest influence on me are:

a. a person's tone of voice

b. understanding other people's ideas and their way of thinking

c. my ability to perceive the other person's true feelings

4. The thing that brings the best out of me is:

a. my choice of clothes

b. my emotions

c. my tone of voice

5. Important decisions are based on:

a. my impressions

b. solutions that sound best

c. solutions that I think are best

6 When I think about a holiday that I have had, I mainly think of:

a. the sight of beautiful countryside and seashore

b. the sounds

c. that wonderful sensation of freedom and holidays

Visual			Auditory			Kinesthetic	
No.	Point		No.	Point		No.	Point
1C			1A			1B	
2C			2A			2B	
3B			3A			3C	
4A			4C			4B	
5C			5A			5B	
6A			6B			6C	
Total			**Total**			**Total**	

(This test is not necessarily a conclusive description of your primary representation system).

9.2 How rapport, pace and lead are used

Imagine that you are having a discussion with a particularly aggressive person. He constantly hurls abuse at you, and he is very angry. Once you have identified this person's behavior, you can pace by reflecting his anger (e.g., by using many kinesthetic words and phrases). After that you can defuse the situation by moderating your use of body language and verbal expressions.

If you can then lead this person over into another lead channel, for example visual, to see the situation from your side, his or her aggression is no longer possible. Just try to cast your mind back to a situation when you yourself were extremely annoyed or very angry with another person. Try to remember images from that situation and recall the sound of voices. Pay attention to the way in which you reacted to your feelings of anger. Those feelings are now disappearing because you are leading over into another channel. Try to smile at the same time. The whole thing becomes impossible, and your state of mind changes immediately.

Try to modify your behavior slowly and see if the other person responds. Does this other person adopt a similar pattern of behavior and imitate your body language, your talking speed and tone of voice, etc.? If this does not happen, you should revert to ordinary pacing and try to re-establish rapport. You can use leading to influence other people's emotions, opinions, decisions and attitudes.

For example, if you feel that the other person's body language indicates depression or a bad mood, you can achieve a psychological and emotional bond by matching (pace). When you have done that you can gradually modify your body language so you display greater vitality and contentment.

9.2.2 WHY LEARN ABOUT REPRESENTATIONS AND STRATEGIES?

Strategies used in a person's representation system provide a link to their mental activity, their view of the world, and produce an effective tool for establishing rapport. When we analyze a person's strategy, we gradually encourage him to display the behavior pattern he uses. We can then "reflect" it back to him, without of course him being consciously aware of it. This function is a type of "slow duplication," and the way in which we do this is by asking a number of questions relevant to the strategies we would like to find out about.

The questions are designed in such a way that the person expresses himself through his representative systems: pictures (visual), words (auditory) or emotions (kinesthetic).

Let us have a look at the example below:

If you are in the process of selling your house and are negotiating with Jesper Ianen, it is appropriate for you to know Jesper Ianen's strategy when purchasing property. Don't forget that purchasing property is a behavior pattern just like all other behavior patterns, no different from having a bath or going for a run. Everything that we embark upon in life can be broken down into smaller units, courses of action and habits. A strategy is like a formula. Once you know Jesper Ianen's formula for purchasing property, you establish rapport. Knowing the strategy is the same as having a detailed road map of the other person's thinking behavior in a specific sphere.

If you know Jesper Ianen's formula for the purchase of property you will know the correct combination for "releasing the lock." Do everything in the correct sequence, in the right order, and "open, sesame." There are a number of questions you should ask to get representative answers. The questions given here as examples are in no way key questions and may easily be elaborated upon, processed and adapted to any given situation.

"Can you tell me about a time when you bought a house and were extremely satisfied and enthusiastic about the purchase?"

What you are doing here is bringing Jesper Ianen back to the time when he experienced rapport within a given framework. On this occasion, it will be the purchase of property. Jesper Ianen will cast his mind back and recall a specific event when he purchased a house and the purchase proved to be beneficial. Perhaps it was the time he spent in that house, perhaps it was the improvements he made to that house, perhaps it was something totally different—it does not really matter.   The important thing is to re-produce one of the three possible processes he uses. These are as follows:

- A visual process
- An auditory process
- A kinesthetic process

Regardless of which one he chooses, he will re-produce the situation that gave him a pleasant purchasing experience. He will tell us about this experience in several ways. Firstly, he will tell us about this verbally, and at the same time his physiological behavior will demonstrate that he has retrieved this experience from his memory.

If you ask someone about a perfect birthday present, an important love affair or the loss of a parent, you will have no trouble detecting whether that person has retrieved the memory. His body language will change, his eyes will change expression, and even his breathing may change.   Sometimes this will be very obvious; at other times it will not be so easy to spot. However, something does happen each time.

You have now asked Jesper Ianen the question: "Can you tell me about a time when you bought a house and you were really satisfied and enthusiastic about the purchase?"

It is very likely that Jesper's answer will relate to a specific event and he might say: "Of course, it was the house I bought with my wife and two boys!"

Once he has given an affirmative answer to question number one, you are ready to move on to question number two.

"Jesper, can you tell me what made you decide to buy that house in the first instance?"

1. Was it something you saw? Or

2. Was it something you heard? Or

3. Was there something that moved you—the atmosphere perhaps?

If you word your questions in a representation-specific way, the answers you receive will give you an insight into Jesper Ianen's initial steps when purchasing property.

"Hmmmm, I know this **sounds** funny," he says "but I think the house **rang** a bell with me because it **sounded** so lively. From the moment we entered the property, we could hear the wind in the trees in the garden and the birds **singing,** and it reminded me so much of the place where I grew up."

You now know what Jesper Ianen's initial steps are with his purchasing strategy. His initial strategy involves sound or hearing, so it is auditory. When he wants to buy a house that will be his first criterion.

On to the second step.

"Jesper, after you heard the wind and the birds, what was the next thing you noticed that made you eager to buy that property?"

1. "Was it something you saw? Or

2. Was something you heard? Or

3. Was it something that moved you? Did the house have a certain atmosphere?""Do you mean after the sounds outside?"

"I mean just that!"

"Hmmmm, I am not quite sure ..... Oh yes, it was the **feeling** I picked up when listing to these things. As I mentioned, it was similar to my childhood home. **I felt safe... The sense of security** was fantastic."

Jesper Ianen has now revealed his second strategy - feelings. So we find he uses a kinesthetic strategy. Up until now, we know that Jesper's reactions are based firstly on auditory strategies (a), secondly on kinaesthetic strategies (k).

A K

The next step is simply a repetition of the first two.

"Jesper, after you heard the wind in the trees and felt a sense of security, what was the next thing you remember which pleased you and made you eager to buy the house?"

1. "Was it something you saw?" Or

2. "Was it something you heard?" Or

3. "Was it something that moved you or did the house have a certain atmosphere?"

"It is funny that you should ask me, because it is a while since I have **seen** the old place."

Now you have all the information you need. He looks up to the left to access images he remembers and speaks visually.

"It is a long time since I have seen such a beautiful sunset as the one I saw in the sitting room. It was out of this world."

Jesper's third strategic component is of course visual. His overall strategy looks like this: **A K V**

This little formula is pure magic. It is a combination that opens the door to Jesper Ianen's purchasing strategy. Remember one important thing. This strategy you have found out about applies only to Jesper Ianen's purchasing strategy for property. Each human being is unique, so what applies to Jesper does not necessarily apply to anyone else. What should I use this for, you may well ask? This knowledge is to enable you to establish rapport, so once you have done that you will find it easy to influence Jesper into buying your property.

9.2.3 USING ,THE STRATEGY

As children we love having stories told to us. My six year-old daughter has a goodnight story read to her every evening. It may be Peter Pan or Emil from Lønneberg or something completely different. She has heard the same stories over and over again, but that does not matter because she loves listening to them, even though she knows how they are going to end and their contents.

She knows that Peter Pan can cope with everything, that Captain Claw does not win in the end, and that Emil does not fall off the board. Psychologists have known for years that stories are a powerful tool for instigating change in people. We all tell stories because we all need to. We use stories to convey certain messages. We tell them constantly, sometimes we do not realize that we are doing it. You probably say: "I once knew someone who....." or "Once, a long time ago...." or "I heard that ...."

Using Jesper's strategy the opposite way round is a natural method in this communication process. It works because it is based on long-established thought patterns. Your conscious mind does not register this; however, the subconscious mind, which registers all words and their meaning, has unrestricted access to these principles. We respond to stories because they ring a bell in our unconscious mind. Once we master this new medium of communication we have a particularly potent tool for negotiation, persuasion, influence, agreement and rapport.

We establish rapport with another person by using their strategy within the same framework but in a different context. In the situation with Jesper Ianen, I will show him the house which interests him, knowing well that his strategy was A – K – V. I will discuss the subject of property with him, and I will use stories to reciprocate his experiences when purchasing property.

"Well, Jesper, do you like it? Isn't it nice? When I first saw this property it was as if I could hear the hustle and bustle that belonged to the past. It was just as if I had actually been here a long time ago. It is funny that a house can give you a feeling like this. I sensed that the people who had lived here were warm-hearted, and I was certain that their property was excellent value for the money. If you look at it in this way, you are bound to see what I mean."

By this time I had not only used the strategies, but I had also obeyed the basic rules necessary for rapport. People like those who are similar to themselves. Jesper trusts me and I have risen in his estimation a thousandfold. I am like him. I remind him of himself.

I am simply using Jesper's purchasing strategy A – K– V: first, auditory representation, then kinesthetic representation, and finally visual representation.

Often once is not enough when applying this strategy. You may be in a situation whereby it is a good idea to tell another story. Here is an alternative:

"Do you know what, Jesper, when I came here first, I found some old wood that was used for building a long time ago. You could make this wood produce a fantastic sound. When I knocked the wood into position, it went really well with the area round the house. You know, this is what bothers me about modern houses. They do not make them like they did in the past. It seems to be a lost art. When you look at something as beautiful as this, you can really see it from the perspective of the past."

When should you use rapport, pacing and leading?

You can use these techniques in many situations:

- **When talking to a manager**

- **Handling a difficult customer**
- **In negotiation situations**
- **Convincing other people of your ideas**
- **Building team spirit**
- **Defusing a difficult situation**
- **Giving bad news**

Imagine that you are negotiating with a very difficult and angry person. The cause of the trouble is irrelevant, but in many important conversations, emotions can take over to a degree that is less than constructive. Many communication experts claim that in this type of situation, you should speak calmly and slowly in order to appease the other person. But what happens? We are all familiar with the situation when we are discussing things at home, and the other person is not taking it very seriously, so we get even more worked up. But you should not lean back in your chair with your arms folded either. What you need to do is to pace the other person's body language, tone of voice and talking speed. Once the other person has registered the feelings of empathy coming from you, rapport will be established.

For example, "I know exactly what you mean," or "I would feel the same."

You establish rapport with that person, and gradually you direct him so that he lowers his tone of voice and his body language calms down. Countless studies of successful people show that they consciously or unconsciously have a great talent for establishing rapport with other people. People who are flexible in all three of these areas can have influence on a lot of people, regardless of whether these are public figures or business people and regardless of background. You don't need to be born with a natural talent. If you are determined to use your eyes and your ears, you will be able to initiate rapport very quickly.

What do we do when we want to break the rapport?

Rapport can be broken in situations where we want to:

- **End relationships**
- **Gain attention**
- **Move interest in another direction**

How do we break rapport? Do the opposite to when you are establishing it. Adopt a different posture to indicate the conclusion of a topic, a meeting or a conversation. We all know situations where the other person looks at his watch or places his hands on the edge of the table. The rules of mismatching apply again, and these must take place at a steady speed. You should not break rapport suddenly.

9.3 Eye movement

From the above description of preferences, you already know that eye movement is important when people are expressing themselves. If you notice which direction the eyes move when you ask someone a question, you can pinpoint which category they come under. When you begin to understand these movements, you can then ascertain the "truth" more easily than when you concentrate on their verbal behavior. The eyes represent a person's primary representation system, and it is therefore impossible for them to change with time.

Meaning

If you ask someone to think about the texture of a piece of material and they look downwards and to the right, this will typically be someone whose thought-process is kinesthetic. Those whose thought-processes are visual tend to look upwards, and those in whom they are auditory tend to look sideways. Since eye movements differ according to whether a person remembers or creates pictures, sounds or sensations, they are a great help when it comes to identifying untruths or "fabricated" information.

Visually fabricated

This person constructs a picture of something that he has not seen before. He actually invents it inside his head. In this case the person looks up and to the right. You can ask a question such as: "How would your car look if it were blue?" Conversely, it would be congruous for a visual person to create ideas by looking to the left.

Visually remembered

This person evokes a mental image of something he has seen before. He looks directly and up to the left. To see this, you can ask a question such as "Can you remember what your first sweetheart looked like?"

Auditorily fabricated

These people can create sounds which they have never heard before. You can ask these people: "What would your boss sound like if she had a voice like Bruce Springsteen?" This sort of person looks directly to the right.

Auditorily remembered

This type of person will *remember* a sound, i.e., he actually has heard it before. You can ask him "What did the lion's roar sound like in the zoo?" This type of person looks directly to the left.

Kinesthetic

This type of person uses his sense of touch to register. You can ask this type of person a question such as: "What does it feel like to touch a wet dog?" or "Imagine that you are lying on a soft sandy beach right now!"

Train yourself

Try this out on innocent people in the next few days to see whether you can interpret their signals. After that you can 'test' the validity of their statements. By focusing on representation systems, you will be able to make an instant assessment of whether or not the individual in question is telling the truth. You will not be able to evaluate another person's utterances from a single conversation, but will make a general assessment of the complexity of their overall communication. Is there congruity between verbal utterances and body language? Are their actions consistent? Our prototype for eye movements fits incredibly well with approximately 90 per cent of right-handed people, but don't forget that these are generalizations.

Most people sweat when they are lying. This is actually how lie detectors work by measuring changes in the skin's moisture.

Neuro-linguistic programming belongs in a world of its own and requires independent and integrated education and training, but the actual tools associated with neuro-linguistic programming are there to use as instruments to consolidate and add momentum when we are out there communicating and negotiating. Whenever I have run training courses on proficiency in communicative competence, their success has been tremendous. You can also implement these techniques directly and use them to improve your own style.

CHAPTER 10 - ASSERTIVE BEHAVIOR

Assertion is about personal strength, impact and the ability to assert your rights without infringing on the rights of others. When talking about assertion, we refer to three behavior patterns: assertive, submissive and aggressive.

Assertion means:

- expressing one's needs, preferences and emotions without threatening or punishing others
- acting without undue fear or anxiety
- acting without infringing upon the rights of others
- direct, honest communication between individuals who treat each other as equals and take responsibility for themselves

Assertive signals can be:

- Reciprocal eye contact
- Nodding while the other person is speaking
- Sending out clear listening signals
- No barrier mannerisms
- Smiling—also with the eyes
- Mannerisms which emphasize verbal utterances

Submission means:

- difficulty in maintaining personal rights
- voluntarily renouncing responsibility for oneself

- inviting persecution by taking on the role of victim or martyr

Submissive signals may be:
- Arms folded as a barrier or hugging yourself (drawing)
- Nervous laughter
- Swallowing noises
- Swinging the body
- Reduced eye contact
- Rubbing hands or fiddling with hair
- Sitting hunched up
- Hands in pockets
- Smiling a lot

Aggression means:
- Establishing one's own rights while also infringing upon those of others
- Doing things at the expense of others by running them down or humiliating them
- manipulation, which includes pretense, persecution or subtle forms of revenge

Aggressive signals may be:
- Staring
- Pointing with finger
- Lips pressed together
- Leaning over another person's desk
- Screwed up eyes
- Clenched fists

- Looking away
- Folded arms
- Upright posture
- Hands behind head

With negotiation techniques, we talk about aggressive behavior as being identical to the fighting negotiator, submissive behavior as being identical to the accommodating negotiator, and assertive behavior as being identical to the partnership negotiator.

> *"No one can make you feel insignificant,*
> *without your consent."*
> —*Eleanor Roosevelt*

The opposite of assertive behavior is passive behavior, in which people hide themselves. This represents inner feelings of powerlessness. People hide behind their own feelings; in the same way as aggression, this comes from insecurity. Assertion is about personal development. The purpose of activities and theories in relation to development is to build self-awareness, to teach you assertive communication techniques and teach you how to use them when you find it difficult to behave in an assertive manner. Recognizing that you are not assertive enough is the first step along the way. People who are not honest about their submissive or aggressive behavior have fewer chances of developing. In order to develop, you need to confront yourself and ask yourself questions like "How do you think you show respect for another person?"

As with any other acquired knowledge, you should not immediately start to use your new skills in order to solve large conflicts. Begin in a small way and continuously train yourself to develop expertise. Developing assertiveness skills requires both continuous training—and continuous re-training. It is also a good idea to go on a special assertion training course.

10.1 ASSERTIVE BODY LANGUAGE

Breathing

Breathe calmly. If you are nervous about some situation or other, relax by doing deep breathing exercises: Breathe in through your nose while counting to five and breathe out through your mouth while counting to five. This will help you to acquire a calmer breathing pattern and will make you less nervous.

Clothes and accessories

Your clothes should be pleasant and appropriate to the climate, your surroundings and the occasion. Your clothes reflect you and are a sign of respect for those around you.

Eye contact

Maintain direct eye contact without gazing or staring. Look "outwards" towards others instead of "inwards" towards yourself the whole time. Eye contact helps you to listen and concentrate. It also gives the other person the impression that he is being listened to and valued.

Facial expression

Your facial expression should match what you say and feel. If you are angry, look angry and don't smile; if you are happy, smile, relax your mouth and your jaws.

Hand movements

Use hand movements to be expressive, but not distracting. Be open with your hands. Avoid sitting and fiddling with something or giving way to irritating habits such as biting nails, tapping the table or covering your mouth with your hands.

Personal space

Think about your distance from other people. It should be appropriate to the situation and your relationship with the other person. Distance should feel comfortable; respect the other person's space. If the other person's height makes you feel awkward, suggest you sit down to talk.

Examples of assertive communication

A = Assertive person R = Respondent

By using this skill, you can make yourself heard. If the person you are talking to avoids the subject in an attempt to make you give up your proposals or alter your demands, stick to your subject. People often use this tactic when they want to make another person do something against their will.

EXAMPLE:

A: "I would like you to tidy up those papers that have been lying around the photocopier for almost 8 days."

R: "I don't have time at the moment."

A: "I know that that you are busy, but it is important that the papers are removed now and I would like you to start doing it immediately!"

R: "Can't you wait a few days?"

A: "I know it looks as if next week would be better, but we must have the filing done immediately, and I would like this job to be done first!"

Clearly and precisely

Make your messages clear; do not beat about the bush. Be direct, but polite. You must never assume that the other person will know what you think if you just drop hints. Don't make excuses; do not come out with pretexts or irrelevant replies. Superfluous chatter indicates that you are shy or embarrassed. Do not say "Do you remember that we did some work for you last month? I was wondering whether you received our invoice."

Compare this with the correct assertive way of saying the same thing.

EXAMPLE:

A: "We sent you an invoice on 7th May, payable within 30 days. This money was due last week, but we have not received payment. We would appreciate it if you could pay this in as quickly as possible."

Intuition

Listen to the other person, what he has to say about the situation, and any problems, feelings or opinions. In this way he will be aware that you are listening to him and making decisions about what is important for him. This will stimulate rapport between you.

EXAMPLE:

A: "I would like you to pay the invoice within 8 days!"

R: "I am afraid that we have problems with our administrative system, so the payment may be delayed."

A: "I can see that it gives you problems, but this invoice should have been paid a week ago, and I would very much appreciate it if you could organize payment within 8 days.

Admit to your shortcomings

If you admit your shortcomings, you will be able to handle criticism, and you may be able to cope with disapproval if you think the other person is in the right. The value of this is that you disarm the other person by acknowledging some of what he says without embarking on a discussion about your weaknesses."

EXAMPLE:

R: "Your office looks like a rubbish heap. It is an absolute mess."

A: "Yes, at the moment I feel as if I am in a mess."

R: "You were impossible at the departmental meeting yesterday. What came over you?"

A: "Yes, perhaps I was a little bit difficult. I don't know what came over me."

Use the first person singular (I form)

Using the first person singular shows that you are strong in an assertive way and take responsibility for your actions, your opinions and your methods. It could be that you find it difficult to break the old tradition of using one of the other personal pronouns (for example, *one* or *you*). Using anything other than the first person singular is a way of disguising your thoughts or feelings. With assertive speech, there is no option; the only pronoun that should be used is the first person singular.

EXAMPLES:

A: "I am furious" instead of "You make me furious."

A: "I agree" instead of "You are right."

A: "I do not agree with you" instead of "You are mistaken."

A: "I find it difficult to make up my mind" instead of "It is difficult to decide in those sort of situations, isn't it?"

Assertive listening

Indicate that you are listening by acknowledging the speaker's opinions and feelings both verbally and non-verbally with nods, smiles, shaking head and direct eye contact. Ask relevant questions to clarify what is being said or to elicit more information.

EXAMPLES:

A: "What happened then is......"

A: "What you say is..............."

A: "Well, yes, quite..............."

Negative assertion

The advantage of this skill is to be able to experience negative sides of yourself and accept them without feeling like a victim of the situation. Relevant criticisms can be put to constructive use. Using criticism constructively also shows the person criticizing you that you are thinking about what he has said.

EXAMPLES:

R: "I thought your presentation could have been better."

A: "Yes, you are right there. When I had almost finished I realized that I had not defined my objectives correctly."

R: "You have not been particularly thorough lately."

A: "No, I know that things have not been done properly. I am sorry about that. I will work on this area in the future."

Negative questions

If someone criticizes you, confront that person in order to get him to clarify exactly why he is angry, or dissatisfied with what you have said or done. These are called negative questions, because you have to ask a question which may produce a negative answer. In this way you have the opportunity to save a situation, change your behavior, or create a platform for a better relationship.

EXAMPLES:

A: "You look angry. Is it about something I have said?"

A: "Please, can you tell me why I did not get a pay rise?"

A: "Can you tell me why I was not called for an interview?"

A: "You do not look happy. Are you angry with me?"

Offer to change

When you have accepted constructive criticism, you can offer to change your behavior or your work. This skill is often used with negative questions and negative assertions.

A: "I thought your presentation was too long" (constructive criticism).

A: "I agree with you" (negative assertion). "I will go through it again and cut it down to half the time" (offer change).

A: "You look angry. Has it got anything to do with my presentation today?"

R: "I was not satisfied with your performance. The audience

had lost the thread before you reached the main points, and these were important clients."

A: "I am well aware that it did not go well" (negative assertion). "I will go through the presentation again and see whether I can change anything" (offer change).

Planning results

Set yourself a goal. That is the first thing you need to do, and it is significant when it comes to mastering the techniques you will need to work on in order to achieve your goal. Who are you going to talk to? When? How? If you do not know what the result is going to be, no one will understand your message, no matter how well it is presented. Set yourself both an ideal goal and one which is realistic. At the same time, you must decide on an NBA (next best alternative), one that you are willing to accept.

EXAMPLE:

You would like to have a holiday in August even though the company has asked everyone to take their holidays in July. For you the ideal would be to have three weeks off in August, but in reality you are prepared to cut it down to two. As the NBA, you are willing to pay for the last week.

Positive approach

You can take control of a situation by using positive words to affirm your rights.

- Address yourself positively before embarking on a difficult talk. For example, say out loud to yourself: "I have the right to...," and then enumerate whatever rights are applicable to that problem. For instance, you can tell yourself about your personal qualities: "I am loyal, intelligent, and professional." Do this often.

- Use emphatic words. Instead of saying "I could...," say "I can..." Instead of phrases such as "I don't have anything against this," say "I don't want to." Don't use words such as "only," "just," "perhaps," or "possibly". Avoid using expressions such as "It is definitely not very important, but...," "I will just ...," or "It is only...:"

Positive questions

Positive questions are the opposite of negative questions. Ask questions to find out why people are pleased about something you have done. This is particularly important when people have praised you. Do not fail to ask the other person to tell you exactly what it was that you did well. This is an investment in the future, and it can help you to enhance your own qualities.

EXAMPLE:

R: "This is the best presentation you have done for a long time. Well done!"

A: "Thank you! That makes me very happy. Can you tell me why you think it is good, so I will know next time?"

Assertive questions

Ask precise questions to get specific information and solve problems.

EXAMPLES:

R: "You have a problem with your behavior." (Is there genuine criticism behind this reproof?)

A: "What do you mean precisely by "a problem with my attitude"?

R: "I am still not satisfied with the result."

A: "Have you any suggestions for how I can make it better?"

R: "I cannot accept your offer. It is too high."

A: "What is acceptable to you?"

Request change in behavior

Ask the other person to change his behavior if he has done something that upsets you. This skill is often used to give constructive criticism or to reconcile yourself with reproof.

EXAMPLES:

A: "I am angry with you for not giving me that message from Mr. Nielsen this morning.

"From now on I would like you to write messages down rather than relying on your memory" (constructive criticism with suggestion of change of behavior).

A: "Please don't tell me off in front of the customer."

Respect other people

Appreciate other people. When you criticize someone, reject someone's request or say "no," you should show them that you are not attacking them personally; you are saying something specific about the way they are acting or the proposal that they are suggesting, but not themselves.

EXAMPLES:

R: "Shall we go out to eat after work?"

A: "I don't feel like eating out this evening, but why don't we have a chat some other time after work?" (You are rejecting the proposal, but showing that you would like to meet this person some other time.)

A: "I am pleased that you have been so quick in getting the hang of everything, but I find it a nuisance that you arrive late. Can you do your best to be here by 8:30 a.m.?" (Respect followed by constructive criticism and request for change)

Self-awareness

Modesty and arrogance are not good strategies, but often it is not enough just to give positive feedback. You should tell other people about their qualities, abilities and achievements; otherwise they might never know that they exist. This can be done at staff meetings, interviews and when working on projects.

EXAMPLES:

A: "Last year I was elected as best salesperson in the company."

A: "I am fast, efficient, and I know how to motivate myself!"

A: "I am fast and accurate with Word and learn new programs quickly."

Reveal yourself

Acknowledge your feelings and express them. It is important to use the "I" form.

If you find it difficult to use assertive forms such as "No" or to ask another person for constructive criticism, it is a sign that your assertive potential is being blocked by emotion. If you acknowledge and express your emotions, being direct will come more easily to you. This provides an outlet for unpleasant feelings and will help you to open up. At the same time, the person you are speaking to can see that you are human. This can be used in hundreds of situations.

EXAMPLES:

A: "I don't like to ask you this, but please can you give me back the money you borrowed from me last week?" (Say how you feel when you ask someone.)

A: "It makes me angry when you pick holes in my work. I would like to know what is good and what is bad." (Say how the other person's behavior is affecting you.)

A: "I feel pressurized when asked to participate in three meetings a week. I would actually prefer to go to just one." (Say how the request or the expectation affects you before you say "No.")

A: "I am surprised that it takes so long to complete the presentation. What is the problem?" (Express your feelings towards the other person's behavior before you try to find a solution.)

A: "I am pleased that you have decided to work here." (Express your positive feelings.)

Find out for yourself how assertive you are. On the next page you can do a test to find out your own level of assertion.

10.1.2 SELF-ASSESSMENT QUESTIONNAIRE FOR ASSERTION EVALUATION.

When you are assertive

Put a ring round the statement that applies to you in the following situations.

1. You are at a meeting, and some people ask your opinion

on a controversial question that is very important to you. Would you:

　　a. Openly say what you feel?

　　b. Prefer to discuss it after the meeting?

　　c. Before you give your opinion on the subject, say to everyone that they will probably not agree?

2. You are with a colleague at a restaurant and find that your soup is cold. Would you:

　　a. Act as if nothing was wrong in order to be polite?

　　b. Refuse to pay the bill?

　　c. Ask them to give you another bowl of soup?

3. You are thinking about applying for a job at a place where a friend has just left. Would you:

　　a. Go to the boss and show him where your talents lie?

　　b. Ask the boss to see you so you can tell him that you are interested?

　　c. Wait for the job to be advertised and apply through the usual channels?

4. When you communicate with managers at a higher level, do you usually:

　　a. Agree with them as often as possible?

　　b. Insist that they take your expert knowledge into consideration?

　　c. Discuss with them and come to an agreement, regardless of the nature of the question?

5. A member of your staff asks to go early once again because of domestic problems. Would you:

a. Sympathize with him and let him go, even though there is an urgent job to be done?

b. Explain that even though you do understand his position, you really need him to be present, especially in situations where everyone is needed?

c. Refuse and say that it has happened too often, and at this precise moment there is a lot to do?

6. A computer salesperson is being supercilious and thinks you lack specific technical skills. Would you:

a. Tell him what your grades were at school and ask to speak to his boss instead?

b. Let him carry on without saying anything, but buy from somewhere else?

c. Interrupt the salesperson and say that you know many customers do not understand but ...?

7. A colleague shouts at you. Would you:

a. Say that you can see and hear that he is angry and you would like to know why?

b. Wait until he has calmed down?

c. Make it quite clear that he understands how you feel and shout back?

8. You have to give someone notice. Would you:

a. Explain the financial situation and reasons for handing him his notice?

b. Apologize, explain the reasons why, and ask what he thinks and feels about the situation?

c. Give this person a written message and avoid all discussions on the subject?

9. A friend does not listen to what you say. Would you:

a. Stop talking?

b. Talk louder to get more attention?

c. Say to him that it seems that his thoughts are somewhere else?

10. You would like to take an extra week's leave before the holiday year is over, but you have a lot of work to do. Would you:

a. Introduce a proposal for a new work routine with your holiday request?

b. Express clearly your right to a holiday?

c. Say that you are prepared to cancel your holiday if it is necessary?

11. You are offered a job that interests you, but the salary is lower than you expected. Would you:

a. Accept it and be pleased that they chose you?

b. Explain that you thought that the job would be worth more and remind them of what you could contribute?

c. Say "No, thank you" and tell them that it is completely unacceptable?

12. You want to buy several new PCs, but the salesperson will not give you a discount. Would you:

a. Understand the situation and accept the price they offer?

b. Say that even though it is not a big order, there will be quite a few other orders in the future?

c. Say that if you do not have a discount, you will not accept the order?

13. You feel uneasy because you do not have sufficient knowledge about a particular project. Would you:

a. Find an expert and ask for help?

b. Behave as if there were nothing wrong and try?

c. Ask why you have been given the assignment?

14. A supplier invoices you twice for a cheap product. Would you:

a. Decide to pay, as you know what their administrative system is like from past experience?

b. Write to them attaching all necessary information and request a quick solution?

c. Ring them up immediately and tell them how inefficient they are and threaten not to give them any more orders?

15. An assignment which you have delegated is returned with errors. Would you:

a. Say what is wrong and ask for it to be re-done?

b. Not say anything and correct it yourself?

c. Point out the areas you think are good and those that need to be changed?

Score

SUBMISSIVE

Question no:	COMPLIANT	ASSERTIVE	AGGRESSIVE
1	B	C	A
2	A	C	B
3	C	B	A
4	A	C	B
5	A	B	C
6	B	C	A
7	B	A	C
8	B	A	C
9	A	C	B
10	C	A	B
11	A	B	C
12	A	C	B
13	B	A	C
14	A	B	C
15	B	C	A
TOTAL	**160**		

Calculating your score

Put a ring round the answer you have selected for each question. Add up the rings in the three columns and write down the total at the bottom.

10.2 STRESS

Stress affects us in three main ways: It influences our intellect, our physical condition, and our emotions.

Physiologically speaking, submissive and aggressive behaviors are contingent upon stress. Imagine our ancestors, the tough Vikings. Our little Viking friend Thorleif runs through the massive forest on his way back to the homestead. He turns round a corner into a glade, and suddenly in front of him is his worst enemy, Gunhild. What options does Thorleif have now? He can run away or he can fight (submissive or aggressive behavior respectively). Assertive behavior would be deadly for Thorleif! He could not possibly start discussing his basic rights with Gunhild.

Nowadays, in our modern society, our reactions in everyday business life are based on stress. Whenever we are involved in negotiations, a certain amount of stress is always present, and it affects us all to some extent. Listen to what your body is telling you. It sends out clear warning signals. Since all its resources are mobilized for physical activity, your pulse will become more rapid, you will breathe more heavily, you will start to sweat, and your muscles will become tense. At that point you really should take a break. When stress situations affect you emotionally and you feel uncertain, your ability to act rationally is limited. In many conversations, you find that you do not have sufficient information to base your decisions on. You try to use fight or flight as a response to threats, uncertainty and stress. There is no way of remedying this since these feelings come from deep inside you. Your ability to assess a situation is affected by your emotions. If you find yourself in a situation where you feel uncertain or you are threatened or stressed, your rational thought-processes short-circuit, and your response takes on the form of an emotional reaction, which is fight or flight.

You are sitting and waiting for some material that a member of staff has promised you. He has forgotten his promise, and when you remind him his reply is: "Sorry about that. I forgot about you. I can do it for next week." You get angry and answer:

"Don't bother. I will manage without your help."

ASSERTIVE BEHAVIOR

Even though you have adequate time, instead of waiting, you make a quick decision. If your decision proves later to be erroneous and expensive, who, other than members of your staff, will get the blame for this? Your ability to assess the situation is being affected by your emotions. If you end up in a situation where you feel uncertain, threatened or stressed, your reasoning process short-circuits, and you respond with an emotional reaction, i.e., either fight or flight.

Typical signs of physiological stress in body language are:

- Facial tension, raised eyebrows, eyes wide open
- Movements clumsy, mechanical and nervous
- Clenched fists, hands in pockets, on hips or behind back
- Shoulders raised because of muscle tension, and signs of frustration visible
- Stammer, cough, pausing sounds

With our communicative analysis we can measure the effect of stress, i.e., produce identification of the person's behavior under stress and outline a measurable stress threshold at which the person will not work constructively due to the effect of stress. Personally I cannot give answers for how to de-stress. My experience is that we all have different approaches when it comes to the way in which we reduce our stress levels.

Differences and similarities

Look at these three shapes.

What do you see? If I asked you to describe the relationship between these three shapes, you could answer in several different ways.

You could say they are rectangles. You could say that they have four sides. You could say that two of them are upright and one lies flat.

If you gave one of these answers, you are a matcher.

If, on the other hand, you say that all these figures are different from each other, that they do not look like each other, you are a mismatcher.

A matcher looks for similarities, and a mismatcher looks for differences. It is known that mismatchers make up approximately 35 per cent of all people. How is this? Is it of any significance if one person belongs to one category and another person belongs to the other?

Imagine a working relationship between a matcher and a mismatcher. Find out which preference a person has by asking him or her to describe the relationships between objects and situations. Whatever the result is, it does not imply that working together is out of the question, but it is important to define the individual's fundamental characteristics.

Creative brainstorming should be carried out by matchers. They find similarities, opportunities and ideas, whereas mismatchers should work on the practical areas once the creative work has been completed.

The mismatcher will be able to ask critical questions about the actual tasks and problems.

CHAPTER 11 - EMOTIONS AND MOTIVATION

*"Amongst like-minded people, coming sec-
ond is the same as being a loser."*
—*Jeff Kennett, Australian politician*

Success may easily have more to do with motivation, commitment and perseverance than talent.

Don't let perfection ruin things that are good!

The surest way of ruining communication is to try and be perfect. A wise man once said: "Making mistakes is a human right!" We will never be perfect, and attempting to be so will come across as affected. Time and time again I have witnessed occasions when a mistake aroused the sympathies of the person being spoken to or the audience at a presentation. Now, of course we should not start making deliberate mistakes in order to win sympathy. That is just as dangerous as perfection.

One presentation that I attended about one year ago started disastrously. One of my friends was to introduce a new marketing plan for a large organization. For a long time he had not been given the opportunity to display his abilities, and management had obviously given him less important roles within the organization. The event at which he was to hold his presentation was an all-day kick-off. As there were internal incentives for the sales department, a number of other presentations were given before it was my friend's turn. When the time came for him to give his presentation, he got up and walked slowly over to the platform.

On the way he tripped over a chair leg and fell down with a mighty crash. He got up undaunted, brushed himself down, smiled and went up onto the platform and said:

"It is such a long time since I have had the opportunity to make a presentation to the group executive that I am slightly nervous!"

The whole room broke out into convulsive laughter, and he won the most enthusiastic applause of the whole evening. During the rest of his presentation, the audience was at ease and listened attentively. Out of personal curiosity, I asked a representative selection of the audience afterwards which presentation they thought was best, and eight out of ten people mentioned my friend's presentation!

The quality of your life is the quality of your communication.

People buy with their emotions and justify the purchase with facts!

A few years ago, when I was the managing director of a Scandinavian IT listed company, one of my colleagues came to me with a CV delivered by someone who was waiting in reception. We were not looking for extra staff at that time, but I quickly skimmed through the CV. It was a good one, but in no way out of the ordinary. I thought that since this man had taken the trouble to come along in person, I would go and tell him myself that unfortunately there were no vacancies; however, during the first thirty seconds while I was shaking Erik's hand, I learned more about him than I could from reading his CV. We continued our conversation for another hour, and not long after that our organization took him on.

Personal appearance, emotions and behavior mean much more than words on a piece of paper. Erik was aware that he was selling himself, his talents, his personality, his expertise and his trust.

Cast your mind back to five important decisions in your life: further education, buying a house, purchasing a car, your first job, your partner. These decisions are vital and crucial ones to make in life. Were they based mainly on factual information or on emotions? The answer is a simple one. Before you made your mind up, did you find a piece of paper and write down all the advantages and disadvantages of each of them in relation to your conclusion? Only a minority of people take steps to help themselves make rational decisions. This is why decisions are often irrational and thus based on emotion.

Foote, Cone and Belding Involvement table:

Humor

When communicating humor can be used in a number of different ways. First and foremost, we should establish that in the context of presentations, humor can be an invaluable weapon when it is used correctly. It is also possible to use humor as a veil to prevent the other person from noticing specific traits of the dialogue, such as aggression, or to avoid conflict. People also use humor to conceal their true feelings. The schoolboy who makes jokes about his own weight probably uses humor to pre-empt teasing from other children.

When a person arrives at a meeting late and the boss says "I am glad you could come," you should watch out, as this type of humor conceals a serious remark. Every so often I meet a person who comes out with "That is just a joke!" Equally often I realize that what he said was more than "just a joke." Listen to humor and make a mental note of whether it is straightforward or whether there is more to it than meets the eye.

Defensive attitude

No one likes it very much if they are criticized or attacked for their ideas and attitudes. If someone comes up to you and says "You are wrong. Your idea is no good," like most people you will be upset, hurt or defensive. We react by putting up barriers, leaning forward on our chairs and arguing in favor of what we think. The conversation quickly becomes emotional. Try to remember that the attack by this other person is probably based on your *ideas,* not on you. There is nothing to stop you from replying and going into greater detail. So pause a little, and you will then be able to respond to the criticism in a far more constructive manner.

Assume the third position

Try to focus on another person from an "outsider's" point of view. Be an objective third party. Have you noticed how hard it is to solve a bitter conflict with another person when you are in the middle of it? Also, have you noticed how easy it is to see solutions, opportunities and openings in a conflict situation when you are just an observer rather than a participant?

Adopting an empathetic approach, showing people that you empathize with them establishes good communication since it involves listening to people in an effective and sympathetic manner. In empathic communication, it is important to put our own feelings and attitudes on hold. Difficult, isn't it?

What is empathy? What it means and why it is important

Most of us know what ordinary empathy is: identifying and understanding the situation, feelings and motives of another person. Empathy is a powerful tool for establishing rapport with another person. Imagine that Ian says "I submitted this bid in order to increase the company's profit, but the boss was not interested. He said it was inappropriate."

As an empathizing listener, you may answer, "You sound

frustrated because the boss rejected your idea." Ian will definitely agree with you on this. Unfortunately, Ian thinks of himself as a victim, and his relationship with his boss has not improved—quite the opposite. Your answer indicates empathy.

However, it has also backed up Ian's negative opinion of his boss and has led him to see his boss's reaction as the cause of his frustration. You have made his feelings of rejection and bitterness worse. This is as wrong as it is unproductive. Let us look at this story more closely. Ian is blaming his boss for his feelings of frustration, but his boss's behavior is not the cause of his frustration. Ian's way of thinking was the cause of his frustration. Our thoughts create our feelings; other people's reactions don't. We can see this by altering the example.

Imagine that the "report on optimal growth for the company" was produced by Erik, who gave it to Ian and asked him to give the report to the boss. When Ian's boss received the report, his attitude was equally negative. But this time Ian thinks that if the boss accepts the report, it will mean a whole lot of extra work for him without any definite payoff. On this occasion Ian is relieved when the boss rejects the report. The boss's reaction was identical. So it was not the boss's behavior that made Ian feel the way he did. It was the way Ian took it and Jen's interpretation of it as being good or bad. The way in which Ian thinks is up to Ian. He probably does not realize that he has this option. It is important to understand how we evaluate things as being good or bad.

Psychologists have recently found that when we are forming our first impressions, we unconsciously evaluate and categorize everything as being good or bad. We are not conscious of doing this. Many of these immediate evaluations are wrong. To confirm this evaluation, our judgment controls our senses, our ears and eyes. If our subconscious on one occasion evaluates something as being "bad," our senses will select data to support only this judgment, and that is why we will not see other sides to the question. This is how our negative feelings lead us into unnecessary conflicts with others and ruin our relationships.

Let us see how true empathy works if we use it with the example of Ian. When he says "I submitted this bid in order to increase the company's profits, but the boss was not interested. He said it was inappropriate" you could perhaps answer:

"Are you frustrated because you would like to have your ideas recognized and heard?" Ian's mental energy is no longer focused on blaming his boss. It is rather geared towards finding out whether being recognized and heard is what he would like. In this process he discovers what he would really like, which leads to his brain automatically coming up with suggestions for ways of achieving this. True empathy involves looking for the other person's aspirations, rather than supporting that person's negative beliefs. When we ask a person to explain what he would like to achieve, he will change his way of thinking, so his mind will turn to aspirations and away from accusatory thoughts. This is an effective step.

Normal conversations often support only negative aspects and accusations, whereas empathy supports positive options. This makes a world of difference.

What is charisma?

We all know people who we consider charismatic types, but what is charisma? Some people say that it is authority; others think it is the ability to communicate effectively. Some people think it is about sex appeal; others believe that is a kind of electrical discharge! Charismatic people are those who are at ease with themselves. They seem to exude self-confidence; their goals, objectives and their sense of direction seem to radiate from them. Throughout life they make their presence felt in the world. Who do you know who is charismatic? Here are a few names:

- Bill Clinton, ex-president
- Oprah Winfrey
- Sean Connery

To find out whether you have charisma, you should ask yourself a few questions:

What do you believe in? Have you a clear mission and a goal in life? Do you radiate vitality and optimism? Do people recognize you as a role model? Are you sure of yourself? Are you balanced? Are your behavior and demeanor natural? Do you maintain eye contact?

Charismatic people are actually hard to pin down and define, but when you meet someone who radiates charisma, there is no doubt about it. They are usually composed, sure of themselves, and have the ability to listen attentively; their posture is good, they are energetic and their eye contact is distinct. In order to optimize or create charismatic features, you need to consider the way you walk.

Walk in a calm and elegant manner. When you walk, be careful not to shuffle along, but acquire instead an elegant and graceful carriage and posture. It seems that charismatic people are never "stony faced." They have friendly faces, and their facial expressions always adapt to the situation at hand. They always dress in an appropriate manner, and their clothes always suit them. Some 90 per cent of our clients express surprise when they see videos of themselves in simulated negotiation or presentation situations. They often say "I thought I was more self-assured." Ask your friends and family or your colleagues who are closest to you to give you an honest answer to the question, "How do I come across to other people?"

The thing we define as "personal chemistry" in negotiation technique also plays a part in the parameters of interpersonal communication and perception. You go into a room and see a man standing to the right of the table. Within seven seconds, you have formed an impression of this man which has led you to decide whether you would like to talk to him more or whether you find him unattractive and boring.

Focus your energy

We can't help noticing it when we attend a meeting or a presentation and the person in the chair is lively and vivacious. This focused energy comes across as being positive, almost magnetic. It is clear that this person is keen on what he is doing. People who radiate positive energy are involved with their audience or the participants at their meeting, and they believe in what they are saying. Because they believe in what they are saying, you also believe in what they are saying. Cast your mind back to when you were studying. Which teachers can you remember? It will definitely be the teacher who radiated the most energy, enthusiasm and who was also keen on teaching, as opposed to the teacher who, in spite of being very correct, was trivial and boring and chanted his message in a monotonous tone of voice. Proficient communicators use energy, a great amount of energy, and they are driven by it. Who is the best at capturing people's attention and communicating? My daughter Nadine, aged six! Just like other children, she could not care less what other people think of her. She demands attention and a response, here and now. A child's linguistic resources and reserves of energy make him or her an effective communicator. They cry, they scratch, they jump up and down, they gesticulate and shout out what they want.

Positive energy

How can you generate positive energy when you need it before an important presentation or speech? Consult yourself and ask yourself: "What am I thinking about?" Am I focusing on positive things such as 'This is a fantastic opportunity...,' 'I know what I am going to say because...' or 'They have asked me to come to the meeting because...'? In the realms of psychology, this is called the Pygmalion effect, or self-fulfilling prophecy. The Pygmalion effect is named after the legendary Cypriot king who fell in love with the statue which he himself had made. People know that their chances of success are considerably higher if they think positively before a meeting rather than negatively when faced with the same situation. Negative thoughts may be something like. "Hell! This is not going very well, I will get the sack ...," or "Gosh, what if I forget all this right in the middle of my presentation?"

After having given presentations to hundreds of clients, training establishments and companies who have responded with enthusiasm and delight, I still sometimes get stage fright or suddenly think. "What if they do not like me...?"

Before everything gets under way, I convert all negative thoughts into positive ones by switching my mind over to the positive feedback which I have received in the past, or I turn my thoughts to my book and all those hours spent in preparation before the course. For me this is guaranteed to help! After four days' intensive training in negotiation techniques, I am exhausted. Even so, it happens that the course lasts an extra day or that I have to attend an important negotiation or meeting which cannot be changed to another date. In order to focus my energy, I try to "elevate" myself. Before the meeting or the presentation gets started, I press my hands firmly together and close my eyes for about 30 to 40 seconds. By doing this I make myself secrete adrenalin, which I can put to constructive use. Alternatively you can move about: Go for a quick walk before you arrive at the event, get your blood circulation going, and rouse activity in your body. Walk upright with a straight back and elevate yourself.

Affect meter

Affect is a psychological expression which describes emotions, mood and temperament. An affect meter is a visual representation of our psyche and our temperament. If the meter registers 100 per cent, it means you are really keen, enthusiastic and sympathetic. The affect meter oscillates according to how much energy there is in your emotional make-up.

No matter whether you think you can or you think you can't, you are definitely right.

From the time a child is born to when it is two years old, the affect meter is 100 per cent; thus emotional energy is at its maximum. Children have no qualms about expressing themselves. From the ages of two to twelve, the meter gradually oscillates towards the left as the child adapts to the socialization process. From thirteen to nineteen, the teenage years, the meter is "down."

A teenager avoids emotional situations and confrontations. The individual has low self-esteem and a poor self-image for representing his emotions. After that, the meter moves back to about 60 per cent; however, we can learn how to increase the meter reading to make it return to its original position. I have come across people whose affect meter registers absolute zero, right at the bottom.

It appears that they are not capable of raising an eyebrow,

and there is nothing in their chemistry to suggest even a trace of enthusiasm or dynamism. This characteristic has nothing to do with knowledge, intellect or talent; it simply means that awareness in this area has been overlooked or is lacking; however people can be trained in this so they develop and register change on their affect meter. Most people who see themselves on a video take deep sighs and express surprise and horror that it is themselves that they see. For them there is a genuine desire and yearning to come across as being more enthusiastic and genuinely keen; however, changing an inborn habit is difficult.

Motivation

How do we motivate ourselves and other people? Motivation is more than just a few words of praise. It is a basic ability to acquire techniques which need to be adhered to in order produce a favorable response from others as well as a personal sense of achievement. In order to optimize your presentation before an important meeting, it is appropriate to enhance your sense of motivation.

How do we activate our most outstanding senses and enhance our psychological strengths? Many psychologists find that fear is our greatest motivator. We are frightened of losing a friend—what if we do not find a new one? We are frightened of relying on a new job—what if we are fired? We are frightened of starting our own company—what if we go bankrupt? Fear is based upon our instinctive desire to avoid pain, death, loss and similar things. In order to neutralize fear and motivate yourself, you should draw up a list which contains the following:

Write everything down about the situation that you are most scared of. After that, write out the first points about what might happen if the thing you are most frightened of actually occurs. In this way you have named the potential risks and their consequences.

Example:

"What is the greatest risk in leaving your job and becoming independent?"

"During the first three months, I won't get any assignments."

"What happens if you do not get any assignments during the first three months?"

"I will be short of a certain amount of money per month for expenses."

By using this method you will get to grips with your fear. At the very least, you will come to understand exactly what you are frightened of.

Belief in excellence

In order to be motivated, we should believe in what we do, what we say and the way we act. It is no good trying to convince ourselves or other people of a false premise. Your belief must be genuine, real and based on genuine assertions. What is belief? Belief is well-defined, well-organized access to filtering communication with ourselves.

Dr. Benjamin Bloom of the University of Chicago has studied 100 extraordinarily successful young athletes, musicians and students. He was surprised to find that these people did not show a high degree of excellence in the early stages. Instead, most of them received a great deal of attention, guidance and support, and they started to develop after that. The belief that they could make something of themselves preceded some of their other talents. Regardless of pastimes or the area of work which we are involved with, we must remember that people are the greatest resource!

Successful people all display a basic belief in and respect for others. In order to obtain results, we need to be capable of recognizing, learning and looking at other people. For their book *In Search of Excellence,* the American management gurus Thomas J. Peters and Robert H.Watermann researched the basic features that are characteristic of successful organizations. This research found that the common denominator was a declared belief in people as individuals, combined with a considerable ability to concentrate.

REMEMBER:

> *The best weapon against fear is knowledge.*

In our endeavor to nurture our motivation, we must work with things we like. Work should be a game. Do you know anyone who has achieved fantastic results by doing something that they hate? I don't. It is all about combining our interests with what we do and what we like. Pablo Picasso said *"When I work, I relax. When I am not doing anything, or have guests, I am tired!"*

"If you want to be powerful, you must look powerful": True words with modifications. Physiology is a vital element in our attempts to change our behavior. If you make yourself physiologically dynamic and vivacious, your psychological demeanor will follow suit. Physiology and internal representation systems are very much linked to one another. If you alter one of them, you will immediately alter the other. Do you remember a time when you were completely "down"? How did you see the world? Were you psychologically tired and exhausted? Did your muscles ache?

Certainly you experience the world very differently when you are in high spirits and on top of everything. Physiological manipulation is a powerful tool for controlling your state of mind. When you are at low physical ebb, your state of mind is the same. When you are physiologically on the top, your state of mind is the same. You cannot have a physiological state without having a corresponding psychological state. There are two ways of changing your state of mind. The first one is to alter your physiological state. The second one is to change your inner representation system.

If you begin to get tired, it is noticeable because your shoulders start to droop and your muscles feel tired. Your nervous system tells you that you are tired. If you change your physiology to something that makes you strong, you inner representation system will respond by doing the equivalent. If you continue to tell yourself that you are tired, you send an internal message that you are tired, and your body reacts in accordance. Think of a task in front of you which you probably have had difficulty in getting down to or getting to grips with. When people say that they cannot do something specific, I say to them, "Try and pretend to do it!" If the person does not know how to do it, I say "Pretend you know how to do it!"

Think about something you find difficult to do, but which you would like to do. If you knew how to do this, how would you stand or sit? How would you walk? What would your breathing be like? You put yourself in the appropriate physiological situation which you would adopt if you knew what to do. Allow your whole body to tell you. Notice how your mental state has changed between what it was like before and what it is like now. If you have adopted the appropriate physiological state, you will "feel" that you can manage what you thought you could not manage before.

The same applies to our clients before they go up onto the platform for the first time in front of 10-15 people. If they have adopted the appropriate attitude, their confidence will have been built up, and mentally they will be prepared. The combination of their internal representation system and appropriate physiology has made them feel self-assured. This means that they can go "to the chair" feeling very self-confident and produce a professional result. If, on the other hand, someone starts to panic at the last minute, it means that their internal representation system has changed, and they visualize the worst possible scenario. As a result this person is physically overcome by fear, and he "freezes." All his muscles seize up, and there are a lot of other physiological reactions.

CHAPTER 12 - ASKING QUESTIONS

I was once at a conference in Copenhagen when the speaker asked, "Are there any questions?" One of the participants raised his hand and said, "I have doubts about the actual contents of your presentation." The speaker immediately answered, "This question is about the gentleman's wish to discuss the validity of my facts."

The answer which the speaker gave was incredibly humiliating, and what was otherwise a successful presentation developed into a real conflict situation between two losers. How should the speaker have answered the question?

> *"The question is about the source of my*
> *data, which is ...."*

The problem in that situation was that the speaker felt personally criticized by the man asking the question. He felt he was being attacked in the situation, and his response was aggressive. Every day conferences, seminars, courses and meetings take place by their thousands, and included in these events there will usually be a round of questions. Very often the conclusion is the most informative part, as it provides participants with an opportunity to explore the content from their own standpoint.

As I have mentioned previously, the technique of asking questions, and preferably plenty of them, is one of the most important techniques in communication. When we ask relevant questions, we do it primarily to uncover areas that are not clear to us; however, we also ask questions to show that we are interested in what our conversation partner is talking about. Without questions, communication would become non-existent. As I have pointed out in the section on *Presentation,* questions are crucial in presentations so that the speaker can clarify points and make sure that everyone has understood what he was speaking about. But how do you ask the right questions? Well, good questions are related to the ability to listen and to listen properly.

12.1 TYPES OF QUESTION

We are going to look at four different techniques for asking questions: open, closed, leading and follow-up.

12.1.2 OPEN QUESTIONS

Open questions lead on to more information. An example of an open question might be: "How are manuals used in teaching?" This forces the other person to say something other than "yes" or "no." Furthermore, open questions give you the opportunity to receive other information which can be used as a basis for evaluation. Don't ask questions such as "It is important to use body language as a channel of communication. What do you think?" In your introduction, you have already given the "correct" answer, which prevents the other person from contributing his own opinion. Possibly this person may answer, "That is what I thought as well." This does not give you much information. We do not know whether it was said to accommodate your wishes; we don't know whether the person has understood the concept of body language and how he understands it. Instead the question should be: "What do you think are important channels of communication?" On the basis of the study carried out concerning people's tendency to lie, asking an applicant a question like "Are you willing to work overtime?" would be wrong. Instead, we should ask "What is your attitude to overtime?"

12.1.3 Closed questions

Closed questions lead to "yes" or "no" answers and should be used for decisions or for finalizing situations. Use questions such as: "Are you fetching the manuals from the cellar?" *or* "Can you sign the contract today?" A closed question does not open up the possibility for the other person to launch into long explanations, and it limits possible answers to a bare minimum. Closed questions can be rightfully used after a series of open questions or leading questions as a technique for finishing off.

12.1.4 Leading questions

Examples of leading questions include: "Can you imagine yourself not having well trained staff?" or "What time will you fetch the manuals?" instead of the above "Are you going to fetch the manuals?" Leading questions can sometimes be used in a similar way to closed questions, i.e., to explain or to conclude. Here we are sending the other person in the direction we ourselves would like to go. Instead of asking, "Are you going shopping today?" we ask "What time are you going shopping?"

12.1.5 Follow-up questions

When people are talking or discussing something, it often happens that someone asks a question that remains unanswered for a number of reasons. I have noticed that on these occasions the person who has asked the question does not follow this up, but he lets the whole thing lie. When he watches a video recording of this conversation afterwards, it becomes clear to him that some very relevant and important questions remained unanswered.

A politician on television news has some questions put to him. The journalist asks the question, "People say that the unofficial unemployment figures are much higher than the published figures, since they do not take certain categories of people into account. Is this correct?" The politician tilts his head sideways, clears his throat and says, "Christian, we should all join forces and do as much as we can for the job market, and in this way...."

Three minutes later the journalist still has not received an answer to his question about the employment figures. On rare occasions the journalist repeats his question. Politicians have an ingenious way of sidestepping when it comes to questions that they cannot answer! One good rule is to follow up the minute you realize that your original question is not being answered. You should do this immediately, and in order to follow up, you must be good at listening. The best thing is for you to assume full responsibility for the communication. It is possible that your question was unclear. You should also give the other person a chance in case you are the one at fault. Ask "I may have mentioned this before, but how was it with...?"

If the other person still does not give an answer to your question, you can use a technique whereby you go back to the last proper direct answer you received and begin from there. If the person does not respond to any of the above examples, you can either wait or go back to the question, or you can confront him by saying directly, "What are the unemployment figures for Denmark?"

12.1.6 QUESTIONS FOR YOUR AUDIENCE

If you want to put a question to your audience, it is best to address the group as a whole. Wait a couple of seconds before you choose someone to answer your question. When choosing someone, you should be gentle and have an air of humility, as people can feel frightened or provoked in these situations. It is possible that the person who has been asked the question may feel embarrassed, and that is something he will not thank you for. Do not demand an answer; try to *invite* an answer to your question. When you select someone to answer your question, other members of the group will switch off, so it is a good idea to repeat the question so that you update everyone on what is being said and make a point of retaining their concentration.

12.1.7 QUESTIONS FROM THE AUDIENCE

Start your round of questions by inviting questions from your audience in a friendly way and step towards them. In this way you come across as more amenable, and you encourage people to ask questions. We have a tendency to be frightened of questions because we expect objections. Don't forget that you depend on questions, both for feedback and for finding out whether the audience has understood what you are talking about. Raise your hand when you announce that it is time for questions. In this way you indicate that they are all welcome to do the same. Or open the session with total communicative behavior. Remember about pacing. Don't say "I don't know whether there are going to be any questions?" It is best to say; "Now I would like to hear what questions you have. We will begin with the front row." Look directly at the person who is asking the question. It is also a good idea to thank him for asking. Tell him that it was a good question (do not exaggerate). Repeat or re-phrase the question, and maybe use other words to show the person asking it that you have understood—and to make sure that everyone has heard it. Pause a little so that people can absorb what has been said. Direct your answer to the group, not just to the person asking. Find out whether the person asking is satisfied with the answer. Thank him again for asking the question.

What happens if no one answers?

If there are no questions at all, speakers often feel awkward.

What should you do then?

It is not a bad idea to ask the first question yourself, "I have often wondered why...?"

Invite questions by asking something like "What do you think your division will make of it?"

Not able to answer?

Either admit that you cannot answer the question or ask someone else in the group to answer it. Most people will respect those who admit that they do not have an answer at their fingertips; however, it is important to say that you will find out and come back with an answer at a later date. Don't make a hasty response by giving an answer in a confident tone of voice if you do not have sufficient expertise. Your audience will see through this immediately, and it will put you in particularly bad light. It is fine to say that you believe it to be correct, subject to the proviso that you are not completely certain about the validity of your answer.

If you know that there is someone in the audience who is well up on the subject and perhaps knows more about it than you do, it is fine to involve this person and call upon him for assistance. These people are a resource, and everyone will respect you for utilizing their expertise. People can also find it flattering to be asked for help.

Be specific

How much, where, how, why, who, in what way? If you want to know something, you must be specific about what it is you want to know. Avoid "emotional hide-and-seek."

Make the person who you are asking feel special

Information is power. It is like gold dust. It is no good expecting to receive an answer just because you have asked a question. Create an advantage for the person to whom you are asking the question. What is there in it for him if he answers your question and gives you the information that you need? If you have a good idea and you would like to base a business on it and need money, you cannot just go up to someone and say, "I would like a million pounds to implement a new idea." Show him what the money will be used for and what you can achieve both for yourself and for him. The value you create is perhaps only a hope or a dream, but very often it will be enough. If you just come up to me and say, "I could do with a million pounds," my answer would be "There are a lot of others like you!"

Make sure your question is focused, fitting and honest

A guaranteed way of messing things up is to display uncertainty. If you do not know what you are asking, there is no one else who will know! Show that you are sure about what you are talking about. Make your body language and verbal behavior convey that you expect an answer to your question.

Precision with language

A great deal of what we say is based on nothing, on generalizations or on assumptions. This type of communication can be deadly and is also known as superficially structured conversation.

For example, one of your salespeople has handled a client's problem badly. The client rings you up and says "All your salespeople are completely useless! They never give proper advice."

Or you see some noisy young people in the street and you say, "Young people today are very noisy." In both situations and much too often, our conversations are superficially structured. We move from a restricted truth to an unrestricted truth. Perhaps *that* salesperson is useless, but not all your salespeople are useless. Perhaps those young people make a lot of noise, but not all young people do. Next time you hear this sort of generalization, you should repeat the statements. "All your salespeople are useless!" You ask "All?" "No, of course not! Only him!"

"All young people today are noisy!" You might ask, "Are all young people noisy?" "No, of course not, just them!"

Many people have a thing about letting others know they can't do something. "I can't!" When someone expresses this feeling, what signal do you think is being sent to the brain? It is a signal which states definitely that there is something which this individual actually cannot do. If you ask why he cannot do it, he often showers you with answers. On the other hand, if you ask, "What would it be like if you were capable of doing it," you give this person a feeling that there is an opportunity which was not apparent before, and you get him to explore the advantages and the disadvantages. Try out something similar on yourself.

The next time you say to yourself *"I can't!"* you should ask yourself *"What would happen if I could?"*

You will then think up a list of the pros and the cons and consider how this activity could open up new opportunities, which in turn would give you more scope. Just by asking yourself this question, you will begin to consider avenues of possibility. You can then ask yourself, "What is stopping me from doing it now?"

Our language and communicative behavior are full of empty words and generalizations. If someone says to you "I am depressed," he is not telling you anything; he is describing a condition. He is not providing you with any information that you can work with. If someone says to you that he is depressed, you should ask him what it is that makes him depressed. Ask him to say exactly what it is that is upsetting him. "I am depressed because I always mess my work up." Your question should then be, "Do you **always** mess your work up?" No doubt the answer will be, "Oh no, not always, but what happened was ...."

How often have you heard people say "They don't understand me!" or "I don't have a chance against them!" Who are *they*? If it is a large organization, the chances are that there is only one person who makes the decisions. By using the word *they*, we envisage the worst scenario for ourselves. We don't know who "they" are.

Once you have defined who "they" are, you have a real world with real people. If you put forward a new idea at a meeting and Erik, who is always critical, says "Your plan is not practicable," it is no good just saying, "Yes, it is!" You will not establish rapport or open up a discussion if you make a statement like that. A number of people that I meet over-use these expressions: *too much, too expensive, too many*. In relation to what? Once in a while someone says to me "Your course is too expensive." When I answer, "In relation to what?" the answer is often "In relation to other courses I have been on." Find out which specific courses he is talking about, refer to one of them, and ask "In what way is this particular course identical to mine?" "Oh, it's not that!" he says.

"That is interesting! What would you say if you did feel that my course was worth the time and the money you had spent on it?"

"Oh, I would think it was fine, yep, okay I think!" "Tell me precisely what I should do in order to provide you with the information you want?" "I would like to know more about the case-study and the video recordings." "By this do you mean that you would consider it to be more worthwhile and value for money if you received a little more information about it?" He nods and confirms that he agrees. What has happened in this conversation? We brought the level down from the surface structure to the underlying structure. We made this real. We moved from a wave of generalizations to a wave of facts. Now try to focus on the way in which people speak.

Begin by trying to identify the surface structure and the underlying structure. How would you hold a conversation with such people? Watch television. Identify the empty words which are used and ask the questions that were asked above. When you hear statements such as "It is a bad idea," you can answer, "According to whom?" Another variation is when people say, "I think he knows what I am talking about!"

To this you can answer, "How do you know that?"

An important rule is to select a "how" question rather than a "why" question. "How" questions give you reasons, causes and explanations rather than excuses.

12.2 LISTENING

Being a good listener requires more talent than most people realize. Try to think of a very good friend, one you really like or turn to when you have problems. What are this person's characteristics? It is most likely that this person is a good listener. What are the characteristics of a good listener?

Even if you are capable of doing five jobs all at the same time while one of your colleagues is telling you something, it is a good idea to stop everything that you are doing. People find it frustrating if you continue to work while they are trying to tell you something. Always remember to meet the other person's gaze and maintain good eye contact. Even if you look away for a fraction of a second, there is a risk that the other person will think that you are not concentrating on what he is saying. Raise your eyebrows and tilt your head slightly. If you hold your face with one hand and at the same time let one finger touch your cheek, it conveys a non-verbal message which indicates that you are "listening quietly." See the drawing.

Remember to nod appropriately at regular intervals. If you do this too frequently or too fast, it looks as if you are impatient and feel like interrupting. Don't say anything, even when the speaker appears to have finished. A short pause every now and again shows that you are taking in what is being said to you.

Some of the greatest impediments to communication are interruptions and questions. When adults talk to each other, they tend to interrupt one another in mid flow and finish off each other's sentences. They do not have sufficient patience to let the other person finish what he is saying, and they seem to assume they know what the other person is going to say. With children it is different—people give them more time.

This is because we assume that children have more difficulty in expressing themselves and so need more time and attention. We should transfer this listening technique to our conversations with adults. Learn to wait until the other person has finished speaking. Rather than interrupting your speaking partner with a question while he is in mid-flow, you should develop a technique for remembering what you want to ask. For example, it is a good idea to have a notepad available when you are at meetings.

Show empathy and avoid being judgmental. Have you ever been in a situation when you have admitted that you did not know who the European champions were in football, and the person you were talking to says loudly "You are kidding, I thought everyone knew that!" So that people will trust you, you should not judge, argue or make light of what they are saying. On the contrary, make sure you do not correct, criticize or make fun of the person you are talking to. Use an assertive questioning technique.

When asking questions, your body language should be appropriate. Display positive attitudes, nod a little, lean over towards the other person, maintain eye contact and make a point of smiling. Remain at arm's length. In some cultures it is acceptable to stand closer to the person who you are talking to. Touch is acceptable in some cultures. If you know the other person well, it is perfectly all right to touch them lightly, for instance by tapping them on the arm or the back, or by pulling them closer to you.

12.3 BACK DOOR SALES (INFORMATION FROM THIRD PARTY)

Those associated with your opposite number are useful. People such as colleagues, business associates, service staff, managers and others know a great deal about what makes your contact person tick; they also know his good points and bad points. People working in the warehouse, service personnel and those working in production all know what goes on when processing orders and when other routine tasks are being carried out. All these people leak information. They tend not to be familiar with communicative practices and know little about the use of information. That is the reason why they do not give much thought to what they say.

Example:

A purchasing agent visiting your company has inquired about a number of matters which you do not want to comment on. A little later he asks if someone could show him around the factory. During a break after lunch, a young member of staff is assigned the task of showing him the factory. The purchasing agent talks to several people and asks them questions. When he comes to the people operating the machines, he asks: *Do you get a lot of overtime?* The purchasing agent finds out that people tend not to work overtime and that 70 % of production capacity is used at the most. The service engineers are asked: "How are you getting on with the systems which we installed?" He hears that there have been big problems. The staff should have been given better training. The machines have been idle because the staff have not learned how to use them properly, and they also have problems understanding the manuals, which are written in English.

An experienced communicator obtains and makes good use of all the information that you did not want to give him. His questions seem harmless enough, though he should not be allowed to hide behind his "sales pitch" in the way he does. Because we live in an open society and the decision-making process is decentralized, it is easy to find out where you need to go in companies in order to access important information. It is a good idea to have an extensive network of contacts. It is not enough merely to negotiate with a purchasing agent. You should ask to speak to the person who is in charge of maintenance, someone who will use your products and services.

These contacts can do more than just supply you with invaluable information and deepen your insight before negotiations take place; these are also people who can initiate correct handling of your products and services. There is no need to go behind the back of your purchasing agent. You should ask him to help you to make contact with other people in the company who can give you the information you require to arrive at the correct solution.

Similarly, some people use sources of contacts to indoctrinate others. The negotiation table is an arena for testing waters, firing warning shots and issuing threats. For instance, one engineer takes his colleague to one side: *Your competitors have promised that we will go on a course in England.*

In these negotiations the sales engineers are being used as

pawns. All the arguments are aimed at them because they will be the users of the equipment. They are led to believe that the supplier is going to provide a support service and solve all their problems. This will include a course for users, a factory visit, a trip abroad, cakes and coffee and perhaps Christmas goodies. All this contributes to strengthening the bond between supplier and user. If this situation is not what you want, you should have better control of information. Your opposite number should not have free access to contacts within your organization. Staff should be informed about their main role in negotiations, even though they are perhaps never present at the negotiation table.

I am always suspicious if someone needs to tell me that what he is saying is true! Does he lie the rest of the time?

As I mentioned previously, you can learn a lot about a person through his friends, his family and circle of acquaintances. It seems to make sense to check out personal references in the same way as employers check work references.

12.4 LOOK FOR THE MOTIVES - "WHERE IS THE MONEY "

My curiosity is always aroused when I come across people who are controlling, dominate conversations, and display great interest in one particular area. What is their motive? Or to put it in another way for the commercial world: Where is the money?

Example:

The sales director from Exodid Entreprises is negotiating with his client, Andersen Consulting, about an order worth just over 5 million USD.

The sales director says, "Are you able to take partial delivery in September instead of December?"

The Andersen Consulting answers: "Unfortunately we are not

able to because we need to have it in December, as we said before!"

This is typical negotiation communication. What is going wrong? Andersen Consulting forgets to look for the motive. Why did Exodid Entreprises want to deliver as early as September rather than December? What is clear to those of us who are listening to the negotiations and keeping an eye on the body language is that it will be financially advantageous for Exodid if delivery is made early. Even in cases when the contents of what is being said have nothing to do with money, the general gist may suggest some other kind of advantage. This is why you should always try to ascertain the motives of your opposite number. Most of us fail to realize when we are being taken in by lies. All of us are quick to deny any form of unfair play, and if we have a clear conscience, we account for ourselves by saying that we have nothing to hide. When there is something which we would rather not discuss or when we have lied and our opposite number relentlessly questions us on this matter, we react with aggression or anger if he continues to pry. Imagine a wife asking her husband: "Were you out with friends last night?" If he told her quite simply what had happened and what they did, it usually means there is nothing wrong. On the other hand, if the situation is such that he has something to hide, he is likely to give a quick answer "Yes, I was."

12.5 COUNTER QUESTIONS

Another way of evading a question is to ask counter questions. These can be used when there is a question which you do not want to answer or when you would like to find out your counterpart's attitude on the subject!

"How do you think the course is going?"

"I don't know. What is your impression?"

Or

"How do you think the course is going?"

"Why do you ask?"

When someone asks you a counter question, you should note that there may be something that the other person does not want to talk about or something they would rather not reveal. Another reason for asking a counter question is that the person is unsure of your attitude on the subject or lacks confidence in that particular area.

12.6 BEING TOO OPEN

I have mentioned in a number of places in this book that it is important to give information about yourself in order to liven up the conversation. It is amazing to see people opening up when someone starts a conversation by giving information about himself. This tactic can also be misused. You have reason to be on guard if your conversation partner voluntarily gives information about himself or his circumstances during inappropriate parts of the conversation. Evidently this person is trying to "get a hold on you" by giving you information in order to make you drop your defenses.

If, for example, your counterpart starts to say how genuine and honest everyone is in his company, you are right to be taken aback. You need to watch out whenever your conversation partner gives you information which you have not asked for.

12.7 GENERAL BEHAVIOR

Genuine honesty is like any other characteristic—it is consistent.

When you want to assess people, you can do it in all types of environment. Have you noticed who takes the lead at functions? Who is the person who always arranges entertainment? How do they behave with other people? You can use occasions like office parties and private parties to observe other people. Try to read them. Watch the person with the loud voice. How does he talk to others? What is his body language like? Look at the buffet area. Who makes way for other people and who pushes in front of everyone else? Who introduces himself to others? Who comes out with "cheers"? Who makes sure that everyone is comfortable? What type of behavior does this person display and what about that person? How do they act? In what context? Attributes such as concern for others, consistency, team spirit and sympathy for others are brought out in general patterns of behavior, but this is not so with egoism.

The boss: "We are very interested in your qualifications but it is important that you understand that working together and team spirit are vital if you are to be successful in this job!"

Applicant: "That is fine by me; I am particularly good at working with people. I have a great sense of responsibility for others, and I would like to be a team player!"

The boss: "I am pleased to hear that! Have you any other questions about the company or the post?"

The applicant: "Yes, I would like to know when it is possible for me to have my first holiday as I am planning on a skiing trip in the near future."

The above is a typical and frequent example of inconsistency in statements and attitude. The story describes in brief the applicant's lack of common sense and insincerity

12.8 BREAKING PROMISES

All of us have colleagues who promise that the report will be ready on Wednesday, but it has not been delivered by Thursday morning. There is the tradesperson who promised to drop by tomorrow morning to finish his work or the person who says he will soon pay us a visit. Life is unpredictable. The car breaks down, new jobs crop up or your child gets sick. The problem is not that people lie. They would really like to do what they say they are going to do, but they do not give much thought to the consequences of breaking their promise; neither do they consider what the long-term impact of keeping that promise might be. It is just the way these people are. It does not really matter what their intentions are; you cannot have complete confidence in what they say, and it is very unlikely that they will ever change.

Do to others as you would have them do to you!

When you are trying to figure out why your friend or colleague has broken his promise, you should consider the following: Did something unexpected happen which explains why this person did not keep his promise? Has the same promise been made at an earlier date and not kept? Was this promise made in haste? There are some people who don't mean any harm in what they do; they just want to be everyone's friend, and this is why they promise too much. In many cultures not keeping promises is standard behavior, and we are so different in that respect.

We are not always ourselves!

Our general behavior is affected by certain factors such as: health, stress, etc.

Very few people tell strangers about their mental or physical condition when they meet them, but the effects of ill health and other problems can seriously impede communication. If you suddenly notice a difference in someone else's behavior, you should take note. Something significant is about to happen or is happening. In my many years as manager of different companies with many employees, I have developed a talent for registering changes in people.

Just a few minutes after a person has arrived at the office or seconds after I have started a conversation with this person, I register changes in behavior. Whether this is caused by family, health or other personal problems, it is difficult to say. On the few occasions when staff have come to me to hand in their notice, I have frequently known before they have said anything. When we pay attention, we can register another person's behavior by spotting changes in their lifestyle or their actions.

12.9 OTHER PEOPLE READ YOU!

People use all those methods that I have described on you. People try to work out who you are and what you stand for at meetings, in shops, at your child's nursery or school, at the club, and when you are with clients, and they judge you by your behavior, your actions, your values and opinions.

You do have some say in the way others perceive you since it is you who "sets the stage" and chooses the "manuscript." How others read you is incredibly important to your life. If you are a man and single and hope to find the love of your life, you should not leave the house in a torn T-shirt and faded jeans, even if you are only going to the supermarket. When at last you meet the lady of your dreams, she will glance over you in that torn t-shirt and walk off in another direction. Both in the social context and in the work context, it is very important to start off on the right footing. Whenever I am off to a meeting or a teaching assignment, I am always conscious of how I would like others to perceive me. Make a point of keeping my techniques in mind until you feel they are programed into you. You will find them in the section on presentation under Preparation. The same techniques apply in your personal life. You should always ask questions such as "Who is my counterpart?"

In what way will you prepare yourself differently for a meeting with the managing director of a listed company than for a meeting with the project manager on a building site? Most of the time we do think about our appearance, though we do not seem to consider our overall appearance. A perfectly turned-out man in an impeccable suit arrives, but his shoes are scratched, worn out and scruffy! A woman comes into the room in a beautiful Armani business creation, but she is carrying a crumpled and worn-out imitation leather handbag made by an unknown manufacturer. Don't forget that people don't read only your physical appearance. They also read your letters, emails, faxes and take in the way you sound on the phone. Look in the mirror. It never lies. Look at the way you carry yourself, your hair, your clothes and your body language. Rehearse what you want to say until you are satisfied with your overall appearance. Pay attention to what other people say to you. It is exactly the same as when you hear a tape recording of your voice, and you notice how different it sounds: Other people see you differently from the way you see yourself.

- What is my image like? How do I come across to other people?
- How should I look?
- What should I say?
- How should I act?
- What is my purpose?

In my training courses, the great change comes when participants see themselves for the first time on video. Use video recordings to practice what you will do, say and how you will present yourself.

How we learn!

We do not realize that we do not know this!

We have a particular learning pattern. This pattern consists of four levels which we have to pass through in order to learn something.

Level 1 – unaware of incompetence

Imagine a little girl aged two who has self-confidence the size of Mount Everest and talent the size of a ladybird. This little girl— we will call her Nadine—has her eyes on the milk carton on the breakfast table. Nadine has got it into her head to pour the milk into her glass. She has seen her mother and father do it so many times, and it all looks quite simple. With her first feeble attempts, mother and father stop her before there is a deluge of milk on the kitchen floor, and before the tables, chairs and everything within striking range is inundated. Nadine is unaware of being incompetent. She does not realize that she is not capable of pouring the milk into her glass. You too could be in this situation if you have never seen a video recording of yourself at a communications meeting. You do not know that you can't do it.

Level 2 – aware of incompetence

Well, Nadine is not one to abandon an idea. Suddenly the chance is there. Her father is out, and her mother has turned her back on her for a minute. Presto, she grabs the milk carton, and— splash—the carton tumbles over, and everything is swamped with milk. Suddenly Nadine has progressed from level 1 to level 2. She now knows that she is not capable of pouring the milk out of the carton without causing a flash flood. You are faced with the same situation when you watch yourself act and communicate for the first time. You notice your mistakes and can see which areas you should brush up on and improve.

Level 3 – aware of competence

Nadine practices non-stop, under the expert guidance of her mother and father. At last the day arrives when she is capable of pouring milk out for herself without there being any dire consequences. Nadine is now aware of her new skill; however, this new skill requires complete concentration and attentiveness on her part.

Level 4 – unaware of competence

We don't need to consider whether we can.

Nadine is now 6 years old. She can cycle, climb trees, swim and ride a horse. She now pours milk out into her glass every day without giving it a single thought. She has acquired this new knowledge by developing it as a habit. Learning to communicate takes place in the same way. When a person is new to public speaking, his skills will be rudimentary; however his skill will soon develop once he acquires theoretical and practical knowledge. In the end he will no longer need to think about how he should approach it. Compare this to the way you go about your daily activities now, how you drive your car or how you cycle or play tennis. On the whole, this applies to everything we are able to do.

CHAPTER 13 - TECHNIQUES AT MEETINGS

In themselves, meetings can be among the most time-consuming and costly communication activities that you can get involved with. Even if you are involved with meetings for just four hours a week (with some people this is longer), it means you will have spent more than nine thousand hours (more than 365 days) either at meetings or involved with activities associated with them during your working life. We know from various research that has been done that the above figures are probably on the low side. For most people meeting activities take up something in the region 35 per cent of their time at work, and with people in managerial positions, time spent on meetings is estimated to be in the region of 50 per cent, in other words, half their working hours.

Meetings are expensive

We can get a fair idea of how much money organizations spend on this activity by looking at the actual costs involved. Most companies spend between 7-15 per cent of their staff budget on meetings. If the staff budget in your company is USD 1,000,000, it follows that between USD 70,000 and 150,000 is spent on meetings. These figures do not include preparation time, courses or conferences. A relatively large Danish company with a staff budget of USD 1.8 thousand million can expect to spend approximately USD 160 million per year on meetings alone.

Why meetings?

You know the situation yourself–another notice, another

meeting. You grumble to yourself, "Another meeting...." There may well be a good reason for the meeting; however, many meetings are held out of tradition; we usually have our "Monday meeting" every Monday morning. Many meetings are unnecessary; either they are badly planned or the wrong people are invited along, and the result could have been achieved more satisfactorily and more efficiently in another way. However, like it or not, face-to-face meetings using both verbal and non-verbal communication often provide the best way to exchange ideas with others in your group. The same level of communication just cannot be achieved using the written form. Great feats of creativity may be achieved with structured brainstorming at meetings. They often take on a psychological character and sometimes develop into a democratic decision-making process, a sound base where everyone feels part of the group and free to contribute their ideas.

What do you get out of it?

After this chapter you will be able to:

- streamline the demand for documentation and preparation for meetings
- develop the individual's ability to understand matters relevant to decision-making
- develop your talents to enable you to get the best out of meetings
- develop knowledge about delegation of roles and the reason for holding different meetings
- be precise in terms of objectives, agendas and target groups
- understand the psychology of meetings, including the phenomenon of "collective incompetence"
- make a check list

- acquire strategies for guiding the meeting in the right direction
- memorandum for the chairman
- measure how successful a meeting has been
- prepare for a meeting

When is a meeting successful?

There are two main things you need to do in order to assess whether a meeting has been fruitful. The most important is— what happened? Did you achieve the results you expected? Which problems did you solve? Were any decisions made? The second most important one is—how were the problems solved? What were people's attitudes at the meeting? How were the decisions made? Did some individuals dominate the meeting? Was this meeting enjoyable? Were people committed and enthusiastic? The follow-up to the meeting and the decisions made are vital when assessing the purpose of the meeting. Research carried out shows that time lost due to unproductive meetings may cost as much as USD 4.8 million per thousand members of staff.

How do you make a success out of your meetings?

As chairman or participant your joint responsibility is:
- to ensure that meetings begin on time and end as planned
- to plan and draw up practical agendas
- to deal with people who talk too much, interrupt or criticize to maintain a high level of motivation and a sense of participation
- to obtain creative decision-making
- to reach a consensus

- to generate a favorable atmosphere
- to establish rapport and a common purpose
- to develop techniques for solving problems
- to give effective and powerful presentations
- to communicate effectively

Productivity, creativity, efficiency, participation and commitment are the results you desire from your meetings. In order to reach these high standards, it is important to understand and accept the mechanisms that will give you these results. This will not be possible unless you consider how successful your meetings have been up until now.

The many-headed monster

At meetings everyone has their own ideas and objectives that they would like to see implemented, and this is, unfortunately, why so many meetings produce poor results. Let us consider one example:

Mike, the course director in charge, has convened a meeting about the course program for next year.

Mike says, "I really do think we should put up attendance fees for the average student by USD 1,100."

Marianne answers aggressively, "We will lose clients if we do that. What we should do is change our name to make it more appropriate for our area of work."

Mike says, "What about if we increased our fees by only USD 800."

Chris chips in, "I know the name of an excellent person who we could employ as course director."

Marianne says, "How about changing our name? Instead of the Training School, why don't we call it the Training Institute—it sounds more professional."

Paul says something for the first time, "Can't we reduce our budget for this year?"

Is this a scenario you recognize? What was it that went wrong at that meeting? Everyone wanted something to be done and had a proposal to make. Mike saw the problem as being the course fees and felt the solution was to put them higher. Marianne thought the name of the company was the problem. Chris and Paul were thinking about something totally different. Everyone's contribution was perfectly sound and feasible in its own right. One of the most significant discoveries is that the mind can cope with only a few ideas at once. In meetings such as this one, you can process and register only one idea, i.e., in this situation your own. Try and listen to two or more conversations at once. Doesn't work, does it? You can really focus properly on only one. This is not the way for groups to function. The number of participants equals the number of ideas put forward. At different stages of the meeting, each participant focuses on a variety of problems. If each individual goes off in his own direction, we get the many-headed monster. In order to work efficiently, a group must have one **focal point.**

Let us have a look at another example:

Peter Erikssen, project manager at a firm of contractors, has convened a meeting. He opens the meeting by saying, "We are here today because our managing director has asked for our views on the immediate problems related to this assignment. Who would like to begin?"

Dorthe begins, "I think the problem is pilfering from the workplace."

Jonas reacts "I think the solution is to have more surveillance cameras."

Niels chips in sarcastically, "We tried that last year and it did not work."

Jonas answers, "I am sure it would have helped, but they only tried it for a short time."

Dorthe continues, "And then there is the problem of overspending on materials."

Karla suddenly chips in, "Last week, one of my carpenters lost his tool box!"

This meeting is not working at all. No one is getting anywhere. If we try to analyze this snippet, we can see this problem clearly. No one in the group accepts Niel's contribution. In order to have a proper focus, the group must first of all reach an agreement on what is to be discussed. Identifying the difference between the content (the what) and the process (the how) is difficult, though vital, and not following this through is one of the fundamental reasons that many meetings are unproductive.

Imagine a football match without a referee, or a busy crossroads without traffic lights. That is no good at all, and the same applies to meetings. Every meeting of more than four participants needs a leader to channel the communication process and make sure that the group stays on the right track.

Who does what

A great stumbling block at meetings is often the lack of any clear guidelines on roles and responsibilities. You have probably attended meetings where people were unsure about who was doing what, who the chairman was, and who was in charge of the agenda. When people have clearly defined roles at meetings, you can easily accept any permutation of the roles. However, if you arrive at a meeting expecting to raise certain matters, but something else is being discussed, you will raise objections.

The main points for a productive meeting:

- Everyone's attention should be focused on matters on the agenda.
- Everyone should follow the procedures.
- Someone will chair the meeting.
- People will be assigned definite roles within the group.

Group memory

You are bound to be familiar with one or more of the situations mentioned below:

- A participant at a meeting constantly repeats the same point.
- The meeting goes round in circles, covering the same ground over and over again.
- You have a good idea, but you forget it before you have the chance to speak.
- You are overwhelmed by too much information. You don't know what questions to ask, which subjects are the most appropriate, or precisely what the purpose of the meeting is.
- Someone arrives late, and it is necessary to go over what has been said again.

These problems are related to memory.

In the chapter on communication, I have discussed short-term memory as opposed to long-term memory. Short-term memory functions as follows: Imagine you are at home looking for a shirt. First of all, you look in the sitting room, and it is not there. Then you look in the kitchen, and it is not there either. So you go and look in the bathroom, and you still can't find it. Now you have forgotten where you have looked. So you go and look in the sitting room again.

The short-term memory is extremely important in certain areas, such as in communication when you need to remember only what happened the minute before. The way in which we remember is by repetition. You will now have read the sentence before this one, and I am sure you can remember the word *way*, which I used to introduce it. Seeing that you are using your short-term memory right now, you will have no problem recalling only the phrase "seeing that" at this particular moment. Unless you were making a special effort to remember the "way" you will have forgotten it. The way to remember a word is by repeating it.

Your short-term memory has a very limited capacity.

Try and remember this combination: A, H, O, T, L, Q, E, S, A. How much could you remember? Not that much? We know that human beings can retain only seven items in their short-term memory at the same time, unless they use tricks to help their memory. For instance, you can break words up or remember them by association with other things such as names or places.

The essence of this is that people at meetings have the same need for short-term memory that all individuals do. Traditionally the long-term memory is taken care of by the agenda and perhaps a memo book with notes on the conclusions of the matters on the agenda; however, fast input, ideas and creative brainstorming are never formally recorded. It is much more common for people to take their own notes to record what has been said at meetings, which means that if there are more than eight people taking notes during a meeting, there will be eight versions of the minutes, the aim of the meeting and often the conclusion. This practice frequently leads to endless discussions

"I thought that we had agreed that your department would..." or "The conclusion was clear, what we do now is...."

At most meetings there is an abundance of exciting and interesting facts in free flow, but unless some form of collective memory is used, 99.9 % will be lost without it ever coming under discussion. A very simple way of initiating group memory is by using a flip chart and putting one person in charge of note-taking and consciously recording ideas and input from the group.

The psychological value of group memory

Group memory facilitates the free flow of ideas and input. It provides everyone with a solid basis for contributing their ideas and gives them all a sense of motivation. It focuses on positive aspects and, in itself, can make a great difference to the result of a meeting. It enables you, as a participant, to contribute ideas spontaneously which you can see recorded, remembered and then taken up at a later point in time. You will feel a sense of relief at having made a point, and then you will have released mental energy necessary to concentrate on other items on the agenda. Now let us have another look at the meeting at the building site. Here we are going to use these new techniques.

Peter Erikssen, project manager at a firm of contractors, has convened a meeting and opens the meeting by saying, "We are here today because our managing director has asked us to suggest solutions to the immediate problems that have been brought to our notice regarding this assignment. We have jotted down these problems on page two of our group memory. Does everyone agree that we should discuss the problems related to the building site?"

Everyone nods. "Good, let's get going. I will be chairing the meeting, and would you, Anders, please write down people's suggestions on the flip chart? How do you think we should deal with the various points?"

Dorthe: "We could begin by discussing what goes on at the building site and see if we can come to an agreement on some of the problems there."

Niels: "Why don't we just say what comes to mind?"

Eva: "We could just have a brainstorming session in the way they do at my husband's workplace."

Karla: "One of my carpenters lost his tool box last week!"

Peter intervenes, "Okay, Karla, Anders has written this down on the group memory, and I am sure that everyone has a lot to say, but let us wait until we all agree on how we should draw up the list. Is brainstorming a good idea?"

Everyone nods. "OK, so let's have a brainstorming session. With brainstorming, you just come out with your own ideas. Anders will write them down on the group memory so that we can discuss them all one by one later on. Let's make a list of 20 points. Any questions? Ok, let's begin."

Dorthe: "Pilfering from the workplace."

Jonas: "Too much overtime."

Eva: "Four hours overtime per week is not unusual ....."

Peter jumps in: "Stop, Eva, we have agreed not to criticize each other's ideas. Is there anything you would like to have included on the list?"

Eva: "Yes there is, more lockers."

Peter: "Thanks Eva; now it is your turn, Karla."

Karla: "Alcohol at lunch."

Because ideas at this type of meeting are not written down with the name of the person who proposed them, they become the group's ideas than rather those of their originator. The group soon forgets whose ideas they were, which means that they become depersonalized and are no longer associated with personal relationships and potential conflict

Win – win at meetings

I am sure you are familiar with the concept of "win" in other situations. Our extremely popular training course on negotiation technique is actually based upon the win-win technique. This is a technique which makes everyone feel that their requirements have been dealt with and no-one perceives himself to be a loser.

Let's imagine a family of four—father, mother, daughter and son. Every summer they have the eternal discussion on where to go for their holidays. The father and daughter would prefer to go to the beach, whereas the son would prefer to visit the great Swedish forests. The mother has not really got a destination in mind, but she feels more inclined to go along with her son's suggestion because he is the odd one out. If they put it to the vote, it looks as if the outcome will be a beach holiday because the boy will be outvoted. This will upset the son, as he is quite adamant about not wanting to go to the beach.

If they elect one person to decide for them, say the mother, her choice will be the Swedish forests, out of consideration of her son, which will mean that the father and the daughter will lose out. The third alternative is that they don't decide on anything. There is a loser whichever way we look at this situation, and we do not have a win-win situation. In win-win situations, everyone feels as if they have won, but in order to reach a consensus, which leads to a win-win situation, everyone needs to pull together. Consensus means finding a solution that is acceptable to everyone. The solution may not be ideal for you, but in a win-win situation, it will be one you can accept without very strong objections. In this sort of situation the family needs to cooperate and instead of limiting themselves to a win-lose scenario, they should look for alternatives. Instead of just having a beach holiday, they could combine a beach holiday with a week in Sweden. It might be a good idea for them to find another family in the same position as them and consider exchanging a holiday apartment or a holiday cottage, or they could hire a caravan and have a holiday in both places. Don't forget that a vote would still create a win and lose situation here. Voting in the democratic way does nothing to convince opponents that that the proposal put forward by its supporters is acceptable. Those who have voted "no" may well leave the meeting room in a less motivated frame of mind than those who have voted "yes."

Decision method Result

- Strike - Lose/Lose
- Lock-out - Lose/Lose
- Protests - Lose/Lose
- Majority vote - Win/Lose
- Management decision - Win/Lose
- Traditional negotiations - Win/Lose
- Collective co-operations - Win/Win (consensus)

Research has found that when it is important for people to agree on a decision, fewer than half achieve an agreement which produces a win-win situation. If a win-win result is not possible when trying to arrive at a consensus, one can have a **negative vote.**

Imagine a meeting where participants have to make decisions on three different problems, which we will call A, B and C. Using the negative voting style, the chairman says:

"OK, let's vote to see who has strong objections to solution A. Please raise your hands." Three people raise their hand. "Thank you for that. Now let's vote to see who has strong objections to solution B." Two people raise their hand. "Thank you and finally who has strong objections to solution C?" Four people raise their hand.

In this case, the chairman will probably focus on solution B, since only two people were not in favor of it. He will try to convince the two people who found solution B unacceptable by considering their actual objections. The chairman may ask, "What would constitute a difference for you?" "How can we make this solution acceptable to you?" etc. One of the main reasons for using this particular method is that it motivates people and boosts their morale. With this method everyone feels that they are participants and that their views are listened to. People feel that others are taking their ideas and contributions seriously.

The Psychology of Meetings

One of the greatest potential dangers with any meeting is collective incompetence. Sensible individuals are capable of forming very incompetent groups.

Groups can undermine the responsibility of the individual

People often feel more secure making decisions in a plenary group rather than as individuals for the simple reason that in a plenary group the individual can divest himself of any responsibility for its outcome. It is normally more difficult to blame a decision on 14 people than just one, and this is often why decisions made at meetings can leave a lot to be desired. From a psychological viewpoint, people seem to find decisions more convincing and cogent if they are made by fourteen people than, say, Mr. Smith in his little office on the third floor. People who are normally quite sensible seem to leave any sense of judgment they may have at the door when they arrive at a meeting and succumb to the herd instinct. On the whole it is possible to say that groups of people make far more mistakes than individual people do. As individuals, people are reasonably sensible, but as soon as they become members of a group, they are overcome by complete stupidity—why is this?

Collective incompetence

Meetings are by their nature a risky business, more vulnerable to passions, loyalties, persuasion and all types of manipulation than any of the individuals at the meeting. We react to people's ideas and their behavior, regardless of whether it is appropriate or not.

How can collective incompetence be avoided?

All meetings have an effect on time, money and payoff. In order to conduct a meeting as an efficient working procedure, it is necessary to adopt a basic approach.

Be aware:

- Meetings have their limits.
- Respect and understand how groups think, the procedures of meetings and all individuals.
- Cognitive dominance. It is important to be self-critical since we like to nurse our prejudices, and we may have a natural resistance to new ideas.
- Meetings must have clear objectives, measurable progress and prestige.
- Communication and empathy.
- Avoid / localize hidden agendas.
- The competitive phenomenon.
- Do not tolerate time wasters.

Control

Whenever you at a meeting, whether as chairman or participant, it is important that you do all you can to keep everything at bay that may detract from the agenda such as irrelevant matters, conflicting interests, personal preferences and other disturbances. An exception can be when you are obviously dealing with an opponent. A potential danger is negative dynamics as this can affect the behavior of a group. You should try to harness the immense power that a group has. In order to get as much as possible out of your meeting, you must put a check on any elements which may jeopardize it:

- Limit the number and diversity of items.
- Limit the number of participants.
- Insist on proper preparation and brief meetings.
- Make sure the venue is suitable for the purpose of the meeting and the work that needs to be done.
- Learn to say "NO." Bear in mind quality rather than quantity. Who is participating? Is this meeting likely to achieve anything? The effect of a bad meeting is never neutral.

Is this meeting really necessary?

Unnecessary meetings

If you have the authority to convene a meeting, it means you also have the power to decide whether it is actually necessary. If you are summoned to a meeting, you should find out whether it is appropriate for: (1) your role in the company, (2) your boss, (3) your department, (4) your organization (5) you as a person. Unnecessary meetings can be:

- held for the wrong reasons.
- a substitute for work.

- because "Those that rejoice and those that are upset seek the company of others."
- to share responsibility and risks.
- because people feel a need to share information with others.
- because people want to be liked and respected.
- because of a need to show power.
- because they have a tendency to be all-embracing.
- changed meetings— meetings where you have not been told the agenda. These can be full of surprises, and these surprises are not always pleasant.
- a plunge into chaos— the feeling that a meeting is better than no meeting. An impromptu meeting can be much worse than no meeting. Be patient.
- "We have always done it this way"—the routine meeting.

The cost of a meeting

The direct costs are plain to see, but indirect costs can be an eye-opener:

How do you make a choice?

Saying "no" can be an excellent way of avoiding a bad meeting. By saying "no" you can also impose a better structure on the meetings that are held. Even in situations where your chances of influencing people are limited, you should seek specific reasons for saying "no," such as:

- It is not clear to you what you are going to achieve by having this meeting or you are not quite sure what this meeting can achieve.
- Good intentions aside, you are not confident that the meeting

will achieve anything because it lacks official recognition, the combination of people is wrong and it is scheduled for the wrong time.

- It would be easier to achieve the intended purpose by employing other methods and procedures.
- Attending this meeting rules out other more beneficial meetings.
- You are not prepared.
- The chairman is not well enough prepared. He does not know how to run the meeting.
- The wrong people are attending or the right people are not present.
- You cannot run this meeting in such a way that you can achieve your goals, and your absence will mean that it will be postponed.
- The venue is wrong.
- The meeting is a waste of time.

How do you say "no"?
- Ask your counterpart the purpose of the meeting.
- Point out the deficiencies in the meeting.
- Ask whether your presence is necessary.

Strategies for guiding the meeting in the right direction

Identifying what it is that makes meetings unsuccessful can make you feel cynical about many potential-meetings; however, you should never be cynical about the participants. Select your meeting partners more carefully, and give more of yourself to those you have selected. The quality of the meeting is the commitment, the expertise and the structure which is there when people meet.

- Expect a lot out of your co-participants.
- Emphasize the importance of preparation and performance.
- Make realistic demands.
- Use the agenda in the way you would use a road map.
- Communicate effectively and respect other people's communication style.
- Delegate clearly.
- Look for solutions.
- Take charge of the procedure and restrain certain "meeting types."
- Make sure the necessary documents are available for items on the agenda.
- When convening a meeting or when making a decision, use standard documents.

Communication styles

Assess the communication styles of the participants. Note the section on communication.

Aggressive behavior

- Abrupt in dealing with issues and people
- Gives orders/demands/requires
- Interrupts
- Direct eye contact
- Willing to take risks
- Extensive and obvious use of body language
- Impatient

Hesitant behavior

Extroverted behavior

Introverted behavior

- Indirect about dealing with issues and people
- Asks and listens
- Is quiet in groups
- Looks away or down
- Avoids risks
- Passive body language
- Patient
- Shows feelings
- A lot of gestures
- Spontaneous
- Hardly shows feelings at all
- Limited gestures
- Evaluates

The participant at the meeting—who is it?

The late arrival:

Always late for meetings, impedes their progress, wants to be updated and disrupts the general structure of the meeting. Don't confront this person directly in front of the group. It does not help; it just makes him feel humiliated. There can be a lot of reasons why this person arrives late. Perhaps he does not consider the meeting to be important, maybe he does not believe that it will start on time, perhaps he has too much on his plate, or perhaps he is always behind schedule.

There is only one way of getting meetings to start on time, and that is to start the meeting on time. By starting five minutes late, you give the go-ahead for it to start ten minutes late next time. Ask the participants that have arrived whether they wish to begin or wait for the latecomers.

The one who leaves early:

Leaving before the meeting has finished drains energy from the group. Check at the beginning of the meeting to see if any-one needs to leave early. As with the late arrival, the person who leaves early must not be confronted in front of everyone. Find out why this person is behaving in such a way. Are the meetings too long? Or too vague? You may be able to learn something from the person who leaves early.

The scratched record

The "scratched record" repeats the same point again and again. Use the group memory to demonstrate that the point is important for everyone. If this person really seems to be "going over the top" in repeating this point, you can perhaps say, "Let's spend three minutes listening to what Marianne has to say; the floor is yours, Marianne!"

Doubting Thomas

Says all the time "That will never work," "We have never done that before," or "I don't think much of that!" Normally it is healthy to have an analytical and skeptical person in the group, but negative aggression immediately puts a damper on the creative process. Ask the whole group to evaluate how the meeting is proceeding, listen to their comments, and get them to agree on the general procedure. Afterwards use this agreement to admonish anyone attempting any infringement: "Wait a minute, Martin! The whole group, including you, has agreed not to evaluate these issues right now. Wait just like everyone else!"

The head shaker

Most often the "head shaker" says very little, but reacts strongly in a non-verbal manner. The "head shaker" shakes his head, rolls back his eyes, crosses his legs and folds his arms; he bangs books about and pulls his chair back noisily. All these non-verbal behavior patterns say something. Try to ignore the "head shaker." Concentrate on the person who is speaking. Very often the "head shaker" is actually unaware of his habit. You could turn to the "head shaker" and say *"Mike, I notice that you are shaking your head. It looks as if you disagree with what is being said?"* If it seems that the "head shaker" is distracting everyone at the meeting, you should wait until there is a break and talk to him.

The outsider

Usually sits right at the back of the room. He has hesitantly pushed his chair back. This type of person distracts the chairman more than the rest of the group, as he is rarely verbally disruptive. One of the best ways of getting "the outsider" to join in is to ask, "Erik, what do you think of this idea?" It may be a good idea to ask him in the break why he is not participating in the meeting.

The whisperer

Often speaks in whispers to his neighbor. It is really difficult to concentrate if one or more people are whispering during the meeting. There are a lot of chairmen who do not have the courage to confront people like this, and they just let them get on with it.

You could confront people who whisper by asking them if they would like to share their information or whether they realize that only one meeting is being held in this room.

The megaphone

Speaks too much, too loudly and too often. He comes across as being very dominant, and it is very difficult to get him to be quiet. Very often the "megaphone" represents management or one of the other decision-makers.

In your role of chairman, you should stand up and try to move closer to the "megaphone" while he is talking. When you are at an appropriate distance, you should maintain eye contact in order to get him to stop talking and then invite someone else to speak. Alternatively you should confront this person during the break.

The assailant

Delivers personal attacks on another member of the group or on the chairman. If the argument is between two members of the group, you can try to bring this conflict to an end by physically placing yourself between them. Use the group memory to focus on the purpose of the meeting and proceed as normal. If you are the one being attacked, you should try to resist the instinctive urge to speak back and defend yourself. Take one minute to compose yourself. After that, thank the "assailant" for his critical insight and use the boomerang method to turn the subject round to the "assailant" for positive input. "You don't feel that I am doing enough to help you and Chris with the marketing strategies. What do you think I should do?"

The Interpreter

Always talks for other people. "What Dorthe is trying to say is....." Turn to Dorthe and ask her if what the "interpreter" is saying is actually what she thinks! Or you could say to the "interpreter" that he should stop for just a minute so that we could hear what Dorthe herself thinks.

The gossip monger

"I heard that management was planning to...." The gossip monger has always heard something or other. Hours of valuable time at meetings are often wasted because the gossip monger comes out with stories that are true or semi-true. Confront this person or save time by looking into the matter. Ask this person to prove that what he says is true. Where did he get his information from? Is there documentary proof? If you get a vague answer, you should ask the others if they can confirm this. Make sure you get an answer. It is better to spend a little time getting a definite answer and not acting on flimsy evidence.

Mr. know-it-all

Uses seniority, age or level of management to back up his statements.

"Now being a law graduate I am familiar with this area....". "I have been working for this company for 21 years and ....." Accept "Mr. Know-it-all's" expertise, but make it clear that the decision is to be made by the group, though you do appreciate his expert opinion.

Back seat driver

The "back seat driver" can't stop telling you what you should have done. "I would have asked him to submit his bid earlier than that..." Politely but firmly, ask him to be quiet. When a "back seat driver" begins to criticize you or what you are saying, it is often possible to ask him to make suggestions on how things could be done in another way. After that go over the points with the whole group, as this will stop the "back seat driver" in his tracks.

The busy bee

The "busy bee" rushes in and out. He receives faxes and phone calls—has to rush out of the room to talk to someone. The worst thing about this is that very often the "busy bee" is the boss, so he feels free to come and go as he likes. This means that time is often wasted for the whole group. When the busy person has left the room, it can often mean that the whole meeting comes to a standstill or that there is no point in continuing until this person is back. It is usually quite impossible to tackle this person during a meeting in your role as chairman. You should confront him during the break or before the meeting starts to try to persuade him not to accept faxes or telephone calls during the meeting.

The interrupter

He begins to talk before another person has finished what he is saying. On the whole, he is not impolite; he is just impatient and enthusiastic. Like the "megaphone," the "interrupter" is frightened of forgetting what he wanted to say if he does not proclaim it immediately. In your role as chairman, it is up to you to ensure the smooth running of the meeting. Let the person who is speaking finish, but after that you should turn to the "interrupter" and ask him to continue. In this way you can demonstrate to the whole group that everyone has the right to speak.

The pet

"The pet" is the one who always agrees with you. He just always sits there and nods at everything you say and approves of all your ideas and points of view. What is so awful about that? Well, because we never receive an objective response to anything we contribute. We should ignore this person and be objective in assessing everything that is said. "The pet" also speaks directly to you and seldom to other participants. When this happens, get into a position where you can break eye contact to encourage him to communicate with the whole group rather than just you.

Memorandum for the chairman

It takes hard work and experience to become a good chairman. Nevertheless, we have outlined a number of points which can benefit the structure of a meeting:

- Make up your mind in advance what is going to happen at the meeting.
- Limit the number of participants.
- Define your role in relation to the other participants, and choose your strategy.
- Limit the number of subjects for discussion, prepare the agenda, and send it out to everyone in good time.
- Arrive at the meeting early. As chairman you are the "standard bearer."
- Become part of the group without losing your authority.
- Begin punctually. Start by giving a solid positive introduction.
- Include all the new items for the agenda and the minutes as soon as you can.
- State the aims, the objectives and the proposed time. During the meeting, refer to the objectives as often as possible.
- Deal with participants who arrive late.

- It is your task to make participants function as a group.

- Be impartial, or at the very least, demonstrate impartiality in your behavior.

- Separate facts from beliefs and assumptions.

- Keep a careful eye on the time.

- Watch out for emotional outbursts and put an immediate stop to them.

- Encourage everyone to contribute and state their points of view.

- Make participants feel important; be generous with complements.

- Be clear—draw attention to points that people agree on and sort out differences of opinion.

- Take things one at a time.

- Take care of those who are weaker.

- Where possible, break big problems down into smaller problems.

- Keep the meeting going. When you come to a suitable place to stop, you should try to conclude and sum up.

- Finish by showing that the meeting has achieved its aims and let everyone know what the next steps will be. Finish on time and on a positive note.

EXPECTATIONS

When you propose a meeting

As the chairman, it is your duty to look important and make the participants believe that their contributions are important. As a participant, you should sound positive about the purpose of the meeting and about the other participants.

At the start

At the beginning of the meeting, you should express your confidence in everyone present. People pick up lack of trust very quickly. As a participant it is very important that your first remarks are positive ones, even if you intend to be critical about the matters under discussion.

During the meeting itself

Sound positive even when you express disagreement. It is all right to disagree with what is being said, but not all right to disagree with the person saying it. When the meeting has progressed and it is time to move on from one subject to the next, you should make this clear. Sum up and show positive support. Make everyone feel that the meeting has gone well and that results have been achieved.

Solution to problems

Look for solutions and encourage participants to do the same. Everyone should find and evaluate solutions rather than aggravating problems and dwelling on those that have already been identified. It demands a great deal of people to find viable solutions.

At the end

It is an unfortunate fact that the last words of a meeting tend to be those that are best remembered by the group of people. The final comments either give people a sense of achievement or a sense of failure, and people base their expectations of future meetings on the final summing up. As the meeting is drawing to a close, all discussion should have come to an end. The last few minutes should be used for summing up and for giving people an idea of the agenda for the next meeting. Finish the meeting by checking and confirming that the purpose of the meeting has been achieved, even if there is an element of doubt.

Focus attention on the next meeting.

General

Make sure you go along to every meeting in a positive frame of mind. Do not disparage either your partners or the task unless you want to undermine the meeting. If you do that, you will make matters worse. Be very careful not to jeopardize the meeting by bringing your own problems with you.

How can we measure the success of a meeting?

How can you tell if a meeting is going according to plan? Try these activities:

1. Try to remember a recent meeting at your workplace. Did this meeting have a purpose? Did you have an aim? Did you have a plan? Did everyone at the meeting have a clear idea of the aims and their responsibilities in achieving them? How effective was this meeting? What worked and what did not? Was this meeting actually necessary? If you had the opportunity to conduct this meeting again, is there anything you would do differently, and if so what?

2. Write a brief note outlining what is going to happen at a meeting you are going to participate in. In other words: Write the minutes of a meeting before it takes place, and write them before you have specified its aims and objectives. Describe the result based on your definition of success. After the meeting, compare this summary with what really happened.

3. On your way to your meeting, ask yourself the following three questions:
   - What is our aim for this meeting?
   - What do I hope to have achieved by the time I leave this meeting?
   - What will define success and failure at this meeting?
4. Compare the outcome of the meeting with your experience of the meeting.
5. Before each meeting that you chair, you should ask yourself the above questions. Share information with your co-participants before the meeting, and see to it that you contribute to its success. You need to have criteria for determining whether or not a meeting has been successful. Why not use "the parameter for effective meetings" as a frame of reference for successful meetings and unsuccessful meetings?

Detailed preparation means shorter meetings

In order to talk concisely about a subject, you need to think for a long time

Once the meeting is under way, the chances of its success are already reduced. If you spend more of your time on preparation, you spend less of your time on the actual meeting, and your chances of achieving your aims are far greater.

Do your homework

Basically there are no excuses for not doing your homework before a meeting. Not only does it hold the meeting up considerably if you don't prepare, but it also sends out signals to all those present. If you have not done your preparation before a meeting, it signals to the others that you generally do not do preparation for your work. It is a sign that you lack respect for yourself and for others. The meeting specialist ALWAYS knows who has prepared for the meeting and who has not prepared. If you have not done your homework, you should make sure that you do not make it obvious by asking silly questions and coming up with comments, as this will make others feel very embarrassed on your behalf.

Exceeding expectations

We always look up to people who stand out in the crowd. No one will criticize you for being better prepared than everyone else. Being well prepared will never do any harm.

- Doing your homework says a lot about what type of person you are.
- Getting others to do their homework says something about the type of leader you are.
- Giving more than is expected makes you stand out from the crowd in a positive way.

Counting votes

"If I have something on the agenda which is particularly important for me, I always know how people will vote before I go into the meeting"

On the basis of this, you can assess whether the matter is still worth pursuing either by spending a little longer preparing it or by letting it drop if it appears to be to no avail. It is neither illegal nor unethical to sidestep an issue, and sometimes it can be quite necessary.

Parameters for Effective Meetings

When participating

- Do not arrive late. The consequence could be that you are excluded or that you are not updated on what has been happening
- Be prepared. Acquaint yourself with the agenda and structure your input if you have to produce written documents to support what you are saying.
- Mobile phones must be turned off, and they must not be answered if they do ring. Do not interrupt a meeting because of a telephone call unless there is a really good reason for it.
- Do not leave the meeting room.
- Do not slouch back in your chair or doodle. It shows lack of commitment and lack of interest.
- Listen carefully. Contribute by making positive suggestions and inspire others to do the same.
- Accept the need for efficiency and remember that it is the chairman's duty to close the discussion when time is running out.
- Make a concerted effort to ensure that the meeting is a success and that the group works well together.
- Look for the positive aspects and avoid the negative aspects
- Endeavour to be the type of person that you expect others to be.

Success criteria

- Aims and objectives
- Status and performance
- Authority and authorization
- Economics

- Quality and control
- Tools and development
- Deadlines–milestones

Summaries

The following list includes many important and relevant aspects that should be borne in mind in connection with meetings; however, this does not apply to shorter and less formal meetings. All or nearly all these points should be considered when a meeting will have far-reaching effect.

When you are not sure whether you should convene a meeting or participate in a meeting ...

- Think about what you will have achieved by the time the meeting is over.
- Force yourself to justify the meeting in terms of making the best possible use of your time or other people's time.
- Make sure that you are authorized to do what is necessary.
- Make sure that you really need to hold a meeting to achieve what you want to achieve. Consider saying "no." Consider one or several shorter meetings as an alternative and consider dealing with just a few of the proposed items.
- In all cases be willing to take full responsibility for your participation in meetings.

Before the meeting ...

- Make sure that you have the aims clear in your mind.
- Make sure that the aims are clear in the minds of your co-participants.
- Establish specific criteria for measuring success or failure.

- Decide what your personal aim is with the group as a whole and with individual members.

- Reduce the number of participants to the absolute minimum needed to perform the task.

- Evaluate where you stand with regard to your co-participants, those senior to you, your colleagues and those junior to you. In addition, evaluate their probable interests and needs.

- Reduce the number of items and tasks to the absolute minimum.

- Be thoroughly prepared

- Establish an environment appropriate to your aims.

- Consult one of the participants or any other person that you may need to work with in order to achieve your aims.

- Draw up a clear, detailed and appropriate agenda and distribute it along with any other relevant documentation before the meeting.

- Do your homework and be at least one step ahead of your co-participators' expectations.

- Make a preliminary evaluation of all the items on the agenda.

- Vote on the matters that are of critical importance to you.

- Be aware of special traditions, rules and forms of etiquette that apply at the meeting. This is particularly important when the meeting consists of people of mixed nationality or culture.

During the meeting ...

- Approach the meeting and your co-participants in a positive frame of mind.

- Arrive early and establish contact with the key people.

- Sit at the head of the table.

- Throughout the meeting, reflect a positive attitude both towards the task and towards everyone present.

- Make sure someone is taking down the minutes—use a standard document.

- If you are the chairman, you should insist on starting punctually.

- If you are the chairman, you should make sure everyone knows the purpose of the meeting. You should also let everyone know how long it should take to achieve this purpose. This is your most important announcement. Every now and again, repeat the aims of the meeting.

- If you are the chairman you should be prepared to separate the procedure from the items on the agenda for your co-participants. As a participant, you should be on your guard against tendencies to confuse procedure with items on the agenda.

- As chairman you must draw a line between facts and assumptions. Watch out for emotional outbursts and try and get everyone to contribute. Highlight areas of agreement and disagreement, make people feel important, act in the group's best interests and protect the integrity of each individual.

- As a participant you should make clear contributions early on in the meeting with sensitivity and intelligence.

- Break bigger problems down into smaller ones, and if possible deal with each one individually.

- Summarize periodically and make sure that relevant information is included in the minutes.

- Set out your arguments clearly and distinctly. Don't get bogged down with the whys and wherefores.

- Don't waste your energy on matters that are of no importance to you.
- Whatever the state of progress you need to know when to concede a point.
- Always do your best to show courtesy and respect.
- Listen carefully and make it clear that you are being attentive to others.
- Make sure you are present both in body and soul–give your whole self.
- At the end of the meeting, give a summary of what has been achieved and try to ensure participants leave with a sense of pleasure at having participated.
- If the work has been completed, bring the meeting to an end.

After the meeting ...

- Evaluate the meeting in the light of your original aims and according to the criteria for a successful meeting. Continue working towards your goal.
- Share the results with all those who need to know them, including those who have helped in your preparations.
- Immediately follow up on agreements and send out the necessary memoranda.

Analysis of meetings

Think of a typical meeting in which you have recently participated. Read through the points below. Write down what you think is relevant. At the same time, evaluate how long you have spent on each item.

Items on the agenda(Was the agenda logical and were the items dealt with in an effective manner?)

The items that were discussed, but which were not on the agenda

(Were there new items which were not on the agenda, and how thoroughly were they discussed?)

Did you feel that the meeting was beneficial for you and your organization?

Did you feel that there was an exchange of expertise and experience between participants?

Did you feel that the meeting was too long/too short/not with enough breaks/too many breaks?

Were there any time wasters (lack of punctuality, turning up late, broken equipment, distractions, unprepared participants, unnecessary interruptions)**?**

Total length of meeting= _____

EVALUATION FORM

(parameters for effective meetings)

Type of meeting: _____

Chairman: _____

Date: _____

What are the most important factors that contributed to the meeting achieving /not achieving its aims and need for efficiency?

I Chairman Fair Good Outstanding Remarkable.

Well prepared

- Was the chairman prepared and was there a basis for making decisions?

- Were the participants prepared and was there a basis for making their decisions?

- Has the chairman promoted growth and earning capacity for the company?

- Have the participants promoted growth and earning capacity for the company?

- Was the chairman competent to deal with the tasks that need to be carried out and reported on?

- Do the participants respect and are they competent to deal with the tasks that need to be carried out and reported on?

- Does the chairman make demands and give positive and negative feedback to the participants?

- Do the participants demand a lot out of themselves and give positive and negative feedback to each other?

- Is the chairman punctual?

- Did the participants arrive at the agreed time?

EVALUATION FORM

(chairman – CHMN)

Type of meeting: ⎯⎯⎯⎯⎯⎯⎯⎯⎯⎯⎯⎯⎯⎯⎯⎯

Chairman: ⎯⎯⎯⎯⎯⎯⎯⎯⎯⎯⎯⎯⎯⎯⎯⎯

Date: ⎯⎯⎯⎯⎯⎯⎯⎯⎯⎯⎯⎯⎯⎯

II Chairman Fair Good Outstanding Remarkable.

Well prepared

- Is the chairman capable of motivating participants to take responsibility and contribute in an actively communicative manner?

- Is the chairman clear when delegating, giving responsibility and authority to participants?

- Does the chairman appear to be of high integrity and self-confident?

- Is the chairman able to convey his message?
- Does the chairman listen and does he encourage contributions and imitative?
- Does the chairman have the ability to see things from other people's perspective and empathize with their views and arguments?
- Does the chairman manage to run the meeting in accordance with its aims and purpose and achieve results within the time required?
- Has the chairman the ability to identify tasks and problems?
- Are meetings structured, i.e., do they follow an agenda?
- Does the chairman instigate action rather than following other people?
- Is the chairman willing to make decisions?
- Does the chairman have the ability to evaluate and prioritize with consistency and see the whole picture when making a decision?
- Is the chairman able to adapt to changes in conditions? Does he listen to the opinions of others?

EVALUATION FORM

(parameters for effective meetings)

Type of meeting: _____

Chairman: _____

Date: _____

III Chairman Fair Good Outstanding Remarkable.

Well prepared

- Are the participants motivated? Do they take responsibility for the organization, and are they careful to communicate actively?

- Are participants open and willing to undertake work delegated to them at the meeting?

- Do the participants show high personal integrity and self-confidence?

- Are the participants able to express themselves clearly?

- Are participants able to understand situations, views and arguments from the point of view of other people?

- Do participants listen carefully, and do they encourage others when they make contributions and suggestions?

- Are the participants able to contribute to the aims of the meeting?

- Do the participants do anything to ensure that the meeting is well structured and follows the agenda?

- Are the participants willing to make decisions or promote the decisions of others in the meeting?

- Have the participants the ability to influence the meeting while recognizing the needs and ambitions of others?

- Have the participants the ability to make consistent judgments and priorities when decisions have to be made?

CHAPTER 14 - PRESENTATION, NERVOUSNESS AND ANXIETY

The 5 "belts"

Based on my experience going back many years in public presentations, I have categorized speakers and communicators into 5 "belt categories."

1. White belt – the untrained person

The untrained person never holds presentations or gives speeches and tries at all costs to avoid such tasks. The very idea of giving a speech inspires a considerable degree of fear and anxiety. Even on courses where a plenary session introduction is required, he gets nervous. Often the untrained person is extremely shy.

2. Yellow belt – the casual speaker

This could be a salesperson who once in a while finds himself in a situation where he has to give a speech or presentation. He is not overcome by fear at the thought of speaking in front of a group, but would not volunteer to do this. The casual speaker has tried to give speeches, maybe in private, on several occasions.

3. The blue belt – the experienced speaker

This speaker has just moved from the yellow belt up to level 3. He has given quite a few presentations and/or speeches with a certain amount of success. He feels he is on reasonably safe ground when he has to give a presentation, but he needs to spend a long time preparing. He does not have a grasp of the relevant techniques and does not understand the finer details of the task.

4. The green belt - the willing speaker

This speaker gives many presentations and is self-assured, capable and experienced. He is happy to volunteer when people want a speech or presentation, and his extensive experience has taught him the basic techniques necessary for giving successful presentations. He feels tension when he has to give a presentation, but he uses this tension constructively. He has a wide vocabulary and is articulate. His job is likely to be that of manager. Given motivation and experience, he can enter the next level, the black belt.

5. Black belt – the communicator

Communication here is best described as the task at hand. This speaker feels stimulated, enthusiastic and at ease when he talks. He welcomes more or less continuous and positive feedback from the audience. This is someone who is completely competent at turning flight or fight to his advantage. He is always ready and enthusiastic about introducing himself and his ideas. He knows that tenacity will be rewarded. His typical work area will be management, but he is primarily a person who is respected as a motivator as he inspires others through his techniques.

Visualization

The creative side of our brain has difficulty distinguishing between fantasy and reality. This is why we are frightened when we see an unpleasant film or shudder at the thought of something we do not like.

Scientists have found that people can increase their self-esteem by inner visualization. This enhances self-confidence and people's belief in their ability to carry out the task at hand. Self-confidence is built upon experiences of success.

Imagine that you are going to speak in front of 200 important people. These could be clients, colleagues, people from your department, or people who are important to you. First of all, start by considering how your life would be different if you were capable of successfully carrying out a presentation. Think about how much more confident you will be and about the respect that will surround you.

Concentrate on the room where you will be holding your talk. It is actually best if you have been into that room, touched the tables, the chairs, noticed its smell, seen the lighting and absorbed the atmosphere.

Cast your mind back to a time when you had a casual chat with friends or family. See yourself as relaxed and happy. Summon up feelings of self-confidence, pride and composure. Every time you think about yourself speaking at a presentation, you must retrieve that mental image and see yourself as being calm and collected with the people you are talking to.

Visualize yourself next to the overhead projector in front of 200 people. See 200 happy, eager, appreciative faces, each of them waiting with great anticipation for what you are about to say because you and you alone have a message that is going to interest them.

Visualize yourself starting to talk and using your first transparency. Notice this transparency between your fingers; switch on the projector and imagine the beautiful graphics. Give your talk and conclude it. See your audience responding, watch them as they applaud you, and notice that warm feeling of enthusiasm rushing through your body.

Now if you have done a good presentation, you must always recall it every time you give a talk. The process of creating visualized repetition practically enables you to program yourself.

You have in fact carried out your first successful communication presentation.

There are four elements to visualization. Strengthening each of them will accelerate the speed with which you will achieve your main objective.

The first element is **frequency.** How often do you visualize your future objective, your behavior, or the task? People who achieve outstanding results continually visualize what they intend to do. They keep thinking the whole time about what they are going to achieve. They play "the film" over and over again, and by doing this they imagine the final result.

The second element is **precision**. How precisely do you visualize your objective or your task? Less successful people have a vague picture of their objectives. Your initial thoughts are likely to be vague, but as time goes on and you frequently "replay" the film, this will become much clearer in your mind. Finally you will be capable of closing your eyes and seeing a clear and precise goal.

The third element is **intensity.** What degree of feelings do you combine with your mental image when you really want to achieve something? When you are enthusiastic, looking forward to reaching your goal, and believe that you will achieve it, the final result will be achieved more quickly. When the degree of feeling is identical to your mental picture, then you will achieve your result. Unsuccessful people are normally unenthusiastic and unmotivated. They are quite pessimistic, and their energy level is low.

The fourth and final element is **period.** How long are you able to keep the picture of what you want in your mind? The longer you are able to do this, the greater your chances of success. If you have a specific picture of the thing you want, for instance a car, you should get hold of a picture of this car. Put this picture in a visible spot where you can often look at it.

I have heard quite a few people say that visualization is pure humbug, black magic or something supernatural. No, it is really not. Visualization is hard work.

What is the difference between daydreaming and visualizing? Daydreams are a substitute for work. Visualization is work, hard work. For visualization to be successful, you must take care of the basics. It is important that you have prepared your speech, either all of it or some of it. You must know where and when you are going to deliver this speech. It is important that you have some idea about the audience which is going to come and listen to you.

There is a simple reason why visualization is successful. Researchers have noted that our subconscious *is not capable of distinguishing the difference between a real experience and one which you have creatively invented.*

Visualization is not in itself a guarantee for success, but it does give you a visible goal.

I frequently use visualization myself. Before a seminar or a lecture, I run through the procedure 20 times. The first 20 times are inside my head. The last time is reality. This means that I have run every single course many times before it is carried into effect.

What happens if reality does not equate with your visualization? The one thing you can be sure about is that you have done a better job than you would have done if you had not done any visualizing, and not only this, it has given you some additional training.

Do you know what it was that gave Albert Einstein the ability to discover the theory of relativity? He told people that one of the chief reasons was his ability to visualize: "What it would be like to ride on the end of a beam of light?"

Principles of visualization

1. Make your visualization realistic. Think about a real event. Use all your senses to help you get an idea of the location, the spectators, the weather, the lighting, and well, yes, even the food.

2. Make it positive. Hear the applause. Listen to your enthusiastic audience. Notice their friendly response.

3. Do this often. Visualize often, preferably every day. The more often you try and train yourself, the better. Think of an event immediately before you go to sleep. When you do this, your unconscious mind will carry on working on the project while you sleep.

4. Use visualization everywhere. People who are successful within their field visualize either consciously or unconsciously. Use visualization every day and in many different situations.

Verbalization

Verbalization means expressing a purpose or a vision out loud. Standing in front of the mirror and saying "I can do it! I can do it!" several times over is a good way of building your self-esteem. For every time you say this consciously with self-confidence and enthusiasm, your belief in yourself will become stronger.

If you watch a high jumper preparing himself for the championships, you will often see him talking to himself. Any tennis star who has just missed his opponent's serve will go around in deep dialogue with himself. A girl handball team will stand around in a circle before the important match and have group battle cries and slogans. All this is verbalization, which enhances motivation and the objective.

Conversation

Think about your presentation as if you were holding an intimate conversation with your audience—not as a performance. Think about how you speak to individuals in the group. When you concentrate on a conversation with individual members of the group, do you begin to talk in a calmer and more relaxed tone of voice? When our clients start doing this, their presentation gradually changes.

They no longer worry about uncontrolled body language; they move about in a natural way.

They look participants straight in the eye and avoid any audio visual aids, which they would otherwise find indispensable.

Instead of focusing on fear, you should learn to see yourself being met with nods of recognition, smiles or good eye contact from the participants. Imagine your participants as being warm and appreciative and that your presentation finishes with rapturous applause.

Find a friendly face in the group, someone who is nodding and giving you a friendly smile. React to this person's messages and reactions. Look at them often, focus on everything that is positive, send your energy in that direction, and remember—do you use your smile? Try it out. It works miracles!

There are several levels in presentation technique (you can obtain belt levels depending on how skilled you are in this area). Do not throw yourself into large and difficult presentations if you have never done one before.

Begin in a small way; do short presentations. After that, you can move up a level. If you have tested out your presentation level and found that your standard is high, you could soon take on one that is difficult.

Presentation technique, level of proficiency and nervousness are very much related to training and training alone. If you would like to increase your level of proficiency, you should set yourself targets according to the degree of difficulty you dare to embark upon.

Nerves before an important presentation will never disappear completely. You will always be nervous. It is important to handle your nerves by making the fullest possible use of them for your presentation.

When you are nervous, your mind concentrates on the task at hand. There is a lot of positive energy in your nervousness, and this can be turned to constructive use when faced with an audience.

If you find yourself in a situation where you are not at all nervous about your presentation tasks, I am afraid to say that you probably run a great risk of giving a bad and boring presentation.

"Before they get up they do not have any thoughts about what they are going to say; when they speak they do not know what they are saying, and when they sit down they do not know what they have said."

—*Lloyd George*

The audience receives only what you give them

Even though it does not seem like this to you, your audience does not have supernatural powers or telepathic abilities. They cannot see through you and your papers. They cannot hear your thoughts.

The audience receives only what you give them.

What does this really mean?

1. They are not aware of your shaky legs or the butterflies in your stomach.

2. They don't know how nervous you feel.

3. They don't know how you feel.

4. They are not aware of the thousand and one thoughts that are racing through your head.

5. They don't know what you are going to say in 30 seconds' time.

6. They don't know anything except what you tell them.

Preparation

American researchers asked a number of top managers about their reaction to a typical business presentation.

The result: Stimulating 3%, Interesting, 52.2 %, Boring 43.5 %, Unbearable 1%.

Before you start, find out whether a presentation is the proper forum or whether a telephone conversation, a letter or another means of communication would produce a better result.

Bad presentations cost billions!

"The cost of a bad presentation is horrendous. When participants lose interest, important messages are lost, sales are lost, training programs go wrong, company policies are badly implemented and productivity and efficiency are undermined."

When you deliver a bad presentation, you may well waste just one hour of your own life; however, you also waste something like one hour in the lives of, say, 45 participants—thus a total of 46 hours at USD 200, plus expenses such as transport, lost work time, room hire, and equipment, etc. This loss can amount to more than USD 20,000 for just one hour.

Gathering information

Form your opinions on the subject and write them down on a large sheet of paper (preferably with an asymmetrical pattern, brainstorming). Note down anything that comes to mind regarding the subject which you want to talk about. The advantage of an asymmetrical pattern is that it is a working method, which is adapted to the brain's creative way of thinking. In most situations our brains do not work in a strictly logical or systematic way.

Not preparing yourself is the same as
preparing for failure.

Ask yourself questions such as:
- Who are the participants?
- How much do they already know about the subject?
- What would I like to tell them?
- How much time do I have available?

Define your goals

After that, you can reject everything that is not relevant to the notes you first prepared. Decide which headings and sub-sections you would like to use and arrange them systematically.

The structure in your presentation gradually begins to take shape. Remember that you do not have time to talk about everything that you know about the subject. Include only relevant points which can be included within the time you have available. That is very important. If you want to come across as professional, bear in mind that if you are allotted thirty minutes, you should keep to thirty minutes.

The purpose should be written out so that it is clear and easy to understand, as in the examples below:

Main points

- Why are you making a presentation?
- How would you like your audience to react?
- What steps should the audience take after the presentation?

"The purpose of this presentation is to make people aware of the company's new bonus incentives."

"My aim with this presentation is to make all employees aware of customer relationships."

There is a tendency to confuse the concepts of the objective of the presentation with the objectives of the project. They are not the same.

In order to understand the objective of the project, you must ask yourself, "What will happen if the project is a success?" In order to understand the objective of the presentation, you must ask yourself, "What will happen if the presentation is a success?"

One example of the project's objective could be: "We will complete the building by 15th December at the latest." The presentation's objective could be to convince the board of directors of the need for extra subsidies for the building.

Preliminary plan

Here we have an example of a preliminary plan. It is based on reorganization of middle management in the company *AYZ Machines*. We are already aware that we need three meetings, and we have identified the principal ideas for the first presentation followed up by supporting information.

First meeting: principal idea

1. Changes in the contracting market will considerably affect our income potential.
2. We will look into our organization's structure to reduce operational costs.
3. We will not reduce staff numbers.
4. Based on the proposed ideas, each department manager will present his own recommendations for cutting costs.

First meeting: supporting information (Changes in contractors...)

Principal idea no. 1:

• Sales figures for the last 4 years showing reduction in earnings

• Information regarding our competitors' price structure with bargain prices and turnover

- Market assessment carried out by market research companies, describing future prospects

First meeting: supporting information (We will look into.....)
Principal idea no. 2:

- Expenses over the last 4 years, which show a constant rise
- Estimated expenses in the future, as long as existing administrative expenses are maintained
- Detailed expense factor for a department which has the greatest increase in expenses

First meeting: supporting information (We will not reduce.....)
Principal idea no. 3:

- Departments where employees will be involved and how they will be moved
- Plans for further training of extra personnel

First meeting: supporting information (Based on the......)
Principal idea no. 4:

- Areas where expenses can be reduced or eliminated
- Type

Schedule for the presentation

 As a result of several years' experience with professional speakers and with others giving commercial presentations, both as a participant and as a consultant, I have drawn up a *Schedule for presentation,* based on my work on negotiation techniques, *see appendix A.*

The schedule is a simple method for organizing your presentation, since you can see at a glance that the main themes are supported by gestures, notes, visual aids, examples etc. This is particularly suitable for people who frequently find that they have too much information and find it difficult to be concise.

At the same time, the schedule has been organized so that the principal points in the presentation are listed. In addition to this, you can also use this schedule as a tool to develop your ideas.

Do not use the schedule for the presentation itself. It is not a substitute for notes or any other kind of aid.

One of my clients told me that he works best on his schedule on his way to and from his office. During this time he is capable of compiling a one-hour long presentation in less than 20 minutes.

First of all you should write out the aims of your presentation. "My aims are ...."

The written objective is there as a focal point. Remember that the driving force behind the presentation is the result. Try not to write sentences into the settings, but use only one or two words per setting.

Principal message

As there may only be 3-4 principal messages in your presentation, you can use the remaining place in your schedule for sub-sections.

Visual aids

This column enables you to describe which visual aids you are going to use for the occasion. Allow for only one transparency for two minutes, or at the most, ten transparencies for a 20-minute presentation.

Examples

In order to make your presentation as lifelike as possible, you should introduce actual examples from everyday life, preferably from your own. It is at this point that you can weave in anecdotes, examples and stories which you are going to use in your presentation.

Body Language

Very few people are aware of the need for congruent body language throughout the communication process beforehand. Including simple, expressive mannerisms will make your messages appear even clearer to the gathering.

Since approximately a third of the gathering will be visually oriented (see communication), exhibiting an expressive body language will help quite a few of them to understand your presentation.

As we notice in other places, congruence, i.e., the correlation between verbal and non-verbal communication, is produced when body language and words convey the same meaning. In this way body language supports the spoken word.

> *Many well prepared presentations have*
> *failed in their objective when the speaker*
> *had not attempted to prepare for the reac-*
> *tion of his audience.*

When we asked participants what they remembered about a presentation, which they had attended the day before, all of them seemed to say that they remembered a person with cogent body language.

Notes for distribution

For some presentations, especially very technical ones, you will need to distribute notes. Perhaps you may need to distribute an actual example of the product you are talking about.

Who is your audience?

I will never forget one of my early presentations. I was working as advisory consultant for a large organization, and I had to hold two identical presentations for two different groups on increase in value and how it is generated.

The first group was easy—they were keen and asked relevant questions. They were also very open and interested in what I had to say. The second group had critical comments about everything that I said; they were negative about the whole idea. By the end of the day, I was absolutely shattered.

Just as I stood packing my things, the department director turned up and asked, "How did it go?"

I answered, "It was awful! The first group was understanding and keen to listen, but the second group was churlish and unmotivated in every respect."

"I am not surprised," he answered, "They are our most difficult employees!"

"What do you mean?" I asked.

I was then told that the organization had intentionally put these people together to see whether they could acquire this particular technique. The alternative would be to dismiss this mistrustful group of participants.

After careful consideration, I suggested repeating the presentation for this group. The department director accepted this.

I restructured the program for this group. Experience had told me that the entire group of twelve were uncooperative because of individuals the rest of the group looked up to. I focused my energies on these people with the amended presentation, which emphasized self-esteem, feelings of value, and their own sense of involvement.

My idea bore fruit. The presentation went fantastically well with magnificent results.

This experience taught me to ask questions about the group I am going to give a presentation to, many questions.

Asking the right questions

For big events, courses and conferences, I send out questionnaires which have to be returned to me. Alternatively, I am physically present in the company and speak to representatives of the group which the presentation is geared for. I make it clear to my clients that every answer I receive will be treated with the greatest confidence.

The location

The more you know about the situation at hand, its physical location, the clients requirements, background information and the type of audience, the greater your chances of a successful presentation.

Find out about all relevant data regarding the physical location for the presentation and any contacts that you may need.

This information should help to alleviate any feelings of stress and help you to deliver a top-quality presentation.

Being prepared for emergency situations is vital. You can never tell what might suddenly happen.

- Where is the meeting actually held?
- Who can you approach within the organization if there should be a problem?
- Where will you stay?
- Are there any participants from outside the organization?

The program

I usually hold a pre-analysis day in consultation with one or several of the clients' representatives. On that day the company clarifies its core motives, possibly situations they themselves are not even familiar with. The objectives of the organization could be:

Background information

- What are the actual objectives with the presentation?
- Are there subjects which ought to be avoided?
- Are there other speakers? Should I finish by a specific time?
- Have there been training programs in the recent past?
- Why the interest in this particular program?
- What will happen if this training is not provided?

This establishes the actual tasks/problems which the client has, i.e., situations which we can relate to and thereby use in the presentation.

Participants

- What are the actual problems/challenges?
- What are the 3 biggest problems?
- Please give me 10 trade expressions.

- How were the participants informed about this program?
- Please attach the notice to attend.
- What are they expecting from the program? Happy about it or ...?
- Have they volunteered to come along, or have they been sent?
- Who poses the greatest problems in my group?

Knowing who the participants are going to be will help you to target your message accurately, and combined with that you minimize the chances of the group asking tricky questions.

- Please send copies of the most recent internal newsletters or other printed matter.
- Who is your main competitor?
- Compared to other organizations, what are the special qualities of your organization?

Remember that knowledge is power!
- And this comes from asking questions.
Many questions

Some people send questionnaires out to participants beforehand in order to gain an insight into aspects such as their expectations, anxieties, and the typical presentation environment. This information helps clarify relevant and important information when planning the presentation.

Four basic questions and answers are of interest to you when you hold a presentation:

1. How nervous are they about holding talks or presentations?

2. Who is their typical audience?

3. What is their level of previous training?

4. What would they like to get out of the presentation or the course?

Those participating in the presentation or the course can benefit tremendously by having material sent to them before the presentation takes place, perhaps 1-2 weeks beforehand. This is what we call pre-training, thus training before the presentation or the course itself. The course itself is the principal part, and we call the follow-up "post-training."

Why is it an advantage to have material sent out with a view to pre-training? Participants have a chance of getting to know me and my methods and log onto my way of thinking, as well as familiarize themselves with the purpose of the presentation. All necessary information is distributed, and the motivation of the participants is heightened. One suggestion for the contents of the training program can be as follows:

Each presentation situation is unique. The agenda varies, speakers are different, and so is the audience; the primary target group varies from one event to another. People's reactions fluctuate because of mood, attitudes and many other things. So ask questions—a lot of questions.

Based on experience, here are a few examples of presentations:

- An overview of a company
- Presentation of an offer to management
- Participation in client presentation
- Internal presentations for departments or staff groups
- Product demonstrations for clients
- Presentation of data for clients
- Welcoming suppliers and introducing company needs and requirements
- Actively participating in negotiations
- Submitting reports on projects

There are of course thousands of other examples.

Notes

Why not use "a post card"? Write the main heading in capital letters (You should be able to read these from a distance). Under each of these headings, write two key words which will remind you of what you are going to say.

Use a short introduction for each subject, one for summing up and one for your conclusion. Make sure that the order is logical. If you have prepared your ideas correctly, words will just come naturally to you. If you need quotations, these should be written on a separate card.

Another good technique is "mind-mapping." Use large sheets of paper and colors. This is a slightly more difficult technique to apply because for most people it is a completely new way of thinking. We can, however, recommend this technique, as it is particularly effective once you have the hang of it.

Regardless of which method you use, you should be able to use catchwords.

If you have to distribute technical drawings or specific data, you should use hand-outs.

A proficient speaker is a person who is
capable of reducing a half-hour presentation
to 8 minutes.

Structure

A well-structured presentation has three main parts:

1. Beginning/introduction
2. Middle part/main part
3. Conclusion/summing-up

Tell them what you want to say.
Let them know.
Then tell them what you have told them

When you begin to prepare your presentation, your objectives should include one or several of the following:

To inform

You want to give information about a process or a procedure, about how the new IT-system works, about what is necessary for the new campaign or on working hours in August. The purpose of a report-presentation is also to inform.

Informative presentations instruct and give guidance by answering the "wh" questions: where, who, what, why as well as how.

Ideally the participants should go away with the impression: "I learned something new."

To entertain

You could be asked to give a light and entertaining speech at an office party or at a function for clients. Remember that this is not just about telling jokes. Talk about yourself in an ironic way. You will discover that the best jokes and stories are those with you as the main character.

At the same time, you must be very careful not to include subjects which may offend participants, for example, religion, weight, skin color, etc.

To motivate

Anything that can encourage participation and motivation is always particularly appropriate at any presentation. As an inspiring speaker, it is not your duty to talk to your participants about their faults and shortcomings, but to direct attention to new methods.

To persuade

Another objective might involve a change of procedure, selling an idea or a product. Persuasion involves using material that is related to fact. It is important that the speaker comes across as being honest and open, someone who participates in the result in addition to being enthusiastic and confident about the new idea or product.

In your discussions, you may need to broach the subject of negative aspects, challenges or objectives.

Structure – informative presentation

Beginning/introduction

A good introduction has three primary purposes:

1. To give participants the chance to settle down. Participants need to listen for a few minutes before they begin to concentrate.

2. To capture the attention of the participants and guide them into the subject you want to talk about.

3. To create an atmosphere and tell the participants why they should listen and what advantages they will receive from being present.

Welcome everyone. Start with a quip if you are able to, or begin by introducing a particularly interesting point about your subject. Don't begin with a question to which you might get an unexpected answer.

Do use humor, but be careful. Humor can bring life and vigor to your presentation, but with humor you can also unintentionally cause offence. Misplaced humor can ruin the whole of your presentation, no matter how fantastic your message may be.

If you really need to use humor, you must make sure that it is a benign type of humor. Never exaggerate humor. One good tip is to use self-irony. Very few people will be offended if you make fun of yourself.

Introduce yourself and your company and state your credentials. Give a clear description of what your aims are with the presentation. Let your audience know as early as possible what you are going to say.

You ought to have reminders on the topics you are including in the middle of your presentation. It is also a good idea to mention how long your presentation is going to last, whether you are going to use any visual aids, and what hand-outs you are going to distribute. Mention when you intend to answer questions and any other "rules" which may apply.

If you would like to give a little more "prominence" to your introduction, you could start by making an apt remark such as:

"Last year you lost USD 2,400,000 because of bad presentations."

"Did you know that the Danes are only in the 17th place when it comes to public health?"

"Development requires change."

"Would you like to make my work twice as easy?"

"When I began this project I felt very optimistic. Now I am over the moon!"

You could tell a story related to the subject or about yourself.

You could tell a joke or an anecdote.

Speakers have used various recordings to capture people's attention at the beginning of their presentations, ranging from the sound of roaring elephants to motorway noises and light shows.

Middle part/main part

While you are talking you should use memory aids, i.e., let your audience know when you have finished one topic and are moving on to the next one.

With each topic, you should order your ideas in a logical sequence. It is quite appropriate to answer questions when you have reached the end of each topic.

Conclusion-summing up

Sometimes it happens that a speaker spoils a good address by saying something like "That's it!" or "I don't think there is any more!"

The conclusion may be a type of summing up (though not a repetition of the whole presentation), or quite simply it may be a rounding off of the presentation.

Clearly indicate that you have come to the end of your presentation and don't just let the presentation degenerate into an apologetic anticlimax. Quickly remind your audience about the points you have made. Thank them for coming along.

Eight ways of making your presentation
more interesting:

- Humor
- Remarks
- Personal stories
- Examples and illustrations
- Statistics
- Graphs and graphics
- Expert opinions
- Involving the audience

Other alternatives are:

- Conclude by telling a dramatic story.
- Quote something.
- Look forward.
- Appeal to the participants.
- Obtain acceptance and *commitment* for further action.

- Motivate your audience.
- Just say "Thank you for letting me come along."

Level of attention

In the beginning the level of attention is very high, and then it falls relatively slowly during the first 10 minutes. After that it falls abruptly until after half an hour, it reaches its minimum. It then increases quickly, and during the last 5 minutes it is high again.

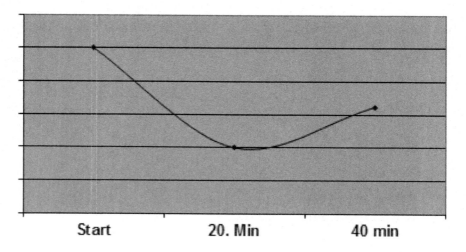

| | Start | 20. Min | 40 min |

Your audience's attention will not increase towards the end unless they are informed that the end is approaching.

The main points which the audience needs to remember are placed at the beginning and at the end. With each topic, the final sentence or illustration is particularly important. Presentations lasting 25-30 minutes have the greatest effect. These receive more attention, though topics that are too short can also impair the presentation.

Be enthusiastic

Enthusiasm, involvement and empathy are key words when trying to use your demeanor to inspire your audience with enthusiasm. I believe in emotion input during presentations, as it is natural. When you reveal your inner being, your real self, your audience will automatically find congruence in your demeanor, find you credible, and listen to you.

Find 2-3 areas in the presentation which really inspire you. Use these actively to improve your own presentation.

Be active

Make demands on your participants. Ask them to participate in physical activity and get them to move about, ideally after lunch. Have a few quick games or challenging tasks to encourage them out of their chairs.

Tell stories

Every presentation, regardless of whether the subject is budgets, product descriptions, sales meetings or courses, is considerably improved by stories, preferably personal stories.

The purpose of your story is to help people to get to grips with the subject and make it simple to understand. They also help you to relate to your audience, create rapport, and make your presentation one to be remembered.

Where does the story come from? Answer: your everyday life. Each and every day something happens in your home, at your office, in the sports club or in a shop, which can be converted and used as a story or an anecdote.

Your own stories should contain situations that your participants can relate to, a story where the audience will say "Me too!"

Time

"My next theme is ...."

"The new development affects ...."

"After this comes ...."

"This leads me on to ...."

This is the way in which we change over to a new section in our presentation. The audience must know with absolute certainty that the former section has finished and that you are continuing onto a new subject area. Instead of saying "OK ...." and continuing, these suggestions are relevant.

Effective presentations do not just have powerful openings and main points–their endings are convincing and spot-on!

Structure - persuasive presentation

Persuasiveness

When you are going to introduce a scheme, which could involve the use of financial resources, or where there may be an alteration of objectives (or both), you should make an extra effort to prepare your presentation thoroughly and introduce it in a professional manner.

You may ask: what is a persuasive and convincing presentation, and does it work? One of the best examples is of course the world of advertising. If you smoke or have smoked in the past, which applies to about half the population of Denmark, you can probably remember the first of the many cigarettes that you smoked. Did it taste nice? I doubt it; quite the contrary, your body protested and told you quite plainly that it would prefer to be spared such a thing. Why did you do it?

You were "The Marlboro Man" or you were taken in by an image, persuasive marketing from manufacturers who told you that it was smart to smoke.

A good persuasive presentation will correlate with the three representative systems described in communication: visual, auditory and kinesthetic. If it is cogent and contains elements of the three representative systems, it will be immensely effective and add weight to what you are saying.

This type of presentation has the same structure as an informative presentation. The difference lies in the way you process the contents while going over the presentation of problems and discussing solutions.

For example, it can be an instance when you try to persuade a person or a group to accept actions which you would like them to perform. This covers everything from selling life insurance to persuading employees about new strategies and agendas. The order of the topics should be "Structure–persuasive presentation technique."

Improvisation

It has been said that a visitor once witnessed Winston Churchill walking backwards and forwards talking to himself. The explanation was that he was preparing an improvised speech. If you have reason to believe that you will be asked to say a few words, try to prepare something beforehand. Unfortunately, the nature of surprise is such that you cannot always prepare yourself as you may suddenly find that you are in the midst of the situation.

Three tips follow:

Firstly: With an improvised speech, no one expects pearls of wisdom or invaluable information. They will be perfectly satisfied with a little bit of friendly small talk (talking about the weather, as we call it). For this reason, you can be quite vague and unspecific without suffering loss of credibility.

Secondly: You can often jog your memory by using mental images which go as far back in time as possible and after that bring the story back to the present. (Structure is used in the same way as with an informative presentation). You can, for example, ask yourself when you first heard about this product/firm/subject and in what context. Can you recall anything happening after that? Where are we now? What about the future?

Thirdly: Remember to take all the time you need. At a maximum you should spend two to three minutes. On such occasions, what you say is normally forgotten after a short time.

Reading a speech

The best advice we can give to those who are planning to read a speech is–don't do it. The spoken word and the written word are two completely different things. When someone reads out a speech, it sounds inauthentic and artificial. Out of habit, people speak much better on the basis of what they understand than directly from detailed and thorough notes.

There can nevertheless be occasions when you need to present a document on behalf of another person. This is an incredibly difficult task, as you need to look at the audience as often as possible in order to put life into your presentation.

It means that your eyes should be five to six words ahead of your voice —a very difficult technique to master. If this applies to you, you can practice by reading out loud from a book or a magazine while looking up as often as you can.

Persuasion: reasons for buying – features and benefits

The art of persuasion

Telling someone something is not the same as selling them something or persuading them about something. It is important to be aware that there is a huge difference between informing people and selling them a product, a service or an idea.

Reasons for buying:

People buy anything, including ideas, for one or several of the following reasons:

- Finance
- Durability
- Utility value
- Image/appearances

- Reliability
- Productivity
- Safety
- Security

They buy because the idea, the service or the product meets a need and gives them an advantage. No one buys products because of their features; they buy them because of their benefits. It is for this reason that when you want to sell something or introduce an idea, a product or a service, you should mention their benefits.

Features and benefits Definition:
A feature describes what things can do.
A benefit describes what a feature can do for someone.

1. Qualify

In order to avoid losing the thread of what you are saying, wandering off the subject or repeating yourself, you should make sure that you talk to the right people. Ask yourself: "Who are they?" "Which department do they come from?" "Do they know who I am and what my occupation is?" Do tell them that you know that they already have quite a bit of knowledge on the subject. This helps you to make contact and establish a rapport.

Remember that you will need to explain any technical details which some of your audience may not be familiar with.

2. Define needs

At least a quarter of your presentation should be confined to defining needs. To give yourself the chance of persuading people, you must make sure that everyone agrees on the problems or disadvantages of the situation at hand. Many ideas are lost because the speaker does not attach much importance to such matters. Before you go on to the next stage, you should ask your audience whether they accept that these problems do exist.

3. Meet needs

At this point your audience will be very keen on hearing how you believe you can solve their problems. You will have built up their expectations. Tell them about your solutions. These solutions ought to be features or descriptions instead of benefits, which will come later on in the structure.

4. Mention benefits

Then explain what your solutions entail and how the company can benefit from them. Attempt to make each benefit an answer to problems, which were defined in step 2.

This is often a good moment to mention expenses—not just costs, but savings. Make sure that you are prepared for objections regarding increase in costs in your preparation.

5. Action

You are ready to recommend how it ought to happen. When all is said and done, this is the intention of your presentation. **Be as positive as you can!**

Summing up of structure

Persuasive presentations

1. Introduction

- Greet everyone, introduce yourself and your company.
- Identify the subject.
- Justify your credentials.
- Make the purpose of your presentation clear.
- Let people know how much time you will spend.
- Let people know how and when you will answer questions.

2. Content

- Outline the situation as it is at present.
- Outline the problem in light of the situation.
- Sum up all the problems and arguments.
- Outline the solutions (ideally the alternative solutions).
- State the advantages and disadvantages of each solution.
- Demonstrate that the advantages of each solution are that they can give the best results.
- Briefly sum up (ideally, you should repeat the topic categories).
- Repeat your intentions.
- Invite questions.

3. Action

- Involve your audience.
- Identify who does what, when, time, etc.
- Reach a final agreement and thank everyone for coming.

Visual aids

An old proverb says, "One picture is worth ten thousand words," or we could change this around a bit and say that a transparency will not replace a twenty-minute speech, but it can add improvements to a presentation and make it more effective.

Visual aids enhance communication because human beings tend not to think in chronological order, but in pictures. The fact is that we absorb graphics faster than words, so verbal presentations can be reduced. It has been found that we have seven times more brain cells available for pictures than we have for sounds and touch!

Your audience will be more attentive when you animate your ideas and your presentations—that is because they are being given both color and perspective. It will also give you a more realistic overview of your presentation, and consequently people will perceive you as being well prepared and professional.

We looked at the way in which we learn in the chapter on "Communication: visual (sight), auditory (sound) and kinesthetic (emotions)."

The professional picture

We should use pictures and symbols to highlight:

- Ideas
- Emotions
- Attitudes and values
- Facts
- Events

Be consistent. Each slide, page or transparency sheet needs to have an identical layout and an identical pattern. Don't begin to vary background and color. Choose a format and stick to it.

Use as few words as possible. The maximum should be six lines with 4 to 7 words per line. More than that confuses people and means that your audience starts to read from the page. Make the transparencies horizontal (A4 placed down).

Use only key words, preferably with color, and keep a lot of empty space on the page so as not to confuse the message. When there are two messages on the same page, make them distinct by using two different colors. If the first message is written in blue, the next one can be written in red. An exception is when using a data projector. PowerPoint, for instance, has multi-media features which give you several additional options for presenting your material besides color.

Typical mistakes

- Too many ideas on one page
- Taking too long over one transparency
- Producing a transparency of a written page
- Too much content on one page, text, pictures and colors

Limit yourself—only one idea for each page. Do not overload with information. It is better to have several pages with just a few points made on each page.

So remember: One page for every two minutes of talking.

Use bullet points to emphasize text. Avoid numbering bullet points, as this may confuse people.

Use just one type face, for instance Times New Roman, which I am using now, or ARIEL like this. Be careful with CAPITAL LETTERS, as it takes longer to read capitals than it does to read ordinary print. Use capitals only with headings.

When you are using bold-faced type, don't use more than two different type-face sizes on the same transparency sheet. The size should be between 26–32". When you insert a logo or another illustration, you should make sure that it is reasonably small and that it is in the same position on each slide or transparency sheet.

When graphic elements are centered, they should be in proportion to one another, which means that they should look symmetrical. The graphic elements are all the objects on the page such as letters, lines, shapes, colors, pictures, and empty areas. A graphic element can look "**HEAVY"** or "light."

Colors

Research has demonstrated the importance of color. Seven thousand presentations were analyzed and evaluated as follows:

People's attention was considerably increased when colors were used rather than black and white. When people were shown a black and white page, their attention was held for eight seconds. When the same people were shown an identical page with colors, their attention was held for 11 seconds. When pictures or photos were placed on the page as background, their attention span increased by 16 seconds per page.

In addition, it has been noted that people memorize faster and are more efficient at remembering the contents of a page when colors are used, in which case attention-span increases by 55 to 78 per cent and audience participation increases by 80 per cent.

It is important, however, to limit the use of color and have a maximum of 3 to 4 colors per page.

Warm, bright colors hold people's attention for longer than cold and dark colors. Use different color variations to designate areas or indicate different sections. Cold colors are: blue, brown, dark green, light green and black. Warm colors are red and orange. Use yellow, orange or light brown to highlight.

It is not advisable to talk for more than ten to twenty minutes without using a visual aid of one kind or another. Visual aids should be used with discretion; do not over-use them.

Swamping your audience with transparencies will not improve your presentation. The aim is for visual aids to supplement what you say, not repeat what you have said.

When you use a board, be careful not to talk into it, but to your audience. Produce your visual aids when you need to refer to something on them and keep them covered up until you are ready to use them.

Erase the information or cover it up until you have finished. If you need to distribute material, you should wait until it is time to refer to it or after you have referred to it.

If you need to use technological resources, you MUST familiarize yourself with the equipment and make sure that it is all in good working order well before your presentation. It is not a bad idea to make sure you have extra equipment available. Very often technical equipment fails, so you should not rely on it completely as you could be in for an unpleasant surprise.

Different types of audio visual aids (AV)
Boards

- Disadvantages
- Chalk dust everywhere
- Not a permanent reference

- You cannot refer back to notes later on in the presentation
- Cannot prepare work or hide it
- Board looks messy when it has been in constant use
- Difficult to write on
- Unpleasant noise

Advantages

- In many training rooms
- Easy to jot things down that crop up incidentally

Flip charts

You should not use a flip chart if there are more than about forty or fifty people present. People often cannot see letters and lines when they are in larger groups, regardless of whether or not you use color. Apart from that, a flip chart can be a staunch ally, especially when used in conjunction with an overhead projector. The flip chart can bring a sense of spontaneity to  your presentation. With these you can record what has been said, write things down, and return to the subject.

If you are right-handed, you should stand to the left of your flip chart so as you do not cover up the area which you are writing on. One frequent mistake is that some people continue to speak while they are writing on it. Stop talking. Pause while you write or draw. This will seem like an eternity to you, but your audience will like it because you are focusing their attention onto the message on the chart.

Use a black or blue felt-tipped pen with a broad point. Don't hesitate to use color to give it some variation and to clarify everything you have written or drawn on the chart.

One little secret: Many professionals prepare by writing things up or by doing their drawings beforehand with a pen. The audience, who of course imagines that the speaker has a natural flair for writing or drawing, never sees this. There are also many speakers who use the pages from the flip-chart for their own notes—again, the audience does not see this.

Disadvantages	Limited space
	Neat handwriting essential
	Tendency to scribble
Advantages	Permanent reference
	Can refer back to points that have been mentioned earlier
	Can be prepared beforehand and remain hidden
	Neat and tidy
	Easy to move
	Easy to use different colors

How to get the best out of audiovisual resources

Remember the following points when you use one or several audio visual aids:

1. Try not to scribble

Lecturers are normally afraid of wasting too much time on writing neatly on the board. Again, it means using up more time than necessary. Write and draw nicely. There is not much worse than bad handwriting and scribbling. Try to write and draw in straight lines in such a way that your writing or your drawing does not slope from one side to the other. Do not write or speak while you are using any kind of support equipment. Spend as much time as you need on writing things down because while you are doing this, your audience will be busy trying to see what you are doing. Never talk into the board or the screen.

2. Use of color

If possible, you may use more than one color, but not more than three. Using more than three can confuse people. Colors arouse people's interest and enhance the speaker's professional image, which tends to be less predominant. Colors are a good way of illustrating the different stages in your presentation.

3. Covering up

Don't let your audience see anything you are going to use before you are ready to use it. It is frustrating for people when they sit there and think about what you have planned to show them and when this is going to happen.

PROJECTORS

Now that there are an increasing number of technological options, direct multimedia presentations are becoming more and more widespread. With data and video projectors, you can use the note-book feature as well as simple programs such as Microsoft PowerPoint.

A bit of advice:

Use multimedia in the same way as you do with overhead projectors. Maintain eye contact with your audience. Never start your presentation by using multimedia equipment; *you* should be active when you introduce your presentation. When it comes to using the equipment, make sure it is interactive with yourself as commentator.

Everything should be straightforward and clear, just as with transparencies. The same rules apply.

Remember that the more electronic equipment you use, the greater the risk of technical breakdown. Be prepared.

Story board

You probably know about this from films. One way of recording ideas and main concepts is to use graphics.

For instance, you can use the left-hand side for writing things down and the right-hand side for drawing.

PowerPoint

PowerPoint presentations have not always been a major force in communications within businesses, but since the 1990s and throughout the 2000s they have been steadily replacing more traditional means of business communication.

Email is still the preferred communication tool in business. After that comes PowerPoint.

As mentioned earlier, there are millions of PowerPoint users in the world and the number is growing rapidly. As a consequence, we also see a growing number of presentations. Even though PowerPoint presentations are produced at a rate not previously seen, the standard of quality and professionalism hasn't changed much. It is actually quite bad when only 4% of all presentations have the professional touches and content that conform with guidelines from leading communication experts.

The situation becomes even more terrifying when you calculate the time spent *preparing* these presentations, and perhaps more importantly, the time spent in their delivery – which means presenter time *plus* audience time. As illustrated earlier, time wasted on presentations means large sums of wasted money every year. This is why there is such great value in improving your PowerPoint presentations, both in preparation and in delivery.

If we compare the two most widely-used means of communication, email and PowerPoint, we do find some major differences. The recipient of an email can choose to ignore or even delete it, if it appears to be irrelevant or a waste of time. When attending a PowerPoint presentation, however, you are likely to be stuck in your seat until the end, hoping you'll eventually leave the room with something useful in tow.

Compared to other common forms of communication, a PowerPoint presentation is different in many ways. For instance, books and bulky reports take many hours, weeks or even months to make ready for distribution. A PowerPoint presentation usually takes less than 24 hours to prepare, often considerably less. Delivery usually takes about 60 minutes, including set-up and take-down.

Similar to a book or report, a PowerPoint presentation very often ends up being a one-way form of communication, with little or no interaction between presenter and audience. It is far more effective, though, where the audience can get involved and become an active part of the presentation.

Audience involvement can be brought about by using open questions, playing games, or through other activities. But beware – unless the content and its delivery are interesting and engaging all on their own, you're not likely to get much willing involvement, no matter what questions you ask or games you offer.

A PowerPoint presentation should to be regarded as the storyboard and screenplay of a great movie in which you are the narrator, the director and the lead character. A great deal of a movie's success also hinges on another vital element: the supporting characters. This is why you need to get your audience involved – they are essentially the supporting characters in the "movie" you are producing. When you achieve this, your audience will leave with the feeling they have learned something and been *part* of the presentation. Hopefully they'll feel they gained much more than they expected. Only then will you leave a lasting impact and be remembered!

Delegate your tasks

Instead of spending most of your time figuring out details such as how to arrange the graphics in your presentation, or how to add tables, as a presenter you need to focus on *how to deliver the most important messages of your presentation.*

The following is a general list of points that will help you manage your time and stay in control while preparing your next presentation:

1. **Draw things out on paper** – lay out what you want your presentation to look like and what you want to include. Rough sketches of graphics, key words and headlines will do. The aim is to get the contents out of your head and down onto paper, so you're better able to *see* what you have and work out what you want to present.

2. **Brainstorm on your message** – decide on your most important points, and how to deliver them in original ways.

Consider images, elements and metaphors that will enhance your message and contents.

3. **Write your manuscript** – as you write, think of ways to make your presentation more dynamic. Write the manuscript in Word while drawing your ideas on a piece of paper.

4. **Adjust the time** you need for your presentation. As a rough rule of thumb, you should plan for one slide every two minutes. (This can vary greatly, though, depending on the type of presentation you're giving.)

5. **Be consistent** with regard to your graphics. Having a clear theme in terms of colors, graphic elements (borders, underlines, etc.), images, tables and so on will add continuity to your presentation and make it look like a single, well-integrated document.

6. **Choose your presentation personality** according to *how* you want to deliver your most important messages (tone, atmosphere, feeling) and the sort of personality you want the audience to see.

7. **Rehearse each part of the presentation.** You don't have to know it all by heart, but you need to remember the presentation's order and overall messages.

8. **Go through the entire presentation,** either by yourself or in front of a test audience (one or more of your friends, family, colleagues).

9. **Proofread** your final presentation and adjust where needed.

10. **Print a copy** of your presentation in case PowerPoint or your computer or projector doesn't work on presentation day.

As the above guide illustrates, a large part of a good presentation lies in the work that goes into preparing the presentation as a whole – rather than just the content and graphics, which people often spend the most time on.

Your personality is 80% of your presentation

In the end, it's not so much about whether your *graphic* presentation is good or bad – that is simply a part of the path to success. The largest factor in deciding whether your presentation is a success or not is *you* – not your PowerPoint, not the participants, not even the words you say. It depends primarily on your "PowerPoint personality."

To be clearer, it is not necessarily your usual personality that is the deciding factor, but rather how you *perform*. And everyone can learn to perform well, even though it takes practice. A good speaker has practiced his presentation – both *how* to present it and *what* it contains. When you have made it absolutely clear in your own mind what you want to share with your audience and how to go about sharing it, it will be easier to do it right, and you'll make a greater impact!

Therefore, by allocating a large part of the total time you spend on your presentation to the preparation stage, and providing you're effective in how you go about preparing, you will be able to give your presentation in a confident, professional and natural manner.

Advice from the worlds best speakers

Here are 12 things you'll see the biggest public speakers do when they deliver a presentation:

1. Learn to get your audiences involved in your presentations – hold on to and build their interest and involvement, and they'll listen to every word.

2. Be passionate about your subject and your presentation, and share that passion with your audience.

3. Save the best for last, and make sure the audience knows there's something more in store for them.

4. Present yourself with a high level of credibility.

5. Show compassion and treat your audience as your equals.

6. Speak loudly, clearly and with confidence

7. Be a real person.

8. Share a bit about yourself and the audience will tend to share, too.

9. Tell *your* story to get the audience involved.

10. Give the audience reason to admire you.

11. Create messages that will help the audience tackle their own challenges.

12. Coach the audience when you're on stage.

Checklist: Seven essential steps to a better presentation

1) Delegate tasks when preparing your PowerPoint slides and your live presentation.

2) Avoid creating entire presentations all on your own. For example, use professionally created graphic content by downloading slides from www.slideshop.com, or use their Design Service.

3) Create the perfect manuscript for your presentation, including catchy wording and eye-catching headlines.

4) Choose and use a personal style when composing and delivering your PowerPoint presentation.

5) Become aware of how you present yourself as a person when on stage.

6) Use metaphors and visual elements to keep the audience interested and make it easier for them to decode your messages.

7) Recycle your best slides.

For additional information on PowerPoint presentations - visit www.slideshop.com for presentation ideas and read Mr. Toke Kruses book Slide Satisfaction on PowerPoint presentation.

Principal idea
Graphic illustration

Welcome. New idea

in training:

How to ensure expansion:

A proportion of turnover for development:

What should be illustrated?

Introduction: You could probably start with a picture, an illustration or with a brief and apposite text. Remember, though, it has to refer to something that you would like your audience to think about. For this you can use pictures or other visuals of personal significance to the audience such as pictures of participants or pictures of their company.

Agenda: Slide no 2 should show the agenda and the aim of your presentation. It will give your audience an idea of what they should expect.

Main points: Go directly to the main section. Use visual representation with your presentation. Use what you consider best, i.e., key words, phrases or graphics.

Conclusion: Don't forget to finish your presentation with a graphic summary. This will give your audience a clear picture of the contents and a deeper insight into the presentation they have just attended.

Success is never an accident!
Take control of the situation

I always arrive at least one and a half hours to two hours before a presentation, and I prefer to turn up the evening before! Why do I do this?

I do it because I like to "get the feel of" the room. I like to find out where the switches are. I like to check to see whether the technicians have assembled the equipment which I requested in my requirement specification. I like to know how the video, the television, the overhead projector and other electronic equipment work. In brief, I like to be in control of loose ends.

You may well say that it is not your responsibility and say that it is your job to give the presentation and deliver your message, and that the responsibility of ensuring that the overhead projector is actually working and has a bulb in it is in the hands of other people! Or ...?

Unfortunately, life is not like that in the real world. If something is not working as it should or if everything goes wrong, it will affect your presentation.

You may well be delivering the most relevant message ever, and you may be backing it up one hundred per cent with factual evidence. What you say may be substantiated by leading experts. You may be producing one of the most professional presentations ever, containing sound and animation, and you perhaps liven it up with your flip-chart. But then ....

If the lunch is cold, the room has faulty air-conditioning, the chairs are hard, if there is not enough parking space, if the overhead projector does not work and then the felt-tip pen is dry, one person will be affected: That is YOU, and it will spoil YOUR presentation.

Arrangement

The room in which you hold your presentation must of course be suitably equipped. Projectors and spaces must be appropriately arranged for your presentation with switches and doors in a safe and convenient place.

If you are to hold an open presentation, i.e., you don't really know how many people are going to attend, it is not a good idea to put extra chairs out. Put them nearby, but out of sight so they can be brought out if they are needed. Nothing is worse than a room with 26 empty chairs. The number of chairs should correspond to the number of participants!

The room that you use must NEVER be too hot. When I submit my requirement specification, I indicate that air conditioning is an essential necessity. Ideally the temperature should be between 18 and 21 degrees. With a group of people, the temperature will rise a little. If it gets too warm, people will get sleepy and find it difficult to concentrate.

Not long ago, I held a course in Haderslev. In the room next to us there was a wedding. The doors between us were not sound-proof, and it affected my presentation.

You can never guess what could happen in the rooms next to yours or on the premises where you are giving your presentation.

Check the doors, and it may be a good idea to put tape over the key holes and other openings so as to get rid of any noise. Put a notice over the doors saying, ""Presentation in progress—do not disturb."

If there are up to sixty people, you can give your presentation without using a microphone. If there are more than that number, you will need to use a microphone or a loudspeaker; otherwise people in the back rows will find it difficult to hear what you are saying.

Make sure that lunch is arranged and fits into the schedule. Find out what happens about lunch if the presentation is delayed.

If you arrive early, you also have the opportunity of meeting some of the participants on a casual basis before the event gets going. This will give you the opportunity to learn a little about their background, where they come from, their company, why they are there and their aims.

You can use this knowledge in the presentation. For instance, address one of them directly regarding problems caused by polluted drinking water. Audiences really enjoy it when a presentation is interactive because it establishes rapport with all the participants.

How should the room be arranged? What configuration should the seating arrangement use to ensure an optimal presentation?

It is important to turn your attention to how everything is arranged and set up. This is of immense psychological value.

Theater seating arrangement

With this set-up there is space for a lot of people, and it's easy for the speaker to assess how many people are present and maintain eye contact. The minus side of this is that participants are not able to communicate with each other. Eye contact between participants is not possible, and audience interaction is severely restricted.

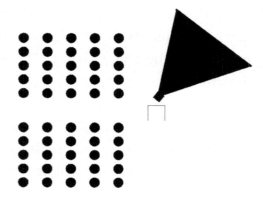

Theatre seating arrangement

Classroom seating arrangement

This set-up is perfect if the room is large and there are not many participants. It will make the event appear "big." The set-up is suitable when people need to take notes, but just as with a theatre seating arrangement, it is difficult for everyone to communicate and establish eye contact.

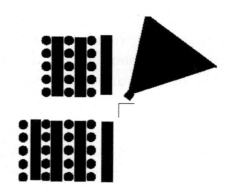

Angular classroom seating arrangement

An alternative set-up to the classroom seating arrangement is when the tables are placed at an angle facing the center. With this set-up, participants are able to communicate and

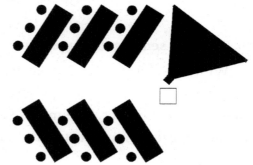

establish eye contact. An added advantage is that participants have a table to write on.

U-shaped or horseshoe arrangement

 I really do recommend this arrangement for courses, seminars, smaller conferences and workshops. Not only can people see the speaker, they also see the speaker, they also see each other, and this facilitates both discussion and non-verbal communication. This type of seating arrangement is suitable for up to sixteen participants.

Good advice!

I have given thousands of seminars, run many courses, presided at meetings and spoken at many conferences. Doing this work has made me develop a clear understanding and a natural ability to define criteria and bring my presentations to life in such a way that I always inspire my audiences, and they go away remembering what I have said–not for just one hour or one day, but for a long time afterwards.

You should choose words that paint pictures. Winston Churchill was a great expert at this technique. He emphasized words and highlighted meaning.

"Iron curtain ..."

"I have nothing to offer other than blood, sweat and tears."

You ask "What are your politics?" You ask "What is your aim?"

Use visual stories with content that binds the audience together. I tell stories that emphasize what I am talking about. I like to include myself in the story so that participants can say "a-ha, that sounds familiar."

One example can be, "It is as big as an elephant." "No human being has such great ape-like mitts that they can carry anything as heavy as that slab."

Speak directly. Always use "you," "us," "we," or the equivalent. Don't be too formal in your speech because people may not understand you. Always repeat what you have to say. Have you ever wondered why songs have a chorus?

Make sure your descriptions, your commands and your guidelines are clear. There must never be any doubt in the minds of your audience about the direction you are going, what you think, when you thought it and why you thought it. You are in the driver's seat!

Check list for effective presentations.
General:

- Look participants straight in the eyes. Maintain eye contact and hold it for 5 seconds.
- You are the greatest authority on things that have happened to you.
- Converse in just the same way as you would with a friend.
- Find out about your audience beforehand. Who are they?
- Think about things that are positive. Forget anything that is negative.
- It is quite natural to be afraid of speaking. Use it to your advantage.
- Establish eye contact with a friendly face. Look for a response.
- Never read your speech.
- Visualize.

During your presentation:

- What is my message?
- What is my aim?
- Keep to the point.
- Support your arguments with transparencies, examples, quotes or demonstrations.
- Keep to the allotted time.
- Plan your final remarks very carefully.
- Don't read from your transparency.
- Turn the overhead projector off when you are not using it.
- Make sure that the overhead projector is working and that you have spare bulbs.
- Use black or blue felt-tip pens with the flip-chart.

Your schedule:

- Use your schedule as a think tank.
- The schedule should focus your thoughts.
- Use only one or two words in each cell.
- Insert the main points.
- Make note of stories, your transparencies and your flip-chart pages.

Preliminary analysis:

- Send out questionnaires to the participants.
- Find out beforehand how the room is set up.
- Find out whether there are subjects that you should not mention.
- Find out beforehand how much knowledge participants

have on the subject.

- Find out if the participants have chosen to attend or if they have been asked to attend.
- When in Rome, do as the Romans do. Use company jargon.

Attract attention:

- Let the host know how you should be introduced. Do not take chances.
- Remember that the first sixty seconds of your presentation are vital.
- By using questions, you force your audience to think in the same way as you do.
- Avoid jokes unless you are a professional comedian.
- Remember to include stories and personal anecdotes.
- Learn to make pauses.
- Be enthusiastic about your own speech.
- Sum up the main points again and again.
- You should choose words that draw pictures.
- Use the words "you," "we," and "us."
- Use words that are positive and cheerful.

Body language:

- Move about in front of your audience. Activity livens up presentations.
- Do not make any unintended movements.
- Always keep your feet pointed forwards.
- Learn to move towards your audience when you want to emphasize a point.

- Acquire a calm and collected manner. Do not fiddle with your watch, your clothes, your hair or your ears.

Visual presentations:

- Pictures and graphics liven up your presentation.
- Each transparency should contain one essential idea.
- 20 per cent of your transparency should be blank, without graphics or text.
- Be consistent with design and impression.
- The message conveyed by the graphics should be easy to understand.
- Use a lot of contrast to enhance readability.
- Spend no more than two minutes on each transparency.

QUESTIONS:

Walk around when people are asking questions.

Make your answers short and to the point.

If you do not know the answer, you must not guess.

Allow your audience to contribute to the answer. Involve them.

Prepare for possible questions.

I hope my words have given you a general insight into communication techniques. I am sorry to say that we have barely touched on many relevant areas. If I were to cover the whole area, I would never stop writing.

I have chosen to focus on areas which are of primary interest. These areas are those where I myself have needed a guiding hand, but have ended up learning by trial and error.

More than anything else, how you will succeed will depend on training. Good luck to you! Remember that you can do anything if you put your mind to it!

Yours sincerely

Keld Ianen

Author, CEO, professor and speaker

Table of Contents

Introducing the "Power of Wow"   3

Focus on the needs of your audience   4

Direct the message   5

Build on a proven success tool   6

Employ your personal advantage   7

Incorporate result-getting techniques   8

Test your visual aid needs   9

Enhance the impact of your visuals   10

Consider visual aid options   12

Eliminate audio-visual distractions   13

Introducing the "Power of Wow"

Congratulations! By requesting this guide, you've shown yourself to be a presenter committed to the "Power of Wow." That's the confidence to walk into a room and quickly have the audience in the palm of your hand.

This mini-guide was prepared to help you continue to build that confidence. It covers winning techniques designed to add the "Power of Wow" to the content, delivery and visuals of your presentations.

Whether you're a beginner, or highly experienced presenter, we're confident you'll find a tip or two in this guide that will make your presentations more impressive and effective in 15 minutes or less.

This guide has been prepared and provided by InFocus with our compliments. As an industry leader, InFocus offers an extensive line of digital projectors and accessories created to enhance your effectiveness as a presenter. We are committed to serving the presentation market in any way we can.

-3-

337

Focus on the needs of your audience

Whatever the subject of your presentation, it's important to understand what your audience wants to gain from attending. The key to winning over an audience is to make their needs and desires the prominent part of your message. Here are some types of audiences you may speak in front of:

Selling goods and/or services

To capture attention, tell listeners what rewards they will personally enjoy using your product or service. Even if you are selling complex technology, your audience wants to know how it can save time, make money, reduce effort, or make them more successful.

Training employees or customers

While you cover the "how to" steps, be sure to interject the personal advantages each customer or employee will gain by having these abilities. The advantages may include working faster, reducing stress and effort, and many others.

Producing investor support

Why your company wants investor money is important. Support can be better built, however, by focusing on the benefits to the investor. These are usually financial, but can also be such things as satisfaction of contributing to an important advancement or being part of historical innovations.

Informing stockholders

The usual goal of this type of presentation, good news or bad, is to reduce investor concerns, or sell stock. If you make these presentations, you are probably already emphasizing your investors' needs. We suggest you review your material to be sure you haven't missed an opportunity to say "you" instead of "we."

Informing the community

Community presentations usually concern something your company has done, or plans to do. To make the work acceptable, be sure to cover the benefits the community (your listeners) will enjoy from the work. Then prove what you say by listing the actions that will create these benefits.

- 4 -

338

Direct the message

Employ this essential practice at every presentation. Mentally put yourself in the audience. Imagine their attitude. Are you glad to be there? Are you comfortable? Understanding how your audience feels gives you the information you need to make an essential connection with them.

Attitude

Is your audience happy to be there, or did you have to convince them to come? As you prepare and present, include a statement showing you understand and share their enthusiasm, or that you're confident you can make them glad they attended — then do so.

Timetable

Is your audience taking a break from work to be with you? Once they start looking at their watches you've lost them. Start and end at a preestablished time. If circumstances cause you to start late, assure your audience you understand the value of their time and that the presentation will end on time. Then speed up, or edit your talk accordingly.

Comfort

Is the room cool, hot, noisy, crowded or uncomfortable in any way? If you have control over making it better, do it. If not, mention the mutual discomfort early in the presentation. It will help your audience relax and you'll create a personal connection with them.

Age

Younger audiences require more visual stimulation. Older audiences may have difficulty hearing or seeing small images. Remember who your audience is, and adjust the presentation accordingly.

Education

The Wall Street Journal is written to a tenth-grade education level.
When preparing, choose language easily understood by the person in the room with the least education and knowledge.

-5-

339

Build on a proven success tool

Are you selling a product? Prospects want to know "what will it do for me?" Are you presenting to stock-holders? Investors want to know how the news will affect their pocketbooks. Are you training employees and customers? They need to know how to accomplish a task, but also what advantages will come from the knowledge. The proven tool salespeople have been using for years is to focus the presentation on benefits. Then cover the facts or features that make those benefits possible.

Benefits are fulfilling basic human desires. These include:

- Make money
- Save time
- Save money
- Save effort
- Gain comfort
- Be appreciated
- Enjoy pleasure
- Be in style
- Be praised
- Feel secure
- Be successful
- Look smart

- Be admired
- Be an individual
- Have beautiful possessions
- Emulate others
- Take advantage of opportunities
- Keep possessions
- Avoid criticism
- Avoid pain
- Avoid loss of reputation
- Avoid loss of money
- Avoid trouble
- Avoid effort

Here are examples of focusing on benefits and supporting them with features:

Benefit: Save time giving branch offices weekly updates. (save time and effort)
Feature: The auto-dial feature can connect up to 25 numbers in 3 minutes.
Benefit: Your dividends will increase by 5% next quarter. (make money)
Feature: Company profits met first quarter projected growth figures.
Benefit: Look like a hero at your next managers meeting. (be praised and appreciated)
Benefit: Use these techniques with confidence. (feel secure, be successful)
Feature: Each technique has been used successfully by experienced presenters nationwide.
Remember the above tips when organizing and presenting your message.

-6-

Employ your personal advantage

As the speaker, you are the center of the presentation. Your visuals and hand-outs are there only to support you. It's important to look and sound comfortable and appear honest and believable. The surest way to do this is to build your presentation around your own personality and style. It's an old adage, but "be yourself" is the secret to success.

Voice

Are you a strong, dynamic speaker? Use your own voice to provide the attention-getting drama and emphasis needed to make important points. Then support them with visuals.

Presence

If you have a strong presence, or are agile and limber, take advantage of who you are. Move around during the presentation. Do live demonstrations, be animated when talking, and use movement to accentuate major issues.

Style

Attempting to be strong and dynamic when you are a warm, softspoken person works against your believability. Write and present your talk from your heart. When you are not in front of an audience, how do you communicate? Use that style in your presentation.

Humor

An amusing anecdote, quote or funny story at the beginning of presentation puts your audience at ease. Humor is entertaining and keeps audience attention. If you are good at telling humorous stories, use this to your advantage. But make sure the stories relate to the subject and don't offend anyone in the room. If you are not known as a good storyteller, don't attempt humor. If your comedic timing is not good, humor can detract more than it adds to your presentation.

Background

Business audiences respect experience and past success. If you have this advantage, use it to establish believability. Then promise your audience that learning through your experience saves them from making the same mistakes in the future.

- 7 -

341

Incorporate result-getting techniques

Here are a few techniques guaranteed to add strength and power to your presentations.

One-on-one contact

Eye contact is the best way to build trust and acceptance with your audience. Treat each person as if you are presenting to him or her personally. Depending on the size of the group, make eye contact with everyone at least once, if not multiple times. If this is not natural to you, it's an important skill to practice and perfect.

Strong, accurate language

Studies have found that delivery has the largest impact on presentations and words a relatively small influence. However, review what you have written and look for the following style errors that weaken what you say.

AVOID USE

Passive Voice/Active Voice
Later it was decided to... Later we decided...
Negative Form Positive Form
Did not have confidence in Mistrusted

Redundant Correct
New breakthrough Breakthrough
Current status Status

Interactive devices

Including audience participation in your presentation commands attention, boosts learning, and builds interest in your subject. Pose informal questions to the audience — Build a relationship with your audience by immediately asking questions about their backgrounds or areas of interest. Then, if you can, adjust your message based on those answers. Integrate topic questions into the talk — Pose questions during the presentation. Ask such things as "what do you think happened next?" "Does anyone know the outcome?" "What is the next step?" Ask whatever is appropriate to your subject. Then call on the audience for answers.

Ask for questions from the audience — If you're a flexible speaker, tell your listeners they can ask questions during the presentation. If not, invite questions at the end. The first option will be more stimulating for the audience.

- 8 -

Test your visual aid needs

Most presentations will be more successful with the addition of visuals.

Studies show that different people rely on different senses to absorb information. Some respond better to audio, while others must see something visually before understanding it. You'll be guaranteed to reach everyone in your audience if you present your material both ways.

How important are visuals in your presentation?

Take this quick quiz and find out.

- ☐ Your product is visual or creates visuals.
- ☐ You have more than two or three major points to make.
- ☐ Your message is controversial or could be misunderstood.
- ☐ You are training and the "how to" involves multiple steps.
- ☐ Your subject is basically dry and needs to be made more exciting.
- ☐ Numbers and/or mathematics are part of your presentation.
- ☐ You are presenting language, terms and other material your audience may not be familiar with.
- ☐ The age or interest level of your audience requires visuals to maintain attention.
- ☐ You are not a strong speaker and need visuals to enliven your message.
- ☐ You want to add powerful emphasis to your major points.
- ☐ Your product is complicated or the material is complex.

If you checked any of the above items, some type of visual support is essential to make your message understood. If you checked many items, your presentation may require dynamic visuals, motion or even sound.

-9-

343

Enhance the impact of your visuals

Here are some tips on making sure your visuals properly support your message.
Use color to influence mood and emotion.
The colors for type, illustrations and backgrounds influence the way they are perceived. Here is a basic guide to using color in your business presentations.

Red - excitement, alert
Green - growth
Yellow - confidence, warmth, wisdom
Purple - dignity, sophistication
White - professionalism, new, innocence
Blue - truth, trust, justice
Black - authority, strength
Orange - action, optimism
Brown - friendliness, warmth
Grey - integrity, maturity

Apply appropriate typestyles for readability.

For hand-outs or take-home material, print the paragraph copy in a serif typestyle. This style has been proven to be 30% easier to read. Type that is projected on a screen, using a slide, overhead or multimedia projector, should be in sans serif type. In the projection process letters lose some of their sharpness, and serif type can look muddy when projected.

This is "**Times New Roman.**" It is a serif type. Notice the tiny scrollwork on the ends of each letter. This is "Helvetica." It is a sans serif type. It does not have the tiny scrollwork on the ends of each letter.

-10-

344

Include photographs to inject realism.
The more true to life you make the issue you are presenting, the better your audience will understand and identify with it. Remember the impact you can add by using photos or video of people on location, using products or talking to the audience.

Insert illustrations to clarify or emphasize.
If your product is complex, an illustration lets you simplify the way it looks. Call-outs can be added to point out major features. Also, illustrations allow you to show exploded views or views normally not seen, such as product interiors.

Add motion, sound or music when necessary.
Just because you can, doesn't mean you should. Add animation, sound effects or music to enliven your presentation when it's appropriate. Animation is valuable when you need to attract attention, demonstrate how something works, or tell a story without words. Animation without purpose detracts from your message.

Keep charts and graphs simple.
Charts and graphs that are used to support a point should be simple and instantly understood. Audiences are confused by complex visuals.

Here are examples of the wrong and right ways to design charts and graphs.

WRONG: Multiple graphic elements force the audience to study the chart in order to understand it.

RIGHT: Combining sales figures into a single graphic element makes the point instantly

WRONG: Using both lines and bars in the same chart will make it busy and confusing, and muddy your message.

RIGHT: Charts can dramatically support your point when complex information is visually simplified.

Consider visual aid options

Here are the primary advantages and disadvantages of most common visual aids.

Flip charts

Advantages

The simplicity eliminates the possibility of mechanical problems. Requires only an easel, which is available in most settings. Using a marker, you can draw or write on the pages during the presentation and make it interactive. A darkened room is not required.

Disadvantages

Creating images is time-consuming as visuals must be drawn on paper, or drawn and mounted on boards. Too small to be effective with a large audience.

Slides

Advantages

Excellent for photographic images and other art. It's now easy to make attractive slides of charts, graphs and other material on a computer. The slide projector is portable enough to travel.

Disadvantages

Slides require a longer lead time for production and are not intimate enough for small conference rooms or office settings.

Advantages

Presentations can be easily written, revised, and personalized to each audience as you travel. By allowing the use of sound and movement you can make your visuals alive and dynamic.

Disadvantages

Requires computer knowledge and experience.

Eliminate audio-visual distractions

Annoying distractions can irritate your audience and reduce the effectiveness of your message. Try to avoid these common problems.

Poor advance work

Check the facility and equipment thoroughly before your audience arrives. Set up your equipment, then make sure your visuals can be seen clearly from any seat in the room. Find light switches and know in advance how they should be set while visuals are being shown.

Awkward room layout

Determine where you will stand or walk while the visuals are being viewed. Will you be in the way? Do you plan to use pointers or slide changers? If so, where will you be when using these? Don't be your own audio-visual distraction.

Distracting equipment

Be sure you carry backup parts necessary to make your equipment work — extra light bulbs for projectors, batteries for computers, markers for boards, or grease pencils for overhead cells. Bring a long extension cord in case outlets are far away. Equipment difficulties make you look unprepared.

Overusing visuals

Visuals should support and emphasize important points; they should not be the presentation. "You" are the heart of the communication. Relying on visuals too much prevents you from connecting with your audience.

Under-using visuals

An old adage states "tell me once, tell me twice, tell me three times, then maybe I'll believe you." No matter what your subject, your purpose is to affect the attitude of your audience. If you underuse visuals, you miss an excellent opportunity to repeat your important points.

-13-

347

Slideshop.com - Copyright: Keld Jensen - Keldjensen.com

CPSIA information can be obtained
at www.ICGtesting.com
Printed in the USA
FSOW04n0421030815
9339FS